Coll

GLASGOW

C000158074

Published by Collins
An imprint of HarperCollins*Publishers*
77-85 Fulham Palace Road, Hammersmith, London W6 8JB

www.collins.co.uk

Copyright © HarperCollins*Publishers* Ltd 2005

Collins® is a registered trademark of HarperCollins*Publishers* Limited

Mapping generated from Collins Bartholomew digital databases

This product uses map data licensed from Ordnance Survey ® with the
permission of the Controller of Her Majesty's Stationery Office.
© Crown copyright. Licence number 399302

The contents of this publication are believed correct at the time of printing.
Nevertheless, the publisher can accept no responsibility for errors or omissions,
changes in the detail given, or for any expense or loss thereby caused.

The representation of a road, track or footpath is no evidence of a right of way.

Printed in Hong Kong

ISBN 0 00 718987 7   RI11726 NDB
Imp 001

e-mail: roadcheck@harpercollins.co.uk

Contents

Key to map pages	4-5
Key to map symbols	6-7
City centre maps	8-15
Map pages	16-85
Rail network map	86-87
Index to street names	88-128

Key to map pages

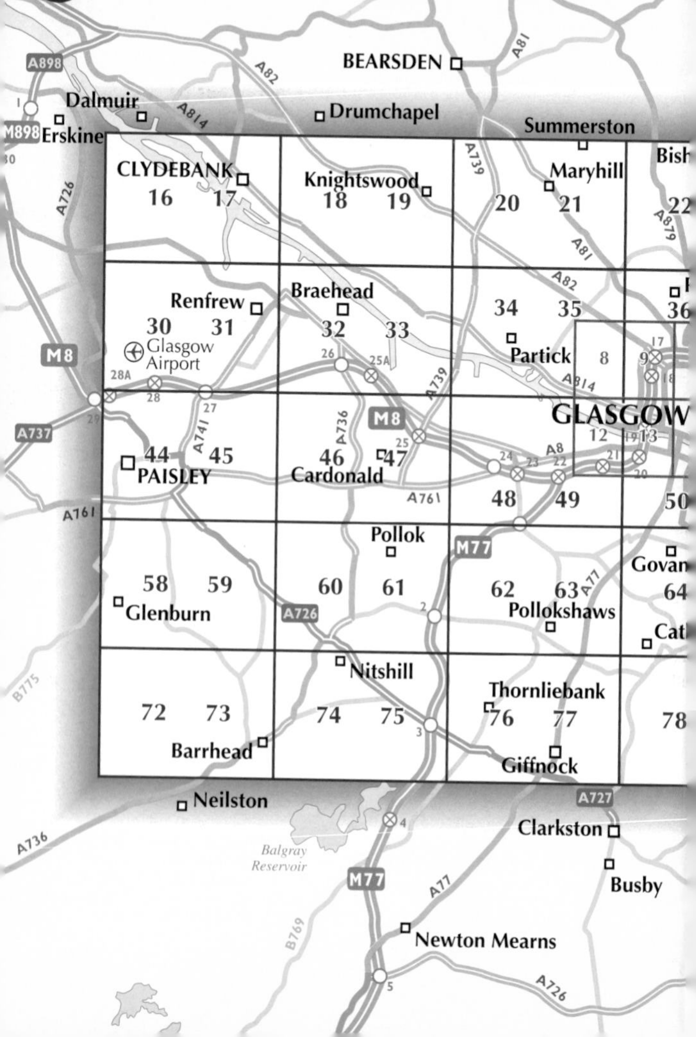
Milngavie
A809
A807
A81
BEARSDEN
A82
A898
Dalmuir
A814
Drumchapel
M898
Erskine
Summerston
CLYDEBANK
16
17
Knightswood
18
19
A739
Maryhill
20
21
Bish
22
A726
A879
A81
A82
Renfrew
30
31
Glasgow Airport
Braehead
32
33
34
35
36
Partick
8
9
M8
28A
28
27
26
25A
A739
A814
GLASGOW
12
13
A737
29
A741
44
45
PAISLEY
A736
M8
46
47
Cardonald
25
24
23
22
A8
21
20
A761
48
49
50
A761
Pollok
M77
58
59
Glenburn
60
61
A726
62
63
A77
Pollokshaws
Govan
64
Cat
B775
2
72
73
Barrhead
Nitshill
74
75
3
Thornliebank
76
77
Giffnock
78
A727
Neilston
4
Clarkston
A736
Balgray Reservoir
M77
A77
Busby
B769
Newton Mearns
5
A726

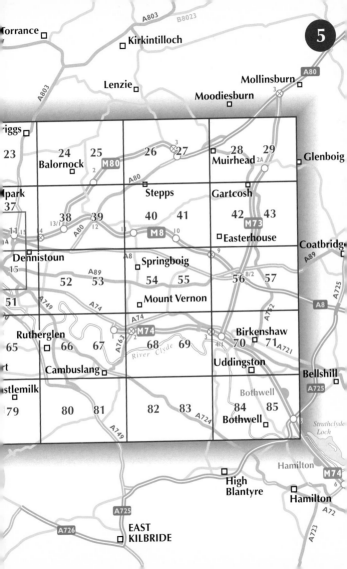

6 Key to map symbols

M8 — Motorway

■ ■ ■ — Motorway under construction

A74 — Primary road dual / single

A89 — A Road dual / single

B763 — B Road dual / single

— Other road dual / single

■ ▭ ▯ — Road under construction

- - - - — Road tunnel

→ — One-way street

Toll — Toll

— Restricted access street

— Pedestrian street

= — Minor road

::::::::: — Track

_FB_ — Footbridge

- - - - - - - - — Footpath

— Unitary authority boundary

— Postcode boundary

— Railway line

—✕— Level crossing

⊐ ⊏ — Railway tunnel

—✦— Main railway station

—✦— Other railway station

Ⓢ — Subway station

— Bus / Coach station

- - - - - - - - Pedestrian ferry

Leisure / Tourism

Shopping / Retail

Administration / Law

Education

Hospital

Industry / Commerce

Notable building

Major religious building

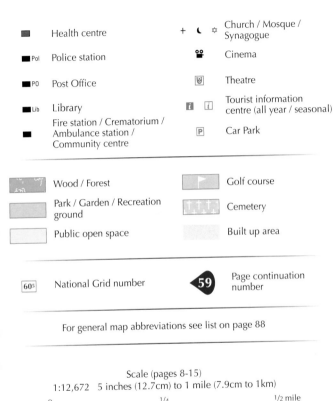

7

▪ Health centre	+ ☾ ✡	Church / Mosque / Synagogue
▪Pol Police station	🎥	Cinema
▪PO Post Office	🎭	Theatre
▪Lib Library	ℹ️ ℹ️	Tourist information centre (all year / seasonal)
▪ Fire station / Crematorium / Ambulance station / Community centre	Ⓟ	Car Park

Wood / Forest	▶	Golf course
Park / Garden / Recreation ground		Cemetery
Public open space		Built up area

60⁵ National Grid number   **59** Page continuation number

For general map abbreviations see list on page 88

Scale (pages 8-15)
1:12,672 5 inches (12.7cm) to 1 mile (7.9cm to 1km)

0 ———— 1/4 ———— 1/2 mile
0 ———— 1/4 ———— 1/2 ———— 3/4 kilometre

Scale (pages 16-85)
1:20,000 3.2 inches (8 cm) to 1 mile (5cm to 1km)

0 —— 1/4 —— 1/2 —— 3/4 —— 1 mile
0 —— 1/4 —— 1/2 —— 3/4 —— 1 —— 1 1/4 kilometres

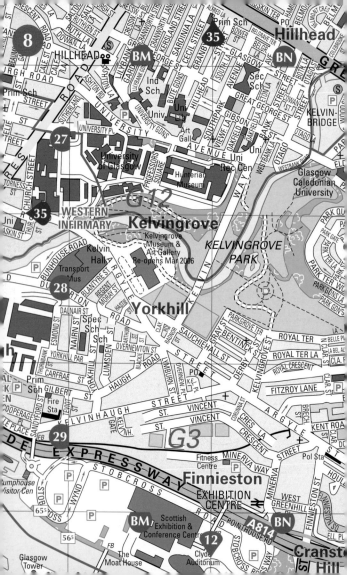

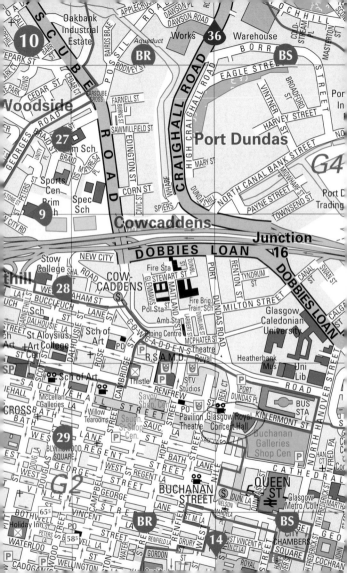

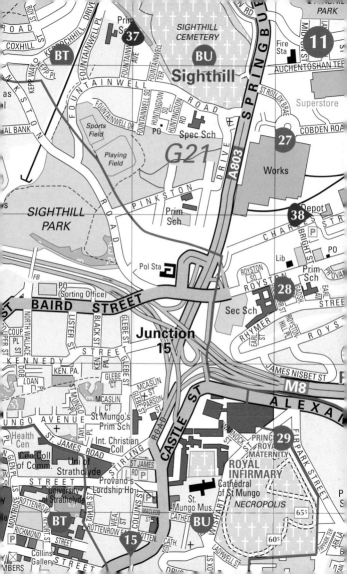

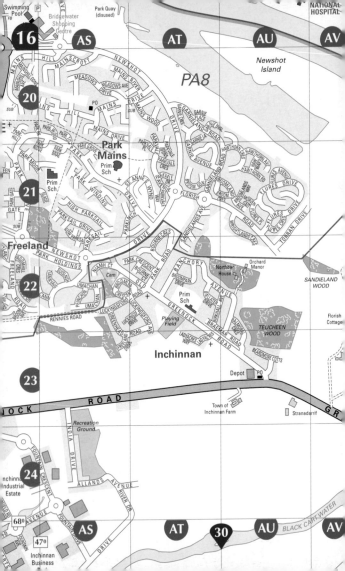

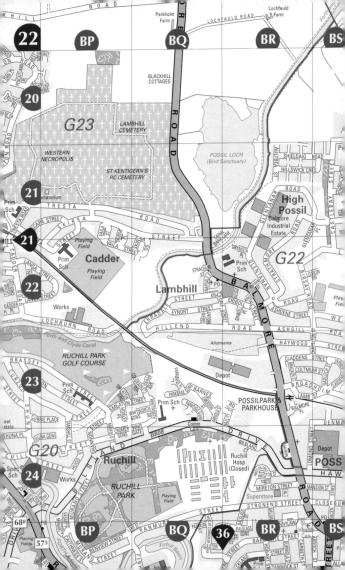

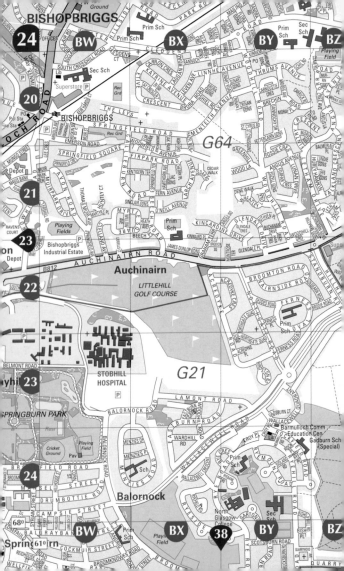

20

21

PA3

Marnock 22

23

24

Leckethill

BIRKENSHA

Football Ground

MIDTON COTTAGES

Cloverhill

Avenuehead Farm

AVENUEHEAD ROAD

ROAD

ACAVEL

T ELLEN COURSE

Club House

GLENBOIG ROAD

Primary School

SOUTH

EAST GATE

HEW OVAL

GARNSIDE ROAD

DINTRA PL

GLENBOIG RO

GAYNE

CHAPTAIN

CRAILING

CHESTNUT

MAR

Johnston House

JOHNSTON B804 ROAD

Johnston Farm

Bothlin Burn

Playing Field

ROAD

INCHNOCK AVE

ASHTON

BROWNLAND COURT

LOCHSIDE

MOWBRAY

PENDEECE

JARDINE TER

MANOR ROAD

KIRKHILL ROAD

WOODNEUK RD

WOODNEUK

BEARSDEN

EASTGATE

GREEN

Rec. Ground

Junction 2a

WOODLAND RESERVE

Ga

68⁹

71⁵

Prim Sch

P

GARTCOSH

Gartcosh Business Interchange

MT73

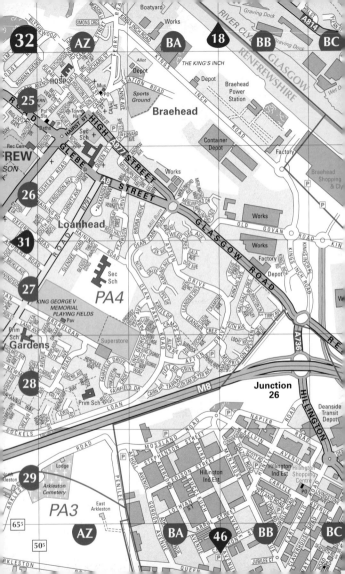

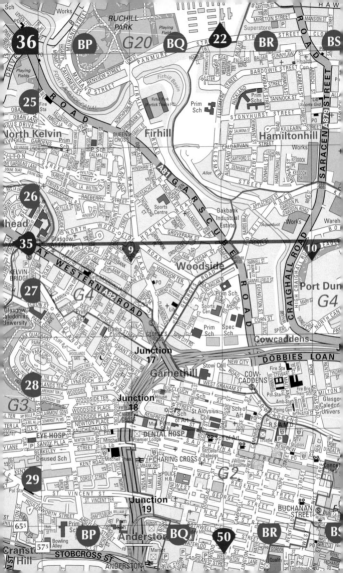

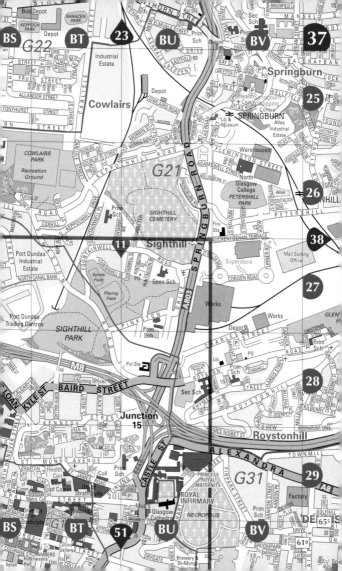

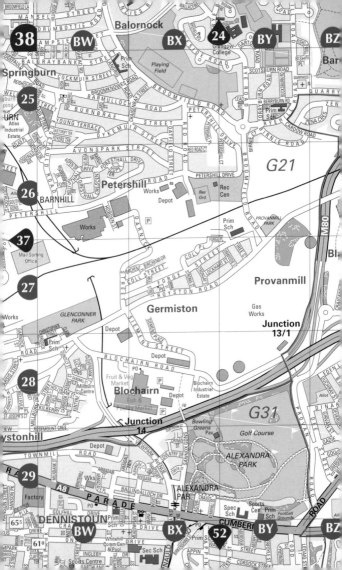

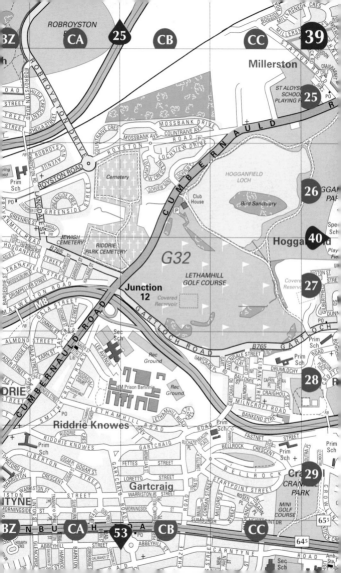

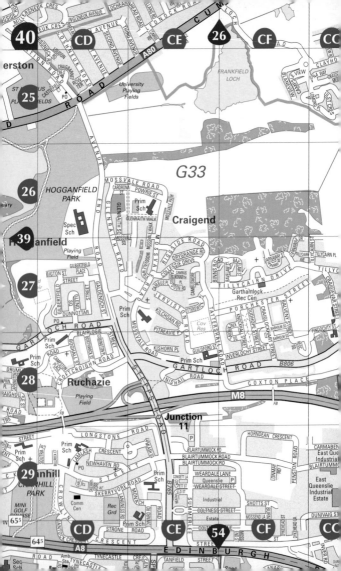

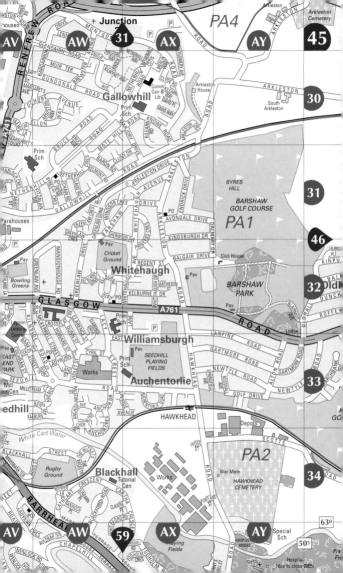

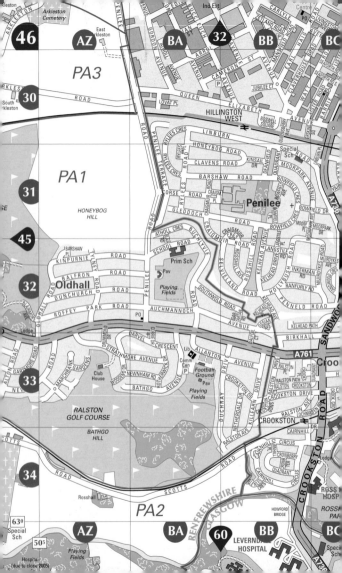

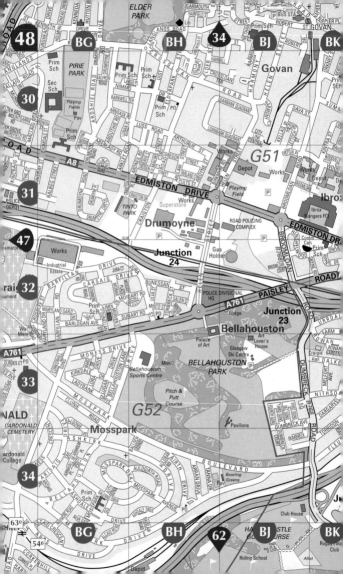

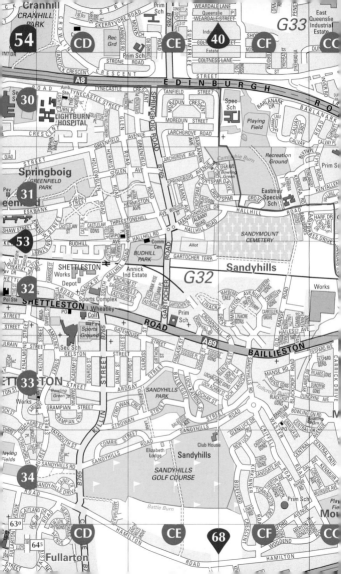

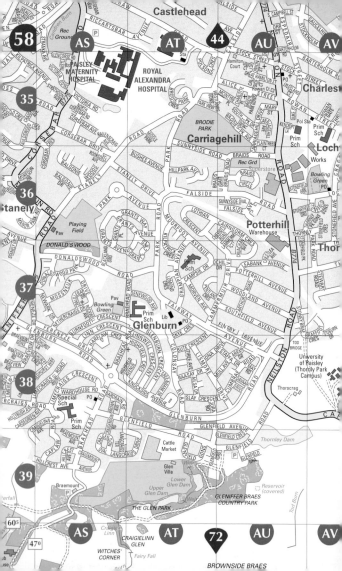

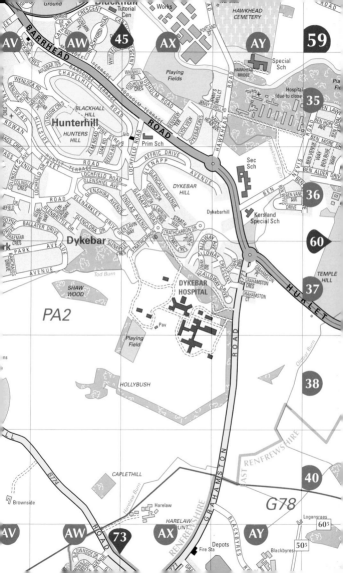

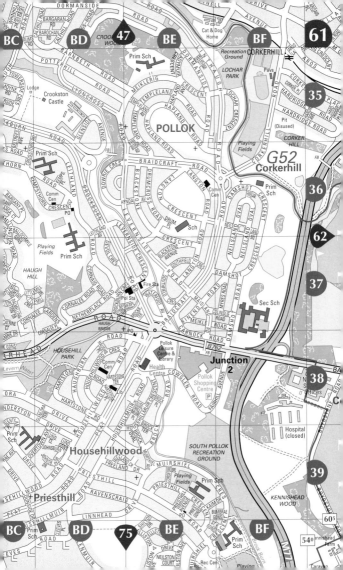

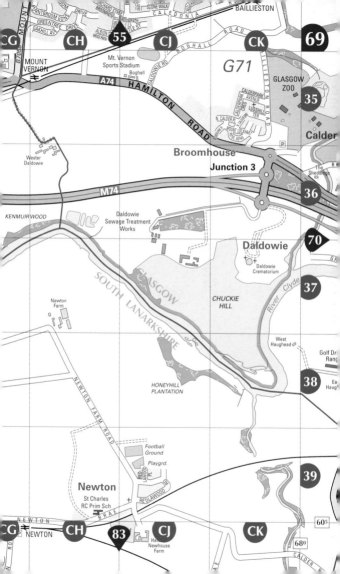

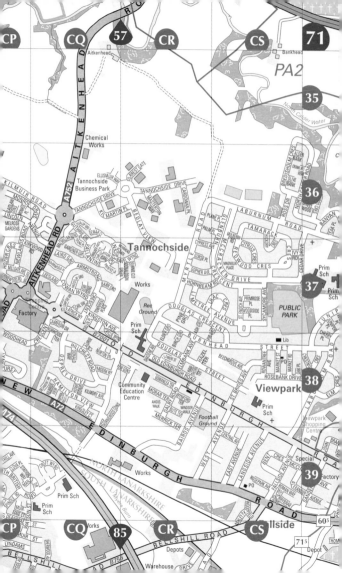

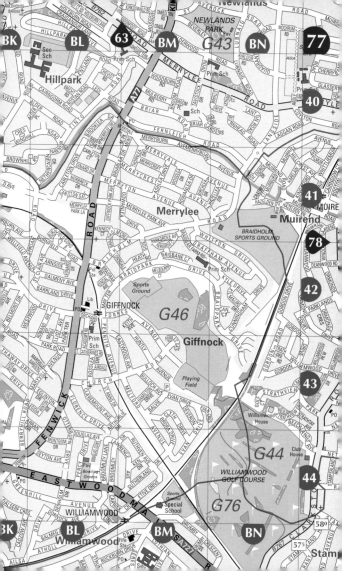

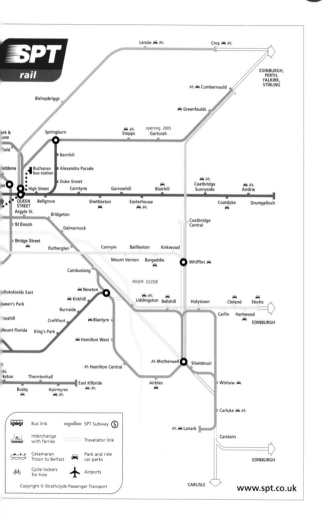

General abbreviations

All	Alley	Ctyd	Courtyard	Int	International	Rds	Roads
Allot	Allotments	Dep	Depot	Junct	Junction	Rec	Recreation
Amb	Ambulance	Dev	Development	La	Lane	Res	Reservoir
App	Approach	Dr	Drive	Las	Lanes	Ri	Rise
Arc	Arcade	Dws	Dwellings	Lib	Library	S	South
Av/Ave	Avenue	E	East	Lo	Lodge	Sch	School
Bdy	Broadway	Ed	Education	Ln	Loan	Sec	Secondary
Bk	Bank	Elec	Electricity	Lwr	Lower	Shop	Shopping
Bldgs	Buildings	Embk	Embankment	Mag	Magistrates	Sq	Square
Boul	Boulevard	Est	Estate	Mans	Mansions	St.	Saint
Bowl	Bowling	Ex	Exchange	Mem	Memorial	St	Street
Br	Bridge	Exhib	Exhibition	Mkt	Market	Sta	Station
Cath	Cathedral	FB	Footbridge	Mkts	Markets	Sts	Streets
Cem	Cemetery	FC	Football Club	Ms	Mews	Sub	Subway
Cen	Central, Centre	Fld	Field	Mt	Mount	Swim	Swimming
Cft	Croft	Flds	Fields	Mus	Museum	TA	Territorial Army
Cfts	Crofts	Fm	Farm	N	North	TH	Town Hall
Ch	Church	Gall	Gallery	NTS	National Trust	Tenn	Tennis
Chyd	Churchyard	Gar	Garage		for Scotland	Ter	Terrace
Cin	Cinema	Gdn	Garden	Nat	National	Thea	Theatre
Circ	Circus	Gdns	Gardens	PH	Public House	Trd	Trading
Cl/Clo	Close	Govt	Government	PO	Post Office	Twr	Tower
Co	County	Gra	Grange	Par	Parade	Twrs	Towers
Coll	College	Grd	Ground	Pas	Passage	Uni	University
Comm	Community	Grds	Grounds	Pav	Pavilion	Vil	Villas
Conv	Convent	Grn	Green	Pk	Park	Vil	Villa
Cor	Corner	Grns	Greens	Pl	Place	Vw	View
Coron	Coroners	Gro	Grove	Pol	Police	W	West
Cors	Corners	Gros	Groves	Prec	Precinct	Wd	Wood
Cotts	Cottages	Gt	Great	Prim	Primary	Wds	Woods
Cov	Covered	Ho	House	Prom	Promenade	Wf	Wharf
Crem	Crematorium	Hos	Houses	Pt	Point	Wk	Walk
Cres	Crescent	Hosp	Hospital	Quad	Quadrant	Wks	Works
Ct	Court	Hts	Heights	RC	Roman Catholic	Yd	Yard
Cts	Courts	Ind	Industrial	Rd	Road		

District abbreviations

Abbots.	Abbotsinch	Both.	Bothwell	Glenb.	Glenboig	Ruther.	Rutherglen
Baill.	Baillieston	Camb.	Cambuslang	Inch.	Inchinnan	Thornlie.	Thornliebank
Barr.	Barrhead	Chry.	Chryston	Kirk.	Kirkintilloch	Udd.	Uddingston
Bears.	Bearsden	Clark.	Clarkston	Mood.	Moodiesburn		
Bishop.	Bishopbriggs	Gart.	Gartcosh	Muir.	Muirhead		
Blan.	Blantyre	Giff.	Giffnock	Neil.	Neilston		

Post town abbreviations

Bell.	Bellshill	Coat.	Coatbridge	Pais.	Paisley
Clyde.	Clydebank	Ersk.	Erskine	Renf.	Renfrew

A

Abbey Cl, Pais. PA1	44	AU32	Abercorn Pl, G23	21	BN20	Academy Rd, (Giff.) G46	77	BL
Abbeycraig Rd, G34	42	CM28	Abercorn St, Pais. PA3	44	AV31	Academy St, G32	54	CD
Abbey Dr, G14	34	BG25	Abercrombie Cres,			Achray Pl, Coat. ML5	43	CS
Abbeygreen St, G34	42	CM28	(Baill.) G69	57	CP32	Acorn Ct, G40	51	BV
Abbeyhill St, G32	53	CA30	Abercromby Dr, G40	51	BV31	Acorn St, G40	51	BV
Abbey Mill Business			Abercromby Sq, G40	51	BV31	Acre Dr, G20	21	BK
Cen, Pais. PA1	45	AV33	Abercromby St, G40	51	BV32	Acredyke Cres, G21	24	BY
Abbotsburn Way,			Aberdalgie Gdns, G34	41	CK29	Acredyke Pl, G21	24	BY
Pais. PA3	30	AT29	Aberdalgie Path, G34	41	CK29	Acredyke Rd, G21	24	BX
Abbotsford Av,			Aberdalgie Rd, G34	41	CK29	Acredyke Rd, (Ruther.)		
(Ruther.) G73	66	BX38	Aberdour St, G31	52	BY30	G73	65	BV
Abbotsford Pl, G5	14	BR32	Aberfeldy St, G31	52	BY30	Acre Rd, G20	20	BK
Abbotsford Rd, Clyde. G81	17	AX20	Aberfoyle St, G31	52	BY30	Adams Ct La, G1	14	BR
			Aberlady St, G51	48	BG30	Adamswell St, G21	37	BU
Abbotsinch Retail Pk,			Aberneithy St, G31	52	BY30	Addison Gro,		
Pais. PA3	31	AV29	Aberuthven Dr, G32	54	CD34	(Thornlie.) G46	76	BH
Abbotsinch Rd, Pais. PA3	30	AU27	Abigail Pl, (Blan.) G72	68	CM44	Addison Pl,		
Abbotsinch Rd, Renf. PA4	31	AV25	Aboukir St, G51	35	BG29	(Thornlie.) G46	76	BH
Abbot St, Pais. PA3	45	AV31	Aboyne Dr, Pais. PA2	59	AV36	Addison Rd, G12	35	BM
Abbott Cres, Clyde. G81	18	AZ21	Aboyne St, G51	48	BH31	Addison Rd,		
Aberconway St,			Acacia Dr, (Barr.) G78	73	AW40	(Thornlie.) G46	76	BG
Clyde. G81	17	AY21	Acacia Way,			Adelphi St, G5	15	BT
Abercorn Av, G52	32	BA29	(Camb.) G72	82	CG40	Admiral St, G41	12	BN
			Academy Pk, G51	49	BL33	Advie Pl, G42	64	BR

Street	Page	Grid
fric Dr, Pais. PA2	59	AX36
ton Dr, Renf. PA4	32	BA27
St, G41	63	BN37
gnew La, G42	64	BQ36
kenhead Rd, G42	50	BX34
kenhead Rd, G44	64	BS39
ean Dr, G32	54	CG33
ean Gdns, G32	54	CG33
sa Dr, (Both.) G71	85	CQ41
sa Dr, (Ruther.) G73	79	BX40
sa Dr, Pais. PA2	58	AT38
sa Av, G53	31	AY27
nslie Rd, G52	33	BC29
rdale Av, (Giff.) G46	77	BL43
lie Gdns, (Ruther.) G73	81	BZ41
lie La, G12	34	BK25
lie Rd, (Baill.) G69	55	CJ34
lie St, G12	34	BJ26
link Ind Est, Pais. PA3	30	AU29
lour Rd, G43	77	BN40
Dr, G52	48	BH34
threy Av, G14	34	BK26
kenhead Av, Coat. ML5	57	CR33
kenhead Rd, (Udd.) G71	71	CQ36
ken St, G31	52	BY30
asdair Ct, (Barr.) G78	73	AY43
pany Av, G32	54	CE31
pany Dr, (Ruther.) G73	66	BX39
pany Quad, G32	54	CE31
pany St, G40	52	BW33
pany Ter, (Camb.) G72	81	CA42
bert Av, G42	64	BQ36
bert Br, G1	14	BS32
bert Br, G5	14	BS32
bert Cross, G41	50	BP34
bert Dr, (Ruther.) G73	80	BX40
bert Dr, G41	63	BL35
bert Rd, Renf. PA4	64	BO36
bion Gate, Pais. PA3	44	AT31
bion St, G1	15	BT31
bion St, (Baill.) G69	55	CH34
bion St, Pais. PA3	44	AT31
bion Wks Ind Est, G13	18	BA22
caig Rd, G52	62	BG35
der Bk, (Udd.) G71	71	CS36
der Ct, (Barr.) G78	73	AY44
der Gate, (Camb.) G72	82	CG40
derman Rd, G13	19	BE23
derman Rd, G13	18	BB21
der Pl, G43	77	BK40
der Rd, G43	77	BK40
dersyde Gdns, (Udd.) G71	70	CN38
dersyde Pl, (Blan.) G72	84	CL44
exander Av, (Udd.) G71	71	CS39
exander Cres, G5	50	BS33
exander St, Clyde. G81	17	AY21
exandra Av, (Stepps) G33	26	CF23
exandra Ct, G31	38	BX29
exandra Cross, G31	52	BX30
exandra Dr, Renf. PA4	32	AZ26
exandra Par, G31	38	BU29
exandra Pk St, G31	52	BX30
ord St, G21	37	BT26
red La, G12	35	BM26
red Ter, G12	35	BN26
gie St, G41	64	BP37
ce St, Pais. PA2	58	AU35
an Av, Renf. PA4	32	BA28
ander St, G22	36	BS25
ands Av, (Inch.) Renf. PA4	16	AS24
an Glen Pl, G4	11	BT29
Allan Pl, G40	52	BX34
Allan St, G40	66	BX35
Allanton Av, Pais. PA1	46	BA33
Allanton Dr, G52	47	BD32
Allen Way, Renf. PA4	32	AZ28
Allerdyce Ct, G15	18	BA20
Allerdyce Dr, G15	18	BB20
Allerdyce Rd, G15	18	BB20
Allerton Gdns, (Baill.) G69	55	CH33
Allison Dr, (Camb.) G72	67	CC39
Allison Pl, (Gart.) G69	42	CN25
Allison St, G42	64	BQ36
Allnach Pl, G34	42	CN29
Alloway Av, Pais. PA2	59	AX37
Alloway Cres, (Ruther.) G73	79	BV40
Alloway Cres, Pais. PA2	59	AX37
Alloway Dr, (Ruther.) G73	79	BV40
Alloway Dr, Pais. PA2	59	AX37
Alloway Gro, Pais. PA2	59	AY37
Alloway Rd, G43	63	BM39
Alma St, G40	52	BW32
Almond Av, Renf. PA4	32	BA27
Almond Rd, G33	26	CE24
Almond St, G33	39	BZ28
Alness St, G52	47	BF34
Alpine Gro, (Udd.) G71	70	CP38
Alton Rd, Pais. PA1	45	AY35
Altyre St, G32	53	CB34
Alva Gdns, G52	62	BG35
Alva Gate, G52	48	BG34
Alyth Gdns, G52	48	BG34
Amisfield St, G20	21	BN24
Amulree Pl, G32	53	CC33
Amulree St, G32	54	CD32
Ancaster Dr, G13	20	BH23
Anchor Av, Pais. PA1	45	AW33
Anchor Cres, Pais. PA1	45	AW33
Anchor Dr, Pais. PA1	45	AW33
Anchor Wynd, Pais. PA1	45	AW34
Ancroft St, G20	36	BQ26
Ancrum St, G32	54	CD32
Anderson Dr, Renf. PA4	32	AZ25
Anderson St, G11	36	BK27
Anderston Cross Cen, G2	13	BQ30
Anderston Quay, G3	13	BP31
Andrew Av, Renf. PA4	32	BA26
Andrew Dr, Clyde. G81	17	AY21
Andrew Sillars Av, (Camb.) G72	82	CD30
Andrews St, Pais. PA3	44	AT31
Angela Way, (Udd.) G71	70	CP39
Angle Gate, G14	33	BF25
Angus Av, G52	47	BD33
Angus Av, (Bishop.) G64	24	BY21
Angus Gdns, (Udd.) G71	70	CP39
Angus La, (Bishop.) G64	24	BZ20
Angus Oval, G52	47	BD33
Angus Pl, G52	47	BD33
Angus St, G21	37	BU25
Angus St, Clyde. G81	18	BA21
Angus Wk, (Udd.) G71	71	CR38
Annandale St, G42	50	BR34
Annan Dr, (Ruther.) G73	66	BZ38
Annan St, G42	64	BQ37
Annbank Pl, G31	51	BV31
Annbank St, G31	51	BV31
Anne Av, Renf. PA4	32	AZ25
Annette St, G42	64	BQ36
Annfield Gdns, (Blan.) G72	83	CK44
Annfield Pl, G31	51	BV30
Annick Ind Est, G32	54	CE33
Annick St, G32	54	CD32
Annick St, (Camb.) G72	82	CF40
Anniesland Cres, G14	19	BC24
Anniesland Ind Est, G13	20	BG21
Anniesland Rd, G13	19	BD24
Anniesland Rd, G14	19	BC24
Anson St, G40	51	BV33
Anstruther St, G32	53	CB33
Anthony St, G2	13	BQ30
Anwoth St, G32	53	CC34
Appin Cres, G31	52	BX30
Appin Rd, G31	52	BX30
Appin Ter, (Ruther.) G73	81	BZ41
Appleby St, G22	36	BR26
Applecross St, G4	36	BR26
Appledore Cres, (Both.) G71	85	CQ42
Apsley St, G11	34	BJ27
Aranthrue Cres, Renf. PA4	31	AY25
Aray St, G20	21	BM22
Arbroath Av, G52	47	BD33
Arcadia Pl, G40	15	BU32
Arcadia St, G40	15	BU32
Archerfield Av, G32	67	CC35
Archerfield Cres, G32	67	CC35
Archerfield Dr, G32	67	CC35
Archerfield Gro, G32	67	CC35
Archerhill Av, G13	18	BC21
Archerhill Cotts, G13	18	BC21
Archerhill Cres, G13	18	BD21
Archerhill Gdns, G13	18	BC21
Archerhill Rd, G13	18	BC21
Archerhill Sq, G13	18	BB21
Archerhill Ter, G13	18	BC21
Ardardie Dr, G32	68	CE37
Ardbeg Av, (Bishop.) G64	24	BY20
Ardbeg Av, (Ruther.) G73	81	CA42
Ardbeg La, G42	64	BQ35
Ardbeg St, G42	64	BQ35
Ardconnel St, (Thornlie.) G46	76	BH41
Arden Av, (Thornlie.) G46	76	BG43
Ardencraig Cres, G45	79	BV43
Ardencraig Gdns, G45	80	BW43
Ardencraig Pl, G45	79	BV42
Ardencraig Quad, G45	79	BV43
Ardencraig Rd, G45	79	BS44
Ardencraig St, G45	80	BW42
Ardencraig Ter, G45	79	BV43
Arden Dr, (Giff.) G46	76	BK43
Ardenlea, (Udd.) G71	70	CP38
Ardenlea St, G40	52	BX34
Arden Pl, (Thornlie.) G46	76	BG43
Ardessie Pl, G20	21	BM24
Ardfern St, G32	53	CC34
Ardgay Pl, G32	53	CC33
Ardgay St, G32	53	CC33
Ardgay Way, (Ruther.) G73	80	BX42
Ardgowan Av, Pais. PA2	44	AV34
Ardgowan Dr, (Udd.) G71	70	CP38
Ardgowan St, Pais. PA2	58	AV35
Ardholm St, G32	53	CC32
Ardlaw St, G51	48	BH31
Ardle Rd, G43	77	BN40
Ardlui St, G32	53	CB33
Ardmaleish Cres, G45	79	BU43
Ardmaleish Dr, G45	79	BT43
Ardmaleish Rd, G45	79	BT43
Ardmaleish St, G45	79	BT43
Ardmaleish Ter, G45	79	BU43
Ardmay Cres, G44	64	BS38
Ardmillan St, G33	39	CB29
Ardmory Av, G42	65	BT38
Ardmory La, G42	65	BU38
Ardmory Pl, G42	65	BU38
Ardnahoe Av, G42	65	BT37

Name	Page	Grid
Ardnahoe Pl, G42	65	BT37
Ardneil Rd, G51	48	BH31
Ardnish St, G51	48	BG30
Ardoch Gdns, (Camb.) G72	67	CB39
Ardoch Gro, (Camb.) G72	67	CB39
Ardoch Rd, G22	36	BS25
Ard Rd, Renf. PA4	31	AX25
Ardshiel Rd, G51	48	BG30
Ardsloy La, G14	33	BC25
Ardsloy Pl, G14	33	BC25
Ard St, G32	53	CC33
Ardtoe Cres, G33	27	CG24
Ardtoe Pl, G33	27	CG24
Arduthie Rd, G51	48	BG30
Ardwell Rd, G52	48	BG34
Argyle St, G2	13	BQ30
Argyle St, G3	8	BM28
Argyle St, Pais. PA1	44	AT33
Argyll Arc, G2	14	BS30
Argyll Av, (Abbots.) Pais. PA3	30	AT28
Argyll Av, Renf. PA4	31	AX25
Argyll Rd, Clyde. G81	17	AY20
Arisaig Dr, G52	48	BG34
Arisaig Pl, G52	48	BG34
Ark La, G31	51	BV30
Arkleston Cres, Pais. PA3	45	AX30
Arkleston Dr, Pais. PA3	45	AX31
Arkleston Rd, Pais. PA1	45	AX31
Arkleston Rd, Pais. PA3	45	AX30
Arkleston Rd, Renf. PA4	31	AW29
Arkle Ter, (Camb.) G72	81	CB42
Arklet Rd, G51	48	BG31
Arlington Pl, G3	9	BP28
Arlington St, G3	9	BP28
Armadale Ct, G31	38	BW29
Armadale Path, G31	38	BW29
Armadale Pl, G31	38	BW29
Armadale St, G31	52	BW30
Armour St, G31	15	BU31
Armstrong Cres, (Udd.) G71	71	CQ37
Arngask Rd, G51	48	BG30
Arnhall Pl, G52	48	BG34
Arnhem St, (Camb.) G72	82	CF40
Arnholm Pl, G52	48	BG34
Arnisdale Pl, G34	41	CJ29
Arnisdale Rd, G34	41	CJ29
Arniston St, G32	53	CB30
Arniston Way, Pais. PA3	45	AW30
Arnold Av, (Bishop.) G64	24	BW20
Arnold St, G20	22	BQ23
Arnol Pl, G33	55	CH30
Arnott Way, (Camb.) G72	67	CC39
Arnprior Cres, G45	79	BT42
Arnprior Quad, G45	79	BT41
Arnprior Rd, G45	79	BT41
Arnprior St, G45	79	BT41
Arnside Av, (Giff.) G46	77	BL42
Arnwood Dr, G12	20	BJ24
Aron Ter, (Camb.) G72	81	CB42
Aros Dr, G52	61	BF35
Aros La, G52	61	BF35
Arran Dr, (Giff.) G46	77	BK43
Arran Dr, G52	48	BH34
Arran Dr, Pais. PA2	48	AU38
Arran Rd, Renf. PA4	32	AZ27
Arran Way, (Both.) G71	85	CP43
Arrochar Ct, G23	21	BM21
Arrochar Dr, G23	21	BM20
Arrochar St, G23	21	BM21
Arrol Pl, G40	52	BX33
Arrol Rd, G40	52	BW33
Arrol St, G52	46	BA30
Arrowsmith Av, G13	19	BF21
Arthur Av, (Barr.) G78	73	AX44
Arthurlie Av, (Barr.) G78	73	AY43
Arthurlie Dr, (Giff.) G46	77	BL44
Arthurlie Gdns, (Barr.) G78	73	AY43
Arthurlie St, G51	48	BH30
Arthurlie St, (Barr.) G78	73	AY43
Arthur Rd, Pais. PA2	58	AU37
Arthur St, G3	8	BM28
Arthur St, Pais. PA1	44	AS32
Arundel Dr, G42	64	BQ38
Ascaig Cres, G52	61	BF35
Ascog St, G42	64	BQ35
Ascot Av, G12	20	BH23
Ascot Ct, G12	20	BJ23
Ashburton La, G12	21	BK23
Ashburton Rd, G12	20	BJ23
Ashby Cres, G13	20	BG20
Ashcroft Dr, G44	79	BU40
Ashdale Dr, G52	48	BG34
Ashdene St, G22	22	BR22
Ashgill Pl, G22	22	BS23
Ashgill Rd, G22	22	BR22
Ash Gro, (Bishop.) G64	24	BX20
Ash Gro, (Udd.) G71	71	CR37
Ashgrove St, G40	66	BW35
Ashkirk Dr, G52	48	BG34
Ashlea Dr, (Giff.) G46	77	BM41
Ashley Dr, (Both.) G71	85	CR40
Ashley La, G3	9	BP28
Ashley Pk, (Udd.) G71	85	CS40
Ashley St, G3	9	BP28
Ashmore Rd, G43	78	BP40
Ashmore Rd, G44	78	BP40
Ashton Gdns, (Gart.) G69	29	CJ34
Ashton La, G12	8	BM27
Ashton Rd, G12	8	BM27
Ashton Rd, (Ruther.) G73	66	BW36
Ashtree Rd, G43	63	BL37
Ashvale Cres, G21	38	BU24
Ash Wk, (Ruther.) G73	80	BY42
Ashwood Gdns, G13	20	BH24
Ash Wynd, (Camb.) G72	82	CG41
Aspen Dr, G21	38	BW26
Aspen Pl, (Camb.) G72	82	CG40
Aster Dr, G45	80	BW42
Athelstane Rd, G13	19	BE22
Athole Gdns, G12	35	BL26
Athole La, G12	35	BL26
Atholl Av, G52	58	BA29
Atholl Cres, Pais. PA1	46	BA31
Atholl Gdns, (Ruther.) G73	81	CA42
Atholl Ter, (Udd.) G71	71	CP36
Atlas Ind Est, G21	37	BV25
Atlas Pl, G21	37	BV26
Atlas Rd, G21	37	BU25
Atlas St, Clyde. G81	17	AX21
Attlee Av, Clyde. G81	18	BA20
Attlee Pl, Clyde. G81	18	BA20
Attow Rd, G43	76	BK40
Auburn Dr, (Barr.) G78	74	AZ44
Auchenbothie Cres, G33	25	CA23
Auchencrow St, G34	42	CM29
Auchengill Pl, G34	42	CM28
Auchengill Rd, G34	42	CL28
Auchinlea Retail Pk, G34	41	CH28
Auchinlea Rd, G34	41	CH28
Auchinlea Way, G34	41	CH28
Auchinleck Av, G33	25	CA22
Auchinleck Cres, G33	25	CA22
Auchinleck Dr, G33	25	CA22
Auchinleck Gdns, G33	25	CA22
Auchinleck Rd, G33	25	CB22
Auchinloch St, G21	37	BV27
Auchmannoch Av, Pais. PA1	46	BA31
Auckland St, G22	36	BR25
Auldbar Rd, G52	48	BH34
Auldbar Ter, Pais. PA2	59	AW37
Auldburn Pl, G43	62	BK38
Auldburn Rd, G43	62	BK38
Auldearn Rd, G21	24	BY20
Auldgirth Rd, G52	48	BH34
Auldhouse Gdns, G43	63	BK38
Auldhouse Rd, G43	63	BL38
Auldhouse Ter, G43	63	BM38
Auld Kirk Rd, (Camb.) G72	82	CE40
Aultbea St, G22	22	BR22
Aultmore Gdns, G33	55	CH31
Aultmore Pk, G33	55	CH31
Aultmore Rd, G33	55	CH31
Aursbridge Cres, (Barr.) G78	74	AZ43
Aursbridge Dr, (Barr.) G78	74	AZ43
Aurs Cres, (Barr.) G78	74	AZ43
Aurs Dr, (Barr.) G78	74	AZ44
Aurs Glen, (Barr.) G78	73	AY44
Aurs Pl, (Barr.) G78	74	BA43
Aurs Rd, (Barr.) G78	74	BA42
Austen Rd, G13	20	BG24
Avenel Rd, G13	20	BG21
Avenue End Rd, G33	40	CD25
Avenuehead Rd, (Chry.) G69	29	CQ25
Avenuepark St, G20	35	BN25
Avenue St, G40	52	BW31
Avenue St, (Ruther.) G73	66	BX37
Aviemore Rd, G52	62	BG35
Avoch St, (Thornlie.) G46	76	BG41
Avonbank Rd, (Ruther.) G73	65	BV37
Avondale Dr, Pais. PA1	45	AX31
Avondale St, G33	39	CC28
Avon Rd, (Giff.) G46	77	BK44
Avon Rd, (Bishop.) G64	24	BW21
Avonspark St, G21	38	BW26
Aylmer Rd, G43	64	BP39
Ayr St, G21	37	BU26
Aytoun Rd, G41	49	BM34
Azalea Gdns, (Camb.) G72	83	CG41

B

Back Causeway, G31	53	BZ31
Back Sneddon St, Pais. PA3	44	AU32
Bagnell St, G21	23	BV24
Baillie Dr, (Both.) G71	85	CQ42
Baillieston Rd, G32	54	CF33
Baillieston Rd, (Udd.) G71	55	CK34
Baillie Wynd, (Udd.) G71	71	CQ37
Bainsford St, G32	53	CB31
Baird Av, G52	32	BA30
Bairds Av, (Udd.) G71	71	CR37
Bairds Brae, G4	36	BR26
Baird St, G4	11	BU29
Baker St, G41	63	BN36
Bakewell Rd, (Baill.) G69	55	CJ32
Balaclava St, G2	13	BQ30
Balado Rd, G33	55	CG30
Balbeggie Pl, G32	54	CE33
Balbeggie St, G32	54	CE33

Name	Map	Grid
Ibeg St, G51	48	BG31
Iblair Rd, G52	48	BH34
Icarres Av, G12	21	BL24
Icomie St, G33	39	CC28
Icurvie Rd, G34	41	CJ27
Idinnie St, G34	41	CK29
Idovan Cres, G33	41	CH29
Idovan Path, G33	55	CH30
Idovie Rd, G52	47	BE34
Idragon Rd, G34	41	CJ30
Idric Rd, G13	19	BE23
Idwin Av, G13	19	BF21
Ierno Dr, G52	48	BG34
Iifluig St, G34	41	CH28
Ifour St, G20	21	BM23
Ifron Rd, G51	48	BG30
Ifron Rd, Pais. PA1	46	AZ32
Igair Dr, Pais. PA1	45	AX32
Igair Pl, G22	36	BR24
Igair Ter, G32	54	CD32
Iglass Gdns, G22	36	BR25
Igonie Dr, Pais. PA2	58	AS36
Igonie Rd, G52	58	BG33
Igonie Wds, Pais. PA2	58	AS36
Igownie Cres, (Thornlie.) G46	76	BJ43
Igraybank St, G21	37	BV25
Igray Cres, (Barr.) G78	74	AZ43
Igrayhill Rd, G21	23	BV24
Iintore St, G32	53	CC32
Iiol La, G3	9	BP28
Iiol St, G3	9	BP28
Ilaig Cres, (Stepps) G33	26	CE24
Ilantay Quad, G45	80	BW42
Ilantay Rd, G45	80	BW42
Ilantay Ter, G45	80	BW42
Ilantrae Ct, G3	13	BP30
Ilantyne Av, G52	46	BC30
Ilater Dr, Pais. PA2	59	AV36
Ilater Dr, (Inch.) Renf. PA4	16	AT22
Ilater Pl, G5	51	BT33
Ilater Rd, G13	14	BS32
Ilindalloch Dr, G31	38	BW29
Iloch Gdns, G52	48	BH34
Iloch (Ruther.) G73	66	BZ37
Ilochmyle Cres, G53	61	BC37
Ilochmyle Dr, G53	61	BC36
Ilochmyle Gdns, G53	61	BC36
Ilochmyle Pl, G53	61	BC37
Ilogie Rd, G44	64	BR38
Imartin Rd, G23	21	BM20
Imerino Pl, (Bishop.) G64	24	BZ21
Imoral Cres, (Inch.) Renf. PA4	16	AU22
Imoral Dr, G32	68	CD37
Imoral Dr, (Camb.) G72	81	CA40
Imoral Gdns, (Udd.) G71	70	CP36
Imoral Gdns, (Blan.) G72	84	CL43
Imore Pl, G22	22	BR23
Imore Rd, G22	22	BR22
Imore Sq, G22	22	BR24
Iornock Rd, G21	24	BW24
Iornock Rd, (Bishop.) G64	24	BW23
Iruddery Pl, (Bishop.) G64	24	BZ21
Ishagray Av, G11	34	BG26
Ishagray Dr, G11	34	BG26
Ishagray La, G11	34	BH27
Baltic La, G40	52	BW34
Baltic Pl, G40	52	BW33
Baltic St, G40	52	BW33
Balvaird Cres, (Ruther.) G73	66	BW38
Balvaird Dr, (Ruther.) G73	66	BW38
Balvenie St, G33	40	CF27
Balvicar Dr, G42	64	BP36
Balvicar St, G42	64	BP36
Balvie Av, G15	18	BC20
Balvie Av, (Giff.) G46	77	BM43
Banavie Rd, G11	34	BJ26
Banchory Av, G43	76	BK40
Banchory Av, (Inch.) Renf. PA4	16	AT22
Bangorshill St, (Thornlie.) G46	76	BH41
Bankbrae Av, G53	61	BC39
Bankend St, G33	39	CC28
Bankfoot Dr, G52	47	BD33
Bankfoot Rd, G52	47	BD33
Bankhall St, G42	64	BR35
Bankhead Av, G13	18	BC23
Bankhead Av, Coat. ML5	57	CS33
Bankhead Dr, (Ruther.) G73	66	BW38
Bankhead Pl, Coat. ML5	57	CS33
Bankhead Rd, (Ruther.) G73	65	BV39
Banknock St, G32	53	CA31
Bank Rd, G32	68	CE37
Bank St, G12	8	BN27
Bank St, (Camb.) G72	67	CC39
Bank St, (Barr.) G78	73	AY43
Bank St, Pais. PA1	45	AV33
Bannatyne Av, G31	52	BX30
Bannercross Av, (Baill.) G69	55	CJ32
Bannercross Dr, (Baill.) G69	55	CJ32
Bannercross Gdns, (Baill.) G69	55	CJ32
Banner Dr, G13	19	BE20
Banner Rd, G13	19	BE20
Bantaskin St, G20	21	BL22
Banton Pl, G33	55	CJ30
Barassie Ct, (Both.) G71	85	CP43
Barbae Pl, (Both.) G71	85	CQ42
Barberry Av, G53	75	BD43
Barberry Gdns, G53	75	BD43
Barberry Pl, G53	75	BD43
Barcaldine Av, (Chry.) G69	27	CK21
Barclay Sq, Renf. PA4	31	AX28
Barcraigs Dr, Pais. PA2	59	AV37
Bard Av, G13	19	BD21
Bardowie St, G22	36	BR25
Bardrain Rd, Pais. PA2	58	AS38
Bardrill Dr, (Bishop.) G64	23	BU20
Barfillan Dr, G52	48	BG32
Barfillan Rd, G52	48	BG33
Bargany Ct, G53	61	BC36
Bargany Pl, G53	61	BC36
Bargany Rd, G53	61	BC36
Bargaran Rd, G53	47	BD34
Bargarron Dr, Pais. PA3	45	AW30
Bargeddie St, G33	39	BZ27
Barholm Sq, G33	40	CF27
Barlanark Av, G32	54	CE30
Barlanark Cres, G33	54	CF30
Barlanark Dr, G33	54	CF30
Barlanark Pl, G32	54	CD31
Barlanark Pl, G33	54	CG30
Barlanark Rd, G33	54	CF30
Barlia Dr, G45	79	BU42
Barlia Gdns, G45	79	BU42
Barlia St, G45	79	BU42
Barlia Ter, G45	79	BU42
Barloch St, G22	36	BS25
Barlogan Av, G52	48	BG32
Barlogan Quad, G52	48	BG32
Barmulloch Rd, G21	38	BW25
Barnbeth Rd, G53	61	BD35
Barnes Rd, G20	22	BQ23
Barness Pl, G33	39	CC29
Barnes St, (Barr.) G78	73	AX43
Barnflat St, (Ruther.) G73	66	BX36
Barns St, Clyde. G81	17	AY21
Barnton St, G32	53	CA30
Barnwell Ter, G51	48	BG30
Barochan Rd, G53	47	BD34
Baronald Dr, G12	21	BK23
Baronald Gate, G12	21	BK23
Baronald St, (Ruther.) G73	66	BX36
Baron Rd, Pais. PA3	45	AW31
Barons Gate, (Both.) G71	84	CN41
Baron St, Renf. PA4	31	AY27
Barony Dr, (Baill.) G69	55	CK31
Barony Gdns, (Baill.) G69	55	CK32
Barony Wynd, (Baill.) G69	55	CK31
Barra Av, Renf. PA4	31	AY28
Barrachnie Av, (Baill.) G69	55	CJ31
Barrachnie Ct, (Baill.) G69	55	CH31
Barrachnie Cres, (Baill.) G69	55	CH32
Barrachnie Dr, (Baill.) G69	55	CJ31
Barrachnie Gro, (Baill.) G69	55	CJ31
Barrachnie Pl, (Baill.) G69	55	CJ31
Barrachnie Rd, (Baill.) G69	55	CH32
Barrack St, G4	15	BU31
Barra St, G20	21	BL21
Barrbridge Rd, (Baill.) G69	57	CR33
Barr Gro, (Udd.) G71	71	CQ37
Barrhead Rd, G43	62	BG38
Barrhead Rd, G53	60	BB39
Barrhead Rd, Pais. PA2	45	AV34
Barrie Rd, G52	46	BC30
Barrington Dr, G4	9	BP27
Barrisdale Rd, G20	21	BM21
Barrland Dr, (Giff.) G46	77	BL42
Barrland St, G41	50	BO34
Barrmill Rd, G43	76	BJ40
Barrowfield St, G40	52	BW32
Barr Pl, Pais. PA1	44	AT33
Barr St, G20	30	BQ26
Barrwood St, G33	39	CA27
Barscube Ter, Pais. PA2	59	AW35
Barshaw Dr, Pais. PA1	45	AW31
Barshaw Pl, Pais. PA1	45	AW31
Barshaw Rd, G52	46	BA31
Barterholm Rd, Pais. PA2	58	AU35
Bartholomew St, G40	52	BW34
Bartiebeith Rd, G33	54	CG30
Bassett Av, G13	19	BD21
Bassett Cres, G13	19	BD21
Bathgate St, G31	52	BW31
Bathgo Av, Pais. PA1	46	BA33
Bath La, G2	9	BQ29
Bath St, G2	9	BQ29
Batson St, G42	64	BR35
Battlefield Av, G42	64	BQ38
Battlefield Gdns, G42	64	BQ37
Battlefield Rd, G42	64	BQ37
Battle Pl, G41	64	BP37
Battles Burn Dr, G32	67	CC35
Battles Burn Gate, G32	67	CC35
Battles Burn Vw, G32	67	CC35
Bavelaw St, G33	40	CF27
Beaconsfield Rd, G12	20	BK24
Beard Cres, (Gart.) G69	29	CP24
Beardmore Cotts, (Inch.) Renf. PA4	16	AU23

Name	Pg	Grid
Beardmore Way, G31	52	BX31
Bearford Dr, G52	47	BD32
Bearsden Rd, G13	20	BH23
Bearsden Rd, (Bears.) G61	20	BH23
Beaton Rd, G41	63	BN35
Beattock St, G31	53	BZ32
Beaufort Av, G43	63	BL39
Beaufort Gdns, (Bishop.) G64	23	BU20
Beauly Pl, G20	21	BM23
Beauly Pl, (Chry.) G69	28	CM20
Beauly Rd, (Baill.) G69	55	CJ34
Beaumont Gate, G12	35	BL26
Beckfield Dr, G33	25	BZ22
Beckfield Gro, G33	25	BZ22
Bedale Rd, (Baill.) G69	55	CH33
Bedford La, G5	14	BR32
Bedford St, G5	14	BR32
Bedlay Vw, (Udd.) G71	71	CR36
Beech Av, G41	49	BK32
Beech Av, (Baill.) G69	55	CJ32
Beech Av, (Camb.) G72	67	CB39
Beech Av, (Ruther.) G73	89	BY41
Beech Av, Pais. PA2	59	AW36
Beech Cres, (Camb.) G72	83	CG41
Beech Gdns, (Baill.) G69	55	CJ32
Beech Gro, (Gart.) G69	29	CQ24
Beechgrove Av, (Udd.) G71	71	CS38
Beechgrove St, G40	66	BX35
Beechlands Av, G44	77	BN43
Beech Pl, (Bishop.) G64	24	BX21
Beech Rd, (Bishop.) G64	24	BX21
Beechwood, (Ruther.) G73	66	BY39
Beechwood Dr, G11	34	BH25
Beechwood Dr, Renf. PA4	31	AX28
Beechwood Gdns, (Mood.) G69	29	CP20
Beechwood Gro, (Barr.) G78	73	AY44
Beechwood Pl, G11	34	BH25
Beecroft Pl, (Blan.) G72	84	CN44
Beil Dr, G13	18	BB22
Beith St, G11	34	BK28
Belgrave La, G12	35	BN26
Belgrave Ter, G12	35	BN26
Belhaven Pk, (Muir.) G69	28	CL22
Belhaven Ter, G12	35	BL25
Belhaven Ter, (Ruther.) G73	66	BY39
Belhaven Ter La, G12	35	BL25
Belhaven Ter W, G12	35	BL25
Belhaven Ter W La, G12	35	BL25
Bellahouston Dr, G52	48	BG34
Bellahouston La, G52	48	BG33
Bellairs Pl, (Blan.) G72	84	CL44
Belleisle Av, (Udd.) G71	70	CN39
Belleisle St, G42	64	BR36
Bellevue Pl, G21	37	BV28
Bellfield Cres, (Barr.) G78	73	AX41
Bellfield St, G31	52	BW31
Bellflower Av, G53	75	BD42
Bellflower Gdns, G53	75	BE42
Bellflower Pl, G53	75	BE42
Bellgrove St, G31	51	BV31
Bellrock Ct, G33	54	CD29
Bellrock Cres, G33	39	CC29
Bellrock St, G33	39	CC29
Bellscroft Av, (Ruther.) G73	65	BV38
Bellshaugh Ct, G12	21	BL24
Bellshaugh Gdns, G12	21	BL24
Bellshaugh La, G12	21	BL24
Bellshaugh Pl, G12	21	BL24
Bellshaugh Rd, G12	21	BL24
Bellshill Rd, (Udd.) G71	85	CP40
Bell St, G1	15	BT31
Bell St, G4	15	BT31
Bell St, Clyde. G81	18	AZ22
Bell St, Renf. PA4	32	AZ25
Bellview Ct, Renf. PA4	32	AZ25
Bellwood St, G41	63	BN38
Belmont Av, (Udd.) G71	70	CN38
Belmont Cres, G12	35	BN26
Belmont Dr, (Giff.) G46	77	BK42
Belmont Dr, (Ruther.) G73	65	BX38
Belmont Dr, (Barr.) G78	74	AZ44
Belmont La, G12	35	BN26
Belmont Rd, G21	23	BV23
Belmont Rd, (Camb.) G72	81	CA41
Belmont Rd, Pais. PA3	45	AW31
Belmont St, G12	35	BN26
Belmont St, Clyde. G81	17	AX21
Belses Dr, G52	47	BE32
Belses Gdns, G52	47	BE32
Belstane Pl, (Both.) G71	85	CQ42
Beltane St, G3	9	BP29
Beltrees Av, G53	61	BC35
Beltrees Cres, G53	60	BC36
Beltrees Rd, G53	60	BC36
Bemersyde Av, G43	76	BK40
Ben Aigan Pl, G53	75	BF41
Ben Alder Dr, Pais. PA2	60	AZ36
Benalder St, G11	35	BL28
Ben Buie Way, Pais. PA2	60	AZ36
Bencroft Dr, G44	79	BU40
Bengairn St, G31	52	BY30
Bengal St, G43	63	BL38
Benhar Pl, G33	53	CB30
Benholm St, G32	53	CB34
Ben Hope Av, Pais. PA2	60	AZ35
Ben Lawers Dr, Pais. PA2	60	AZ35
Ben Ledi Av, Pais. PA2	60	AZ35
Ben Loyal Av, Pais. PA2	60	AZ35
Benmore St, G21	23	BV23
Bennan Sq, G42	65	BS35
Benn Av, Pais. PA1	45	AW33
Ben Nevis Rd, Pais. PA2	59	AY36
Benny Lynch Ct, G5	14	BS32
Ben Oss Pl, G53	75	BE41
Bent Cres, (Udd.) G71	71	CS39
Benthall St, G5	51	BT33
Bentinck St, G3	8	BN28
Bents Rd, (Baill.) G69	55	CK32
Ben Uird Pl, G53	75	BF41
Ben Vane Av, Pais. PA2	59	AY36
Ben Venue Way, Pais. PA2	60	AZ36
Benview St, G20	36	BP25
Benview Ter, Pais. PA2	59	AX35
Ben Vorlich Dr, G53	75	BF41
Ben Vorlich Pl, G53	75	BF41
Ben Wyvis Dr, Pais. PA2	59	AY36
Berelands Cres, (Ruther.) G73	65	BU38
Berelands Pl, (Ruther.) G73	65	BV38
Beresford Av, G14	34	BG25
Berkeley St, G3	8	BN29
Berkeley Ter La, G3	9	BP29
Berkley Dr, (Blan.) G72	84	CL44
Bernard Path, G40	52	BW33
Bernard St, G40	52	BW33
Bernard Ter, G40	52	BW33
Berneray St, G22	23	BS22
Berriedale Av, (Baill.) G69	55	CJ33
Berryburn Rd, G21	38	BY25
Berryhill Dr, (Giff.) G46	76	BK43
Berryhill Rd, (Giff.) G46	77	BK44
Berryknowe Av, (Chry.) G69	28	CL22
Berryknowes Av, G52	47	BE32
Berryknowes Dr, G52	47	BF3…
Berryknowes La, G52	47	BE3…
Berryknowes Rd, G52	47	BE3…
Bertram St, G41	63	BN3…
Bervie St, G51	48	BH3…
Berwick Dr, G52	47	BE3…
Berwick Dr, (Ruther.) G73	66	BZ3…
Beverley Rd, G43	63	BM3…
Bevin Av, Clyde. G81	18	AZ2…
Bideford Cres, G32	54	CF3…
Biggar St, G31	52	BX3…
Bigton St, G33	40	CD2…
Bilsland Ct, G20	22	BR2…
Bilsland Dr, G20	22	BP2…
Binend Rd, G53	61	BE3…
Binnie Pl, G40	15	BU3…
Binns Rd, G33	40	CE3…
Birch Dr, (Camb.) G72	68	CE3…
Birchend Dr, G21	38	BW2…
Birchend Pl, G21	38	BW2…
Birchfield Dr, G14	33	BD2…
Birch Gro, (Udd.) G71	71	CR3…
Birch Knowe, (Bishop.) G64	24	BX2…
Birchlea Dr, (Giff.) G46	77	BM4…
Birch Pl, (Camb.) G72	83	CH4…
Birchwood Av, G32	54	CG3…
Birchwood Dr, Pais. PA2	59	AW3…
Birchwood Pl, G32	54	CG3…
Birdston Rd, G21	24	BY…
Birgidale Rd, G45	79	BT4…
Birgidale Ter, G45	79	BT4…
Birkdale Ct, (Both.) G71	85	CP4…
Birkenshaw Ind Est, (Udd.) G71	70	CN…
Birkenshaw St, (Gart.) G69	29	CS3…
Birkenshaw St, G31	52	BX…
Birkenshaw Way, Pais. PA3	30	AU…
Birkhall Av, G52	46	BB…
Birkhall Av, (Inch.) Renf. PA4	16	AT…
Birkmyre Rd, G51	48	BH…
Birmingham Rd, Renf. PA4	31	AX…
Birness Dr, G43	63	BM…
Birnie Ct, G21	38	BY…
Birnie Rd, G21	38	BY…
Birnock Av, Renf. PA4	32	BA…
Birsay Rd, G22	22	BR…
Bishopmill Pl, G21	38	BY…
Bishopmill Rd, G21	24	BY…
Bishopsgate Dr, G21	23	BU…
Bishopsgate Gdns, G21	23	BU…
Bishopsgate Pl, G21	23	BU…
Bishopsgate Rd, G21	23	BU…
Bishop St, G3	13	BQ…
Blackburn Sq, (Barr.) G78	74	AZ…
Blackburn St, G51	12	BM…
Blackbyres Ct, (Barr.) G78	74	AZ…
Blackbyres Rd, (Barr.) G78	59	AY…
Blackcroft Gdns, G32	54	CF…
Blackcroft Rd, G32	54	CF…
Blackfaulds Rd, (Ruther.) G73	65	BU…
Blackford Rd, Pais. PA2	45	AW…
Blackfriars St, G1	15	BT…
Blackhall La, Pais. PA1	45	AV…
Blackhall St, Pais. PA1	45	AV…
Blackhill Cotts, G23	22	BQ…
Blackie St, G3	8	BM…
Blackland Gro, Pais. PA2	58	AS…
Blacklaw La, Pais. PA3	44	AU…
Blackstone Av, G53	61	BE…
Blackstone Cres, G53	61	BE…
Black St, G4	11	BT…
Blackthorn St, G22	23	BU…
Blackwood St, G13	20	BG…
Blackwood St, (Barr.) G78	73	AX…
Bladda La, Pais. PA1	44	AV…

Street	Page	Grid
ades Ct, (Gart.) G69	29	CQ23
aeloch Av, G45	78	BS44
aeloch Dr, G45	78	BR44
aeloch Ter, G45	78	BR44
airatholl Av, G11	34	BJ26
airbeth Dr, G44	64	BR38
aireth Rd, (Ruther.) G73	80	BW40
air Dr, G20	21	BL22
air Cres, (Baill.) G69	55	CJ34
airdardie Dr, G15	19	BD20
airdardie Rd, G13	19	BD20
airdardie Rd, G15	19	BD20
airgowrie Rd, G52	47	BE33
airlogie St, G33	40	CE29
antyre Ferme Rd, (Udd.) G71	70	CL39
antyre Mill Rd, (Both.) G71	85	CP44
antyre Rd, (Both.) G71	85	CQ43
antyre St, G3	8	BM28
aven Ct, (Baill.) G69	56	CL33
awarthill St, G14	18	BB24
enheim Av, (Stepps) G33	26	CF25
enheim Ct, (Stepps) G33	26	CF25
enheim Av, Pais. PA1	44	AT32
enheim Cres, (Stepps) G33	26	CG23
ochairn Rd, G21	38	BZ26
uebell Gdns, G45	80	BW43
yth Pl, G33	54	CF31
yth Rd, G33	54	CG31
ythswood Dr, Pais. PA3	44	AT31
ythswood Retail Pk, Renf. PA4	31	AX25
ythswood Pl, Renf. PA4	17	AY24
clair St, G2	13	BQ30
clair Cres, (Bishop.) G64	24	BW20
clair St, G13	20	BG21
den Ind Est, G40	52	BX30
den St, G40	52	BW33
gany Ter, G45	79	BU43
gbain Rd, G34	41	CJ29
gbaknowe, (Udd.) G71	70	CM37
ghall Rd, (Udd.) G71	69	CJ35
ghall St, G33	40	CD29
ghead Rd, G21	24	BW20
gleshole Rd, (Camb.) G72	67	CA38
gmoor Pl, G51	33	BE28
gmoor Rd, G51	33	BE29
gside Rd, G33	25	CC24
gside St, G40	52	BX33
gton Av, G44	78	BP41
gton Av La, G44	78	BP41
leyn Rd, G41	63	BN35
plivar Ter, G42	64	BS37
plivar Dr, G42	64	BQ37
n Accord Sq, Clyde. G81	17	AX21
ness St, G40	52	BX33
pnhill St, G22	36	BR26
pnar St, G40	52	BW34
nnyholm Av, G53	47	BC34
pnyrigg Dr, G43	76	BJ40
pnyton Av, G13	18	BB23
Borden La, G13	20	BG24
Borden Rd, G13	20	BG24
Boreland Dr, G13	19	BC22
Boreland Pl, G13	19	BD23
Borgie Cres, (Camb.) G72	81	CC40
Borron St, G4	36	BS26
Borthwick St, G33	40	CD28
Boswell Ct, G42	64	BQ38
Boswell Sq, G52	46	BB30
Botanic Cres, G20	35	BM25
Botanic Cres La, G20	35	BM25
Bothlin Dr, (Stepps) G33	26	CF23
Bothlyn Cres, (Gart.) G69	28	CN22
Bothlyn Rd, (Chry.) G69	28	CM21
Bothwell La, G2	13	BQ30
Bothwellpark Ind Est, (Udd.) G71	85	CQ40
Bothwellpark Rd, (Both.) G71	85	CS42
Bothwell Rd, (Udd.) G71	84	CP40
Bothwell St, G2	9	BQ30
Bothwell St, (Camb.) G72	67	CA39
Bourne Ct, (Inch.) Renf. PA4	16	AT22
Bourne Cres, (Inch.) Renf. PA4	16	AT22
Bourock Sq, (Barr.) G78	74	BA44
Bouverie St, G14	18	BA23
Bouverie St, (Ruther.) G73	79	BV40
Bowden Dr, G52	47	BD31
Bower St, G12	35	BN26
Bowes Cres, (Baill.) G69	55	CH33
Bowfield Av, G52	46	BB31
Bowfield Cres, G52	46	BB31
Bowfield Dr, G52	46	BB31
Bowfield Pl, G52	46	BB31
Bowhouse Way, (Ruther.) G73	80	BW41
Bowling Grn La, G14	33	BF26
Bowling Grn Rd, G14	33	BF26
Bowling Grn Rd, G32	54	CF33
Bowling Grn Rd, (Chry.) G69	28	CM21
Bowman St, G42	64	BQ35
Bowmont Gdns, G12	35	BL26
Bowmont Pl, (Camb.) G72	82	CF40
Bowmont Ter, G12	35	BL26
Bowmore Gdns, (Udd.) G71	70	CN37
Bowmore Rd, G52	48	BG32
Boydstone Pl, (Thornlie.) G46	76	BH40
Boydstone Rd, G43	76	BF40
Boydstone Rd, G53	76	BD40
Boyd St, G42	64	BR36
Boylestone Rd, (Barr.) G78	73	AW41
Boyle St, Clyde. G81	18	AZ21
Boyndie Path, G34	41	CK29
Boyndie St, G34	41	CK29
Brabloch Cres, Pais. PA3	45	AV31
Brackla Av, G13	18	BA21
Brackla Av, Clyde. G81	18	BA21
Bracken Ter, (Both.) G71	85	CQ42
Bradan Av, G13	18	BA22
Bradan Av, Clyde. G81	18	BA22
Bradda Av, (Ruther.) G73	80	BY41
Bradfield Av, G12	21	BL24
Braefield Dr, (Thornlie.) G46	76	BJ42
Braefoot Cres, Pais. PA2	58	AU38
Braehead Rd, Pais. PA2	58	AS39
Braehead Shop Cen, G51	32	BC26
Braehead St, G5	51	BT34
Braemar Ct, G44	77	BN41
Braemar Cres, Pais. PA2	59	AV36
Braemar Dr, (Ruther.) G73	81	CA42
Braemar Rd, (Inch.) Renf. PA4	16	AT22
Braemar St, G42	64	BP38
Braemore Gdns, G22	37	BT25
Braemount Av, Pais. PA2	58	AS39
Braes Av, Clyde. G81	18	AZ20
Braeside Av, (Ruther.) G73	66	BY38
Braeside Cres, (Baill.) G69	56	CP32
Braeside Cres, (Barr.) G78	74	BA44
Braeside Dr, (Barr.) G78	74	AZ44
Braeside Pl, (Camb.) G72	82	CD41
Braeside St, G20	36	BP26
Braidbar Fm Rd, (Giff.) G46	77	BM41
Braidbar Rd, (Giff.) G46	77	BL42
Braidcraft Rd, G53	61	BE36
Braidfauld Gdns, G32	53	CB35
Braidfauld Pl, G32	67	CB35
Braidfauld St, G32	53	CB35
Braidholm Cres, (Giff.) G46	77	BL42
Braidholm Rd, (Giff.) G46	77	BL42
Braidpark Dr, (Giff.) G46	77	BM42
Braids Circle, Pais. PA2	58	AU36
Braids Ct, Pais. PA2	58	AU36
Braids Dr, G53	60	BB36
Braids Gait, Pais. PA2	58	AT36
Braid Sq, G4	9	BQ27
Braids Rd, Pais. PA2	58	AU36
Braid St, G4	9	BQ27
Branchock Av, (Camb.) G72	82	CF41
Brandon Gdns, (Camb.) G72	81	CA40
Brandon St, G31	51	BV31
Brand Pl, G51	49	BL31
Brand St, G51	49	BL31
Branklyn Ct, G13	19	BF23
Branklyn Cres, G13	19	BF23
Branklyn Gro, G13	19	BF23
Branklyn Pl, G13	19	BF23
Brassey St, G20	21	BN23
Breadalbane Gdns, (Ruther.) G73	81	BZ41
Brechin Rd, (Bishop.) G64	24	BY20
Brechin St, G3	8	BN29
Bredisholm Cres, (Udd.) G71	71	CS36
Bredisholm Dr, (Baill.) G69	56	CL33
Bredisholm Rd, (Baill.) G69	56	CL33
Bredisholm Ter, (Baill.) G69	56	CL33
Brenfield Av, G44	78	BP41
Brenfield Dr, G44	78	BP41
Brenfield Rd, G44	78	BP41
Brent Av, (Thornlie.) G46	76	BH40
Brent Dr, (Thornlie.) G46	76	BH40
Brent Gdns, (Thornlie.) G46	76	BJ40
Brent Rd, (Thornlie.) G46	76	BH40
Brent Way, (Thornlie.) G46	76	BH40
Brentwood Av, G53	75	BC41
Brentwood Dr, G53	75	BC41
Brentwood Sq, G53	75	BD41

Street	Page	Grid
Brereton St, G42	64	BS36
Bressay Rd, G33	55	CG31
Breval Ct, (Baill.) G69	56	CL33
Brewster Av, Pais. PA3	45	AW30
Briarcroft Dr, G33	25	BZ22
Briarcroft Pl, G33	25	CA23
Briarcroft Rd, G33	25	BZ23
Briar Gdns, G43	77	BM40
Briar Gro, G43	77	BM40
Briarlea Dr, (Giff.) G46	77	BL41
Briar Rd, G43	77	BM40
Briarwood Ct, G32	69	CG35
Bridgegate, G1	14	BS31
Bridge St, G5	14	BR31
Bridge St, (Camb.) G72	67	CC39
Bridge St, Pais. PA1	44	AU33
Bridgeton Business Centre, G40	51	BV32
Bridgeton Cross, G40	51	BV32
Brighton Pl, G51	49	BK31
Brighton St, G51	48	BK31
Brightside Av, (Udd.) G71	85	CP40
Bright St, G21	37	BW28
Brisbane St, (Giff.) G46	77	BM42
Brisbane St, G42	64	BQ38
Britannia Way, Renf. PA4	31	AY28
Briton St, G51	48	BK31
Broadford St, G4	10	BS27
Broadholm St, G22	22	BR23
Broadlie Dr, G13	19	BC23
Broadloan, Renf. PA4	31	AY27
Broad St, G40	51	BV32
Broadwood Dr, G44	64	BR39
Brockburn Cres, G53	61	BD37
Brockburn Pl, G53	60	BC35
Brockburn Rd, G53	61	BC35
Brockburn Ter, G53	61	BE37
Brock Oval, G53	61	BE39
Brock Pl, G53	61	BE38
Brock Rd, G53	61	BE39
Brock Ter, G53	61	BE38
Brockville St, G32	53	CB31
Brodick Sq, (Bishop.) G64	24	BX22
Brodick St, G21	38	BW28
Brodie Gdns, (Baill.) G69	56	CL31
Brodie Pk Av, Pais. PA2	58	AU35
Brodie Pk Cres, Pais. PA2	58	AT35
Brodie Pk Gdns, Pais. PA2	58	AU35
Brodie Rd, G21	24	BZ22
Brookfield Av, G33	24	BZ22
Brookfield Cor, G33	25	BZ22
Brookfield Dr, G33	25	BZ22
Brookfield Pl, G33	25	BZ22
Brookfield Rd, G33	25	BZ22
Brooklands Av, (Udd.) G71	70	CN38
Brooklea Dr, (Giff.) G46	77	BL40
Brookside St, G40	52	BW32
Brook St, G40	51	BV32
Broom Cres, (Barr.) G78	73	AW40
Broomdyke Way, Pais. PA3	30	AT29
Broomfield La, G21	23	BV24
Broomfield Pl, G21	23	BV24
Broomfield Rd, G21	23	BV24
Broomfield Ter, (Udd.) G71	71	CP36
Broomhill Av, G11	34	BH27
Broomhill Av, G32	68	CD37
Broomhill Dr, G11	34	BH26
Broomhill Dr, (Ruther.) G73	80	BX40
Broomhill Gdns, G11	34	BH26
Broomhill La, G11	34	BH26
Broomhill Path, G11	34	BH27
Broomhill Pl, G11	34	BH26
Broomhill Ter, G11	34	BH27
Broomieknowe Dr, (Ruther.) G73	66	BX39
Broomieknowe Gdns, (Ruther.) G73	66	BW39
Broomieknowe Rd, (Ruther.) G73	66	BX39
Broomielaw, G1	13	BQ31
Broomielaw, G2	13	BQ31
Broomknowes Rd, G21	38	BW25
Broomlands Av, Ersk. PA8	16	AT21
Broomlands Cres, Ersk. PA8	16	AT21
Broomlands Gdns, Ersk. PA8	16	AT21
Broomlands St, Pais. PA1	44	AS33
Broomlands Way, Ersk. PA8	16	AU21
Broomlea Cres, (Inch.) Renf. PA4	16	AS22
Broomley Dr, (Giff.) G46	77	BL44
Broomley La, (Giff.) G46	77	BL44
Broomloan Ct, G51	48	BJ32
Broomloan Pl, G51	48	BJ31
Broomloan Rd, G51	48	BJ31
Broompark Circ, G31	37	BV29
Broompark Dr, G31	51	BV30
Broompark Dr, (Inch.) Renf. PA4	16	AT22
Broompark La, G31	51	BV30
Broompark St, G31	51	BV30
Broompark, (Baill.) G69	55	CH34
Brora Dr, (Giff.) G46	77	BM40
Brora Dr, Renf. PA4	32	BA26
Brora Gdns, (Bishop.) G64	24	BX20
Brora Rd, (Bishop.) G64	24	BX20
Brora St, G33	38	BZ28
Broughton Dr, G23	21	BN21
Broughton Rd, G23	21	BN21
Brown Av, Clyde. G81	18	BA21
Brownhill Rd, G43	77	BK41
Brownlie St, G42	64	BR37
Brown Pl, (Camb.) G72	67	CC39
Brownsdale Rd, (Ruther.) G73	65	BV38
Brownside Av, (Camb.) G72	81	CA40
Brownside Av, (Barr.) G78	73	AW40
Brownside Av, Pais. PA2	58	AS38
Brownside Cres, (Barr.) G78	73	AW40
Brownside Dr, G13	18	BB23
Brownside Dr, (Barr.) G78	73	AW40
Brownside Gro, (Barr.) G78	73	AW40
Brownside Ms, (Camb.) G72	81	CA40
Brownside Rd, (Camb.) G72	81	CA40
Brownside Rd, (Ruther.) G73	80	BZ40
Brownsland Ct, (Gart.) G69	29	CP23
Browns La, Pais. PA1	44	AU33
Brown St, G2	13	BQ30
Brown St, Pais. PA1	44	AS32
Brown St, Renf. PA4	31	AX27
Bruce Av, Pais. PA3	45	AW30
Brucefield Pl, G34	42	CM29
Bruce Rd, G41	49	BN33
Bruce Rd, Pais. PA3	45	AW31
Bruce Rd, Renf. PA4	31	AW28
Bruce St, Clyde. G81	17	AX20
Bruce Ter, (Blan.) G72	84	CN44
Brunstane Rd, G34	41	CJ28
Brunswick St, G1	14	BS30
Brunton St, G44	78	BD40
Brunton Ter, G44	78	BP41
Bruntsfield Av, G53	75	BD42
Bruntsfield Gdns, G53	75	BD42
Buccleuch Av, G52	32	BA29
Buccleuch La, G3	9	BQ…
Buccleuch St, G3	9	BQ…
Buchanan Business Pk, (Stepps) G33	27	CH…
Buchanan Cres, (Bishop.) G64	24	BY…
Buchanan Dr, (Bishop.) G64	24	BY…
Buchanan Dr, (Camb.) G72	67	CA…
Buchanan Dr, (Ruther.) G73	66	BX…
Buchanan Gdns, G32	68	CG…
Buchanan Gro, (Baill.) G69	55	CK…
Buchanan St, G1	14	BR…
Buchanan St, (Baill.) G69	55	CK…
Buchanan Ter, (Camb.) G72	81	CA…
Buchlyvie Gdns, (Bishop.) G64	23	BV…
Buchlyvie Path, G34	56	CL…
Buchlyvie Rd, Pais. PA1	46	BA…
Buchlyvie St, G34	55	CK…
Buckingham Dr, G32	68	CD…
Buckingham Dr, (Ruther.) G73	66	BX…
Buckingham St, G12	35	BM…
Buckingham Ter, G12	35	BM…
Bucklaw Gdns, G52	47	BE…
Bucklaw Pl, G52	47	BE…
Bucklaw Ter, G52	47	BE…
Buckley St, G22	23	BJ…
Bucksburn Rd, G21	38	BY…
Buckthorne Pl, G53	75	BD…
Buddon St, G40	52	BY…
Budhill Av, G32	54	CD…
Bulldale Ct, G14	18	BA…
Bulldale Rd, G14	18	BA…
Bulldale St, G14	18	BA…
Buller Cres, (Blan.) G72	84	CL…
Bullionslaw Dr, (Ruther.) G73	66	BZ…
Bulloch Av, (Giff.) G46	77	BM…
Bullwood Av, G53	60	BB…
Bullwood Ct, G53	60	BB…
Bullwood Dr, G53	60	BB…
Bullwood Gdns, G53	60	BB…
Bullwood Pl, G53	60	BB…
Bunessan St, G52	48	BH…
Bunhouse Rd, G3	35	BL…
Burghead Dr, G51	48	BG…
Burghead Pl, G51	34	BG…
Burgher St, G32	52	BY…
Burgh Hall La, G11	34	BK…
Burgh Hall St, G11	34	BK…
Burgh La, G12	35	BM…
Burleigh Rd, (Both.) G71	85	CR…
Burleigh St, G51	34	BJ…
Burlington Av, G12	20	BK…
Burmola St, G22	36	BR…
Burnacre Gdns, (Udd.) G71	70	CN…
Burnbank Dr, (Barr.) G78	73	AY…
Burnbank Gdns, G20	9	BP…
Burnbank Pl, G4	15	BU…
Burnbank Ter, G20	9	BP…
Burnbrae Gdns, G53	61	BF…
Burnbrae St, G21	38	BW…
Burncleuch Av, (Camb.) G72	81	CC…
Burndyke Ct, G51	49	BK…
Burndyke Sq, G51	49	BL…
Burndyke St, G51	49	BK…
Burnett Rd, G33	54	CG…
Burnfield Av, (Thornlie.) G46	77	BK…
Burnfield Cotts, (Thornlie.) G46	76	BK…
Burnfield Dr, G43	76	BK…
Burnfield Gdns, (Giff.) G46	77	BL…
Burnfield Rd, G43	76	BJ…
Burnfield Rd, (Thornlie.) G46	76	BK…

Name	No.	Grid
rnfoot Cres, (Ruther.) G73	80	BZ40
rnfoot Dr, G52	47	BD32
rnham Rd, G14	32	BC25
rnhead Rd, G43	77	BN40
rnhead Rd, (Udd.) G71	77	CR38
rnhill Quad, (Ruther.) G73	65	BV37
rnhill, (Ruther.) G73	65	BV37
rnhouse St, G20	21	BM23
rnmouth Rd, G33	55	CH31
rnpark Av, (Udd.) G71	70	CM38
rns Gdns, (Blan.) G72	84	CL44
rns Gro, (Thornlie.) G46	76	BJ44
rnside Av, (Barr.) G78	73	AX41
rnside Ct, (Ruther.) G73	80	BY40
rnside Rd, (Ruther.) G73	80	BY40
rns St, G4	10	BR27
rntbroom Av, (Baill.) G69	55	CH34
rntbroom Gdns, (Baill.) G69	55	CH34
rntbroom St, G33	40	CF29
rrells La, G4	15	BU30
rrelton Rd, G43	64	BN39
shes Av, Pais. PA2	58	AT36
sheyhill St, (Camb.) G72	81	CC40
te Av, Renf. PA4	32	AZ28
te Cres, Pais. PA2	58	AT38
te Gdns, G12	8	BM27
te Gdns, G44	78	BP41
te Rd, (Abbots.) Pais. PA3	30	AT28
te Ter, (Udd.) G71	71	CT38
te Ter, (Ruther.) G73	80	BW40
tterbiggins Rd, G42	50	BQ36
rebush Rd, G53	61	BE36
res Av, Pais. PA3	45	AW31
res Cres, Pais. PA3	45	AW31
res Rd, G11	35	BL27
ron Ct, (Both.) G71	85	CR43
ron St, G11	34	BJ27
shot St, G22	37	BT25
dder Pl, G20	21	BN22
dder Rd, G20	21	BN22
dder Rd, G23	21	BN22
doc St, (Camb.) G72	82	CD40
dogan St, G2	13	BQ30
dzow St, G2	13	BQ30
dr, G11	35	BK27
irn Av, Renf. PA4	32	BA28
irnban St, G51	47	BF31
irnbrook Rd, G34	42	CL29
ircraig St, G31	52	BY33
irndow Av, G44	78	BP41
irndow Av La, G44	78	BP41
irndow Ct, G44	78	BP41
irngorm Cres, (Barr.) G78	73	AU44
irngorm Cres, Pais. PA2	58	AU36
irngorm Rd, G43	77	BL40
irnhill Circ, G52	46	BB34
irnhill Dr, G52	46	BB34
irnhill Pl, G52	46	BB34
irnhill Rd, (Bears.) G61	29	BH20
irnlea Dr, G51	48	BK31
irns Av, (Camb.) G72	82	CD40
irns Rd, (Camb.) G72	82	CD41
irn St, G21	23	BV23
irnswell Av, (Camb.) G72	82	CE41
irnswell Pl, (Camb.) G72	82	CE41
Cairntoul Dr, G14	19	BC23
Cairntoul Pl, G14	19	BC23
Caithness St, G20	36	BP25
Calcots Pl, G34	42	CL28
Caldarvan St, G22	36	BR26
Calder Av, (Barr.) G78	73	AY45
Calderbank Vw, (Baill.) G69	56	CL34
Caldercuilt Rd, G20	21	BL21
Caldercuilt Rd, G23	21	BL20
Calder Dr, (Camb.) G72	81	CC40
Calderglen Av, (Blan.) G72	84	CL42
Calderpark Av, (Udd.) G71	69	CK35
Calderpark Cres, (Udd.) G71	69	CK35
Calder Pl, (Baill.) G69	55	CK35
Calder Rd, (Udd.) G71	83	CK40
Calder St, G42	64	BR35
Calderwood Av, (Baill.) G69	55	CJ34
Calderwood Dr, (Baill.) G69	55	CJ34
Calderwood Gdns, (Baill.) G69	55	CJ34
Calderwood Rd, G43	63	BM39
Calderwood Rd, (Ruther.) G73	66	BY38
Caldwell Av, G13	19	BC23
Caledonia Av, G5	51	BS34
Caledonia Av, (Ruther.) G73	66	BX37
Caledonia Dr, (Baill.) G69	56	CK34
Caledonian Pl, (Camb.) G72	82	CG40
Caledonia Rd, G5	51	BS34
Caledonia Rd, (Baill.) G69	55	CJ34
Caledonia St, G5	51	BS34
Caledonia St, Pais. PA3	44	AT31
Caledonia Way, (Abbots.) Pais. PA3	30	AT28
Caledonia Way E, (Abbots.) Pais. PA3	30	AU28
Caledonia Way W, (Abbots.) Pais. PA3	30	AT28
Caledon La, G12	35	BL26
Caledon St, G12	35	BL26
Caley Brae, (Udd.) G71	70	CP39
Calfhill Rd, G53	47	BD34
Calgary St, G4	10	BS28
Callaghan Wynd, (Blan.) G72	84	CL44
Callander St, G20	36	BQ26
Callieburn Rd, (Bishop.) G64	24	BW20
Calside, Pais. PA2	44	AU34
Calside Av, Pais. PA2	44	AT34
Calside Ct, Pais. PA2	58	AU35
Calvay Cres, G33	54	CG30
Calvay Pl, G33	54	CG30
Calvay Rd, G33	54	CF30
Cambridge Rd, Renf. PA4	31	AY27
Cambridge St, G2	10	BR29
Cambridge St, G3	10	BR29
Camburn St, G32	53	CB31
Camburn St, G32	53	CB31
Cambus Pl, G33	40	CE27
Cambusdoon Rd, G33	40	CE27
Cambus Kenneth Gdns, G32	54	CF32
Cambuskenneth Pl, G33	54	CF32
Cambuslang Ind Est, G32	67	CC38
Cambuslang Rd, G32	67	CA37
Cambuslang Rd, (Camb.) G72	67	BZ38
Cambuslang Rd, (Ruther.) G73	66	BX36
Cambusmore Pl, G33	40	CE27
Cambus Pl, G33	40	CE27
Camden Ter, G5	50	BS33
Camelon St, G32	53	CB31
Cameron Dr, (Udd.) G71	71	CR38
Cameron St, G52	47	BB32
Cameron St, Clyde. G81	17	AY21
Camlachie St, G31	52	BX32
Campbell Cres, (Both.) G71	85	CR41
Campbell Dr, (Barr.) G78	73	AY43
Campbell St, G20	21	BM22
Campbell St, Renf. PA4	32	AZ25
Camphill, Pais. PA1	44	AT34
Camphill Av, G41	63	BN38
Camphill Ct, Pais. PA2	44	AT34
Camp Rd, (Baill.) G69	55	CK32
Camp Rd, (Ruther.) G73	65	CX32
Campsie Av, (Barr.) G78	73	AY44
Campsie Cres, Renf. PA4	32	BA27
Campsie Dr, Pais. PA2	58	AT37
Campsie Dr, (Abbots.) Pais. PA3	30	AU28
Campsie Dr, Renf. PA4	31	AW29
Campsie Pl, (Chry.) G69	28	CL21
Campsie St, G21	23	BV24
Campsie Vw, (Stepps) G33	40	CF25
Campsie Vw, (Baill.) G69	56	CP32
Campsie Vw, (Chry.) G69	28	CL21
Campsie Vw, (Udd.) G71	71	CQ37
Campsie Vw, (Camb.) G72	82	CG42
Campston Pl, G33	40	CD28
Canal Bk La, G22	22	BQ21
Canal La, Renf. PA4	32	AZ25
Canal St, G4	10	BS28
Canal St, Clyde. G81	17	AX20
Canal St, Pais. PA1	44	AT33
Canal St, Renf. PA4	32	AZ25
Canal Ter, Pais. PA1	44	AT33
Canberra Ct, (Giff.) G46	77	BN42
Candleriggs, G1	15	BT31
Canmore Pl, G31	52	BZ33
Canmore St, G31	52	BZ33
Cannich Dr, Pais. PA2	59	AX36
Canonbie St, G34	42	CM28
Canting Way, G51	49	BL30
Capelrig St, (Thornlie.) G46	76	BH41
Caplaw Rd, Pais. PA2	58	AS39
Caplethill Rd, (Barr.) G78	58	AV38
Caplethill Rd, Pais. PA2	58	AV38
Caprington Pl, G33	39	CC28
Caprington St, G33	39	CC28
Carberry Rd, G41	63	BM35
Carbeth St, G22	36	BR25
Carbisdale St, G22	23	BU24
Carbost St, G23	21	BM20
Carbrook St, G21	38	BW28
Carbrook St, Pais. PA1	44	AS33
Cardarrach St, G21	24	BW24
Cardonald Dr, G52	47	BC34
Cardonald Gdns, G52	47	BC34
Cardonald Pl Rd, G52	47	BD33
Cardowan Dr, (Stepps) G33	26	CG24
Cardowan Pk, (Udd.) G71	71	CR36
Cardowan Rd, G32	53	CB31
Cardowan Rd, (Stepps) G33	26	CG23
Cardow Rd, G21	38	BY25
Cardrona St, G33	40	CD26
Cardross Ct, G31	51	BV30
Cardross St, G31	51	BV30
Cardyke St, G21	38	BW25
Careston Pl, (Bishop.) G64	24	BZ20
Carfin St, G42	64	BR35
Carfrae St, G3	35	BL29
Cargill Sq, (Bishop.) G64	24	BY21
Carham Cres, G52	47	BE32
Carham Dr, G52	47	BE32
Carillon Rd, G51	49	BL32
Carlaverock Rd, G43	63	BM39
Carleith Quad, G51	47	BF30
Carleston St, G21	37	BV25
Carleton Ct, (Giff.) G46	77	BL41

Carleton Dr, (Giff.) G46 77 BL41
Carleton Gate, (Giff.) G46 77 BL41
Carlibar Av, G13 18 BB23
Carlibar Dr, (Barr.) G78 73 AY42
Carlibar Gdns, (Barr.) G78 73 AY42
Carlibar Rd, (Barr.) G78 73 AY42
Carlile Pl, Pais. PA3 44 AU31
Carlisle St, G21 37 BT25
Carlisle Ter, Pais. PA3 44 AU31
Carloway Ct, G33 40 CD29
Carloway Av, (Blan.) G72 40 CL43
Carlton Ct, G5 14 BR31
Carlton Pl, G5 14 BR31
Carlyle Av, G52 32 BB29
Carlyle St, Pais. PA3 44 AU32
Carlyle Ter, (Ruther.) G73 66 BX36
Carmaben Rd, G33 40 CG29
Carment Dr, G41 63 BM37
Carment La, G41 63 BM37
Carmichael Pl, G42 64 BP38
Carmichael St, G51 49 BK31
Carmunnock Rd, G44 64 BR38
Carmunnock Rd, G45 58 BS40
Carmunnock Rd, (Busby) G76 79 BS44
Carmyle Av, G32 54 CD34
Carna Dr, G44 78 BS40
Carnarvon St, G3 9 BP28
Carnbooth Ct, G45 79 BV43
Carnegie Rd, G52 47 BC30
Carnock Rd, G53 61 BE37
Carnoustie Ct, (Both.) G71 85 CP43
Carnoustie Cres, (Bishop.) G64 24 BY20
Carnoustie Pl, G5 13 BP32
Carnoustie St, G5 13 BP32
Carntynehall Rd, G32 53 CB30
Carntyne Ind Est, G32 53 CA31
Carntyne Path, G32 53 BZ30
Carntyne Pl, G32 53 BZ30
Carntyne Rd, G31 52 BY31
Carntyne Rd, G32 53 BZ30
Carnwadric Rd, (Thornlie.) G46 76 BG41
Carnwath Av, G43 64 BP39
Caroline St, G31 53 CA32
Carrbridge Dr, G20 21 BM23
Carriagehill Av, Pais. PA2 58 AU35
Carriagehill Dr, Pais. PA2 58 AU36
Carrick Cres, (Giff.) G46 77 BL44
Carrick Dr, G32 54 CG34
Carrick Dr, (Ruther.) G73 80 BW40
Carrick Gro, G32 55 CG33
Carrick Rd, (Bishop.) G64 24 BY20
Carrick Rd, (Ruther.) G73 80 BW40
Carrick St, G2 10 BQ31
Carrick Way, (Both.) G71 85 CQ42
Carriden Pl, G33 54 CG30
Carrington St, G4 9 BP27
Carroglen Gdns, G32 54 CF32
Carroglen Gro, G32 54 CF32
Carron Ct, (Camb.) G72 82 CF40
Carron Cres, G22 23 BT24
Carron Cres, (Bishop.) G64 24 BX20
Carron Pl, G22 23 BU24
Carron St, G22 23 BU24
Carsaig Dr, G52 48 BG32
Carstairs St, G40 69 BW35
Carswell Gdns, G41 63 BN36
Cartbank Rd, G44 78 BQ41
Cartcraigs Rd, G43 62 BK39
Cartha Cres, Pais. PA2 44 AW34
Cartha St, G41 63 BM38
Cartside Quad, G42 64 BQ38

Cartside St, G42 64 BP38
Cart St, Clyde. G81 17 AX21
Cartvale La, Pais. PA3 44 AU31
Cartvale Rd, G42 64 BP38
Caskie Dr, (Blan.) G72 84 CN44
Cassley Av, Renf. PA4 32 BB27
Castle Av, (Udd.) G71 84 CN41
Castlebank Ct, G13 20 BG23
Castlebank Cres, G11 34 BJ28
Castlebank Gdns, G13 20 BG23
Castlebank St, G11 34 BH27
Castlebay Dr, G22 22 BS20
Castlebay Pl, G22 22 BS21
Castlebay St, G22 22 BS21
Castlebrae Gdns, G44 78 BR39
Castle Chimmins Av, (Camb.) G72 82 CF41
Castle Chimmins Rd, (Camb.) G72 82 CF42
Castlecroft Gdns, (Udd.) G71 84 CN40
Castlefern Rd, (Ruther.) G73 80 BX42
Castlefield Ct, G33 40 CD25
Castle Gait, Pais. PA1 44 AT34
Castle Gdns, (Chry.) G69 28 CP20
Castle Gate, (Udd.) G71 84 CN40
Castlelaw Gdns, G32 54 CD31
Castlelaw Pl, G32 54 CD31
Castlelaw St, G32 54 CD31
Castlemilk Arc, G45 79 BU42
Castlemilk Cres, G44 79 BU40
Castlemilk Dr, G45 79 BU43
Castlemilk Rd, G44 65 BU38
Castle Pl, (Udd.) G71 70 CN39
Castle St, G4 11 BU29
Castle St, G11 35 BL28
Castle St, (Baill.) G69 55 CJ34
Castle St, (Ruther.) G73 66 BW37
Castle St, Pais. PA1 44 AS33
Castleton Av, (Bishop.) G64 23 BU22
Castleton Ct, G45 79 BV43
Cathay St, G22 23 BS21
Cathcart Cres, Pais. PA2 44 AW34
Cathcart Pl, (Ruther.) G73 65 BV38
Cathcart Rd, G42 64 BR37
Cathcart Rd, (Ruther.) G73 65 BU38
Cathedral Sq, G4 11 BU30
Cathedral St, G1 10 BS29
Cathedral St, G4 10 BS29
Cathkin Av, (Camb.) G72 67 CA39
Cathkin Av, (Ruther.) G73 66 BY38
Cathkin Bypass, (Ruther.) G73 80 BZ42
Cathkin Ct, G45 79 BV43
Cathkin Pl, (Camb.) G72 67 CA39
Cathkin Rd, G42 64 BP38
Cathkin Rd, (Udd.) G71 70 CN36
Cathkin Rd, (Ruther.) G73 80 BY43
Cathkin Vw, G32 68 CD37
Cathkinview Pl, G42 64 BQ38
Cathkinview Rd, G42 64 BQ38
Catrine Ct, G53 61 BC37
Catrine Gdns, G53 60 BC37
Catrine Pl, G53 60 BC37
Catrine Rd, G53 60 BC37
Causewayside Cres, G32 67 CC35
Causewayside St, G32 67 CC35
Causeyside St, Pais. PA1 44 AU33
Cavendish Ct, G5 50 BR33
Cavendish Pl, G5 50 BR33
Cavendish St, G5 50 BR33
Cavin Dr, G45 79 BU41
Cavin Rd, G45 79 BU41
Cayton Gdns, (Baill.) G69 55 CH33
Cecil St, G12 21 BM26
Cedar Ct, G20 9 BQ27
Cedar Ct, (Camb.) G72 83 CG41

Cedar Dr, (Udd.) G71 71 CS…
Cedar Gdns, (Ruther.) G73 80 BY…
Cedar Rd, (Bishop.) G64 24 BX…
Cedar St, G20 9 BQ…
Cedar Wk, (Bishop.) G64 24 BX…
Cedric Pl, G13 19 BF…
Cedric Rd, G13 19 BF…
Celtic St, G20 21 BL…
Cemetery Rd, G52 47 BF…
Centenary Ct, (Barr.) G78 73 AX…
Centenary Ct, Clyde. G81 17 AX…
Central Av, (Udd.) G71 71 CS…
Central Av, (Camb.) G72 67 CB…
Central Gro, G32 54 CH…
Central Gro, (Camb.) G72 67 CC…
Central Path, G32 54 CG…
Central Rd, Pais. PA1 44 AU…
Central Sta, G1 14 BR…
Centre, The, (Barr.) G78 73 AX…
Centre St, (Glenb.) … 13 BC…
Ceres Gdns, (Bishop.) G64 24 BZ…
Cessnock Pl, (Camb.) G72 82 CF…
Cessnock Rd, G33 25 CC…
Cessnock St, G51 49 BI…
Chalmers Ct, G40 15 BU…
Chalmers St, G40 15 BU…
Chalmers St, Clyde. G81 17 AX…
Chamberlain La, G13 20 BG…
Chamberlain Rd, G13 20 BG…
Chancellor St, G11 35 BK…
Chapelhill Rd, Pais. PA2 59 AW…
Chapel St, G20 21 BN…
Chapel St, (Ruther.) G73 65 BV…
Chapel St Ind Est, G20 21 BN…
Chapelton St, G22 22 BS…
Chaplet Av, G13 19 BE…
Chapman Av, (Glenb.) Coat. ML5 29 CS…
Chappell St, (Barr.) G78 73 AX…
Charing Cross, G2 9 BP…
Charles Av, Renf. PA4 32 AZ…
Charles St, G21 11 BU…
Charlotte Pl, Pais. PA2 58 AU…
Charlotte St, G1 15 BT…
Chatelherault Av, (Camb.) G72 81 CA…
Chatton St, G23 21 BM…
Cheapside St, G3 13 BP…
Chelmsford Dr, G12 20 BK…
Cherrybank Rd, G43 78 BK…
Cherry Gro, (Baill.) G69 57 CP…
Cherry Pl, (Bishop.) G64 24 BX…
Cherryridge Dr, (Baill.) G69 57 CC…
Cherrytree Dr, (Camb.) G72 83 CC…
Chesterfield Av, G12 20 BJ…
Chesters Pl, (Ruther.) G73 65 BV…
Chester St, G32 53 CC…
Chestnut Gro, (Gart.) G69 29 CC…
Chestnut St, G22 23 BT…
Chestnut Way, (Camb.) G72 83 CC…
Cheviot Av, (Barr.) G78 73 AY…
Cheviot Rd, G43 77 BL…
Cheviot Rd, Pais. PA2 58 AV…
Chirmorie Cres, G53 60 BC…
Chirmorie Pl, G53 60 BC…
Chirnside Pl, G52 47 BE…
Chirnside Rd, G52 46 BD…
Chisholm St, G1 15 BT…
Crighton Grn, (Udd.) G71 71 CC…
Christian St, G43 63 BM…
Christie La, Pais. PA3 44 AU…
Christie Pl, (Camb.) G72 81 CC…
Christie St, Pais. PA1 45 AV…

istopher St, G21 38 BW27
ryston Business Cen, (Chry.) G69 28 CL21
urch Av, (Stepps) G33 26 CM21
urch Av, (Ruther.) G73 80 BY40
urch Hill, Pais. PA1 AU32
urchill Cres, (Both.) G71 85 CR42
urchill Dr, G11 34 BJ26
urchill Way, (Bishop.) G64 23 BV20
urch Rd, (Giff.) G46 77 BL43
urch Rd, (Muir.) G69 28 CL22
urch St, G11 35 BL27
urch St, (Baill.) G69 55 CK33
urch St, (Udd.) G71 84 CN40
urch Vw, (Camb.) G72 82 CG42
cus Dr, G31 51 BV30
cus Pl, G31 51 BV30
cus Pl La, G31 37 BV29
cus Cres, (Udd.) G71 71 CS37
ford Cres, (Ruther.) G73 65 BV39
ford Dr, (Ruther.) G73 65 BV39
y Link Cen, G51 48 BJ30
ic St, G4 10 BR27
ddens Quad, G22 22 BS23
ddens St, G22 22 BS23
irmont Gdns, G3 9 BP28
ir Rd, (Bishop.) G64 24 BZ20
remont St, G3 8 BN29
remont Ter, G3 9 BP28
remont Ter La, G3 9 BP28
remount Av, (Giff.) G46 77 BN28
rence Dr, G11 34 BJ26
rence Dr, G11 34 BJ26
rence Dr, Pais. PA1 45 AW32
rence Gdns, G11 34 BJ26
rence La, G12 34 BK26
rence St, Pais. PA1 45 AW32
rendon Pl, G20 9 BQ27
rendon, (Stepps) G33 26 CF24
rendon St, G3 9 BQ27
ce St, G21 38 BW27
rion Cres, G13 19 BG21
rkston Rd, G13 19 BC21
rkston Av, G44 78 BP41
rkston Rd, G44 78 BP41
k St, Pais. PA3 44 AS31
k St, Renf. PA4 31 AY26
ude Av, (Camb.) G72 82 CG42
ud Rd, Pais. PA3 44 AW31
vens Rd, G52 46 BA31
verhouse Rd, Pais. PA2 45 AW34
verhouse Rd, G52 46 BB30
vering St E, Pais. PA1 44 AS32
yhouse Rd, G33 40 CC25
ypotts Pl, G33 39 CC28
ypotts Rd, G33 39 CC28
yslaps Rd, G3 8 BM28
ythorn Av, G40 51 BU32
ythorn Pk, G40 51 BU32
ythorn St, G40 51 BU31
ythorn Ter, G40 51 BU31
yton Ter, G40 51 BV30
eves Pl, G53 75 BD40
eves Quad, G53 75 BD40
ethorn St, G22 36 BR26
land La, G5 14 BS32
land Av, (Bishop.) G64 24 BW21
rwood St, G32 53 BZ31
veden Cres, G12 21 BK24
veden Cres La, G12 21 BK24
veden Dr, G12 21 BK24
veden Dr, (Ruther.) G73 66 BY39
veden Gdns, G12 21 BK24
veden La, G12 20 BK23

Cleveden Pl, G12 21 BK23
Cleveden Rd, G12 20 BK23
Cleveland La, G3 9 BP29
Cleveland St, G3 9 BP29
Clifford Gdns, G51 48 BK32
Clifford La, G51 49 BL32
Clifford Pl, G51 49 BK32
Clifford St, G51 49 BK32
Cliff Rd, G3 9 BP28
Clifton Pl, G3 8 BN28
Clifton Pl, (Giff.) G46 77 BK42
Clifton St, G3 8 BN28
Clifton Ter, (Camb.) G72 81 CA42
Clincarthill Rd, (Ruther.) 66 BW38
Clincart Rd, G42 64 BR37
Cloberhill Rd, G13 19 BE20
Cloch St, G33 39 CC29
Clonbeith St, G33 40 CG27
Closeburn St, G22 22 BS24
Cloth St, (Barr.) G78 73 AY43
Cloudhowe Ter, (Blan.) G72 84 CL44
Clouston La, G20 35 BN25
Clouston St, G20 35 BM25
Clova Pl, (Udd.) G71 71 CP39
Clova St, (Thornlie.) G46 76 BH41
Cloverbank Gdns, G21 38 BW28
Cloverbank St, G21 38 BW28
Clovergate, (Bishop.) G64 23 BU20
Cloverhill Pl, (Chry.) G69 28 CL21
Clunie Rd, G52 BG33
Cluny Dr, Pais. PA3 45 AW31
Cluny Gdns, G14 35 BG25
Cluny Gdns, (Baill.) G69 55 CJ33
Clutha St, G51 BM31
Clyde Av, (Both.) G71 85 CP44
Clyde Av, (Barr.) G78 74 AZ44
Clydebrae Dr, (Both.) G71 85 CR44
Clydebrae St, G51 35 BK29
Clydeford Dr, G32 53 CA34
Clydeford Dr, (Udd.) G71 70 CN38
Clydeford Rd, (Camb.) G72 67 CC37
Clydeholm Rd, G14 BF27
Clydeholm Ter, Clyde. G81 18 AZ22
Clyde Ind Cen, G3 8 BN29
Clydeneuk Dr, (Udd.) G71 70 CM38
Clyde Pl, G5 8 BO31
Clyde Pl, (Camb.) G72 82 CF41
Clyde Rd, Pais. PA3 45 AX30
Clydesdale Av, Pais. PA3 31 AW28
Clyde Shop Cen, Clyde. G81 17 AY20
Clydeside Expressway, G3 35 BJ27
Clydeside Expressway, G14 35 BG24
Clydeside Ind Est, G14 33 BF27
Clydeside Rd, (Ruther.) G73 BV35
Clydesmill Dr, G32 67 CC38
Clydesmill Gro, G32 67 CC38
Clydesmill Ind Est, G32 67 CC37
Clydesmill Pl, G32 67 CC37
Clydesmill Rd, G32 CB37
Clyde St, G1 14 BR31
Clyde St, Clyde. G81 17 AY21
Clyde St, Renf. PA4 18 AZ24
Clyde Ter, (Both.) G71 85 CQ44
Clyde Tunnel, G14 34 BG28
Clyde Tunnel, G51 34 BG28
Clydevale, (Both.) G71 85 CR44
Clyde Vw, Pais. PA2 59 AX35
Clydeview Ter, G32 68 CD37
Clynder St, G51 49 BK31
Clyth Dr, (Giff.) G46 77 BM43
Coalburn Rd, (Both.) G71 CR40
Coalhill St, G31 51 BX32
Coatbridge Rd, (Baill.) G69 CN32
Coatbridge Rd, (Gart.) G69 42 CO25
Coats Cres, (Baill.) G69 55 CJ32
Coatshill Av, (Blan.) G72 84 CL44

Cobblerigg Way, (Udd.) G71 84 CN40
Cobden Rd, G21 37 BV27
Cobington Pl, G33 40 CD28
Cobinshaw St, G32 53 CC31
Coburg St, G5 14 BR32
Cochno St, Clyde. G81 17 AY21
Cochrane St, G1 14 BS30
Cochrane St, (Barr.) G78 73 AX43
Cochran St, Pais. PA1 45 AV33
Cockels Ln, Renf. PA4 31 AX28
Cockenzie St, G32 53 CC32
Cockmuir St, G21 38 BW25
Cogan Rd, G43 63 BK38
Cogan St, G43 63 BL38
Cogan St, (Barr.) G78 73 AX43
Colbert St, G40 51 BV34
Colchester Dr, G12 20 BJ23
Coldingham Av, G14 18 BA23
Coldstream Dr, (Ruther.) G73 66 BZ39
Coldstream Pl, G21 37 BS26
Coldstream Rd, Clyde. G81 17 AX20
Colebrooke Pl, G12 35 BN26
Colebrooke St, G12 35 BN26
Colebrooke Ter, G12 35 BN26
Colebrook St, (Camb.) G72 67 CC39
Coleridge Av, (Both.) G71 85 CR42
Colfin St, G34 42 CL28
Colgrain Av, G20 22 BQ23
Colgrain Ter, G20 22 BQ23
Colgrave Cres, G32 53 CB34
Colinbar Circle, (Barr.) G78 73 AX44
Colinslee Av, Pais. PA2 59 AV36
Colinslee Cres, Pais. PA2 59 AV36
Colinslee Dr, Pais. PA2 58 AV36
Colinslie Rd, G53 61 BE37
Colinton Pl, G32 54 CD30
Colintraive Av, G33 39 CB25
Colintraive Cres, G33 39 CA26
Coll Av, Renf. PA4 32 AZ28
College La, Pais. PA1 44 AT32
College St, G1 15 BT30
Collessie Dr, G33 CE27
Collina St, G20 21 BL23
Collins St, G4 15 BU30
Coll Pl, G21 38 BX27
Coll St, G21 38 BW27
Colmonell Av, G13 18 BB22
Colonsay Av, Renf. PA4 31 AY28
Colonsay Rd, Pais. PA2 58 AT38
Colquhoun Av, G52 47 BC30
Colston Av, (Bishop.) G64 23 BV22
Colston Dr, (Bishop.) G64 23 BV22
Colston Gdns, (Bishop.) G64 23 BU22
Colston Gro, (Bishop.) G64 23 BV22
Colston Path, (Bishop.) G64 23 BU22
Colston Pl, (Bishop.) G64 23 BU22
Colston Rd, (Bishop.) G64 23 BU22
Coltmuir Cres, (Bishop.) G64 23 BU21
Coltmuir Dr, (Bishop.) G64 23 BU21
Coltmuir Gdns, (Bishop.) G64 23 BU21
Coltmuir St, G22 22 BR23
Coltness La, G33 54 CE30
Coltness St, G33 40 CE29
Coltpark Av, (Bishop.) G64 23 BU21
Coltpark La, (Bishop.) G64 23 BU21
Columba St, G51 48 BK30
Colvend Dr, (Ruther.) G73 80 BX42
Colvend La, G40 51 BV34
Colvend St, G40 51 BV34
Colville Dr, (Ruther.) G73 67 BZ39
Colwood Av, G53 74 BC41

Street	PC	Pg	Grid
Colwood Gdns, G53		75	BC42
Colwood Pl, G53		75	BC42
Colwood Pl, G53		75	BC41
Comedie Rd, G33		40	CG25
Comelypark St, G31		51	BV31
Commerce St, G5		14	BR32
Commercial Ct, G5		15	BT32
Commercial Rd, G5		51	BS33
Commercial Rd, (Barr.) G78		73	AY42
Commonhead Rd, G34		42	CM29
Commore Av, (Barr.) G78		74	AZ44
Commore Dr, G13		19	BC22
Comrie Rd, G33		26	CE24
Comrie St, G32		54	CD34
Conan Ct, (Camb.) G72		82	CF40
Cona St, (Thornlie.) G46		76	BG41
Congress Rd, G3		12	BM30
Congress Way, G3		12	BN30
Conisborough Cl, G34		41	CJ28
Conisborough Rd, G34		41	CH27
Conistone Cres, (Baill.) G69		55	CH33
Connal St, G40		52	BX34
Conniston St, G32		53	CA30
Connor Rd, (Barr.) G78		73	AX42
Consett La, G33		40	CE29
Consett St, G33		40	CE29
Contin Pl, G12		21	BM24
Cook St, G5		13	BQ32
Cooperage Ct, G14		18	AZ23
Cooperage Pl, G3		35	BL29
Coopers Well St, G11		35	BL28
Copland Pl, G51		49	BK30
Copland Quad, G51		49	BK31
Copland Rd, G51		49	BK31
Coplaw Ct, G42		50	BO34
Coplaw St, G42		50	BO34
Copperfield La, (Udd.) G71		70	CO38
Corbett Ct, G32		53	CB34
Corbett St, G32		53	CB34
Cordiner La, G44		64	BR38
Cordiner St, G44		64	BR38
Corkerhill Gdns, G52		48	BG33
Corkerhill Pl, G52		57	BF35
Corkerhill Rd, G52		61	BF36
Corlaich Av, G42		65	BU38
Corlaich Dr, G42		65	BU38
Cornaig Rd, G53		60	BD37
Cornalee Gdns, G53		61	BC37
Cornalee Pl, G53		60	BD38
Cornalee Rd, G53		61	BC37
Cornhill St, G21		24	BW24
Corn St, G4		11	BR27
Cornwall Av, (Ruther.) G73		81	BZ40
Cornwall St, G41		12	BM32
Cornwall St S, G41		48	BM33
Coronation Pl, (Gart.) G69		28	CN22
Corpach St, G34		41	CM28
Corran St, G33		39	CB29
Corrie Dr, Pais. PA1		46	BA33
Corrie Gro, G44		78	BP41
Corrour Rd, G43		63	BM38
Corsebar Av, Pais. PA2		58	AS35
Corsebar Cres, Pais. PA2		58	AS36
Corsebar Dr, Pais. PA2		58	AS35
Corsebar Way, Pais. PA2		44	AS34
Corsehill Path, G34		42	CL29
Corsehill Pl, G34		42	CL29
Corsehill St, G34		42	CL29
Corselet Rd, G53		75	BD42
Corse Rd, G52		46	BA31
Corsewall Av, G32		54	CG34
Corsford Dr, G53		61	BE39
Corsock St, G31		52	BY30
Corston St, G33		38	BZ29
Cortachy Pl, (Bishop.) G64		24	BZ20
Corunna St, G3		8	BN29
Coshneuk Rd, G33		26	CD24
Cottar St, G20		21	BN22
Cotton St, G40		65	BV35
Cotton St, Pais. PA1		44	AV33
Coulin Gdns, G22		37	BT25
County Av, (Camb.) G72		67	BZ38
County Pl, Pais. PA1		44	AU32
County Sq, Pais. PA1		44	AU32
Couper Pl, G4		11	BT28
Couper St, G4		11	BT28
Courthill Av, G44		78	BR40
Coustonholm Rd, G43		63	BM37
Coventry Dr, G31		38	BX29
Cowal Rd, G20		21	BK22
Cowal St, G20		21	BL22
Cowan Cres, (Barr.) G78		74	AZ41
Cowan La, G12		8	BN27
Cowan St, G12		8	BN27
Cowan Wynd, (Udd.) G71		71	CO37
Cowcaddens Rd, G4		10	BR28
Cowdenhill Circ, G13		19	BF21
Cowdenhill Pl, G13		19	BF21
Cowdenhill Rd, G13		19	BF21
Cowden St, G51		47	BF30
Cowdray Cres, Renf. PA4		32	AZ26
Cowglen Rd, G53		61	BE38
Cowlairs Rd, G21		37	BU25
Coxhill St, G21		37	BT26
Coxton Pl, G33		40	CF28
Coylton Rd, G43		77	BN40
Craggan Dr, G14		18	BB23
Crags Av, Pais. PA2		59	AV36
Crags Cres, Pais. PA2		59	AV35
Crags Rd, Pais. PA2		59	AV36
Craigallian Av, (Camb.) G72		82	CF42
Craiganour La, G43		63	BL39
Craigard Pl, (Ruther.) G73		82	BZ42
Craigbank Dr, G53		60	BF39
Craigbarnet Cres, G33		40	CD25
Craigbo Av, G23		21	BM21
Craigbo Pl, G23		21	BM21
Craigbo Rd, G23		21	BM20
Craigbo St, G23		21	BM20
Craigellan Rd, G43		63	BM39
Craigenbay St, G21		38	BX25
Craigend Dr, Coat. ML5		57	CS33
Craigendmuir Rd, G33		40	CG25
Craigendmuir St, G33		38	BZ27
Craigendon Oval, Pais. PA2		58	AS39
Craigendon Rd, Pais. PA2		58	AS38
Craigend Pl, G13		20	BG23
Craigend St, G13		20	BG23
Craigflower Gdns, G53		75	BC41
Craigflower Rd, G53		75	BC41
Craighall Rd, G4		10	BR27
Craighead Av, G33		38	BZ26
Craighead St, (Barr.) G78		73	AX43
Craighead Way, (Barr.) G78		73	AX43
Craighouse St, G33		39	CC28
Craigiebar Dr, Pais. PA2		58	AS37
Craigieburn Gdns, G20		21	BK21
Craigiehall Pl, G51		48	BM31
Craigielea Pk, Renf. PA4		31	AY26
Craigielea Rd, Renf. PA4		31	AY26
Craigielea St, G31		38	BW29
Craigie St, G42		64	BO35
Craigievar St, G33		40	CG27
Craigknowe Rd, (Blan.) G72		84	CL43
Craiglockhart St, G33		40	CE27
Craigmillar Rd, G42		64	BO38
Craigmont Dr, G20		21	BN24
Craigmont St, G20		21	BN23
Craigmore St, G31		52	BY31
Craigmount Av, Pais. PA2		58	AS39
Craigmuir Cres, G52		46	BB31
Craigmuir Pl, G52		46	BA31
Craigmuir Rd, G52		46	BA31
Craigneil St, G33		41	CG28
Craignure Rd, (Ruther.) G73		80	BX41
Craigpark, G31		52	BW30
Craigpark Dr, G31		52	BW30
Craig Rd, G44		78	BQ40
Craigton Av, (Barr.) G78		74	BA44
Craigton Dr, G51		48	BH30
Craigton Dr, (Barr.) G78		74	BA44
Craigton Pl, G51		48	BG30
Craigton Pl, (Blan.) G72		84	CM44
Craigton Rd, G51		48	BH31
Craigvicar Gdns, G32		54	CF34
Craigwell Av, (Ruther.) G73		66	BZ39
Crail St, G31		53	BZ32
Crammond Av, Coat. ML5		57	CS30
Cramond Av, Renf. PA4		32	BA28
Cramond St, G5		65	BT35
Cramond Ter, G32		54	CD32
Cranborne Rd, G12		20	BJ24
Cranbrooke Dr, G20		21	BM23
Cranston St, G3		9	BP29
Cranworth La, G12		35	BM26
Cranworth St, G12		35	BM26
Crathes Ct, G44		77	BN41
Crathie Dr, G11		34	B...
Crawford Av, (Udd.) G71		70	CN36
Crawford Cres, (Blan.) G72		84	CM43
Crawford Dr, G15		18	BB26
Crawford St, G11		34	B...
Crawford Gdns, (Ruther.) G73		80	BY41
Crawfurd Rd, (Ruther.) G73		80	BX41
Craw Rd, Pais. PA2		44	AS33
Crebar Dr, (Barr.) G78		73	AY43
Crebar St, (Thornlie.) G46		76	BG39
Credon Gdns, (Ruther.) G73		80	BY41
Cree Av, (Bishop.) G64		24	BZ20
Cree Gdns, G32		53	CB33
Ceran Dr, Renf. PA4		31	AX28
Crescent Rd, G13		19	BD23
Crescent Rd, G14		19	BD23
Cressdale Av, G45		79	BT42
Cressdale Ct, G45		79	BT42
Cressdale Dr, G45		79	BT42
Cressland Dr, G45		79	BT43
Cressland Pl, G45		79	BT43
Cresswell La, G12		35	BM26
Cresswell St, G12		35	BM26
Cressy St, G51		34	BG29
Crest Av, G13		19	BD22
Crestlea Av, Pais. PA2		58	AU38
Crichton Ct, G45		79	BT44
Crichton St, G21		37	BU26
Criffell Gdns, G32		54	CF34
Criffell Rd, G32		54	CE33
Crimea St, G2		13	BQ30
Crinan Gdns, (Bishop.) G64		24	BY20
Crinan Rd, (Bishop.) G64		24	BY20
Crinan St, G31		38	BX30
Cripps Av, Clyde. G81		18	AZ21
Croftbank Av, (Both.) G71		85	CQ43
Croftbank Cres, (Both.) G71		85	CQ43
Croftbank Cres, (Udd.) G71		71	CP40
Croftbank Gate, (Both.) G71		85	CQ43
Croftbank St, G21		37	BV26
Croftburn Dr, G44		79	BS41
Croftcroighn Rd, G33		40	CD28
Croftend Av, G44		65	BU39
Croftfoot Cres, G45		79	BV41
Croftfoot Dr, G45		79	BV41
Croftfoot Quad, G45		79	BU41
Croftfoot Rd, G44		79	BT41
Croftfoot Rd, G45		79	BT41
Croftfoot St, G45		79	BV41
Croftfoot Ter, G45		79	BV41

ofthead St, (Udd.) G71	85	CP40
ofthill Av, (Udd.) G71	71	CP39
ofthill Rd, G44	79	BU40
ofthouse Dr, G44	79	BU41
oftmont Av, G44	79	BU41
ofton Av, G44	79	BT41
oftpark Av, G44	79	BT41
oft Rd, (Camb.) G72	82	CD40
oftside Av, G44	79	BU41
oftspar Av, G32	54	CE31
oftspar Dr, G32	54	CE31
oftspar Gro, G32	54	CE31
oftspar Pl, G32	54	CE31
oft Way, Renf. PA4	32	AZ28
oftwood Av, G44	79	BT41
oft Wynd, (Udd.) G71	71	CQ39
omarty Av, G43	64	BP39
omarty Gdns, (Clark.) G76	78	BQ44
omarty Pl, (Chry.) G69	28	CM20
ombie Gdns, (Baill.) G69	55	CJ34
omdale St, G51	48	BG31
omer Gdns, G20	22	BP24
ompton Av, G44	78	BN40
omwell La, G20	9	BQ27
omwell St, G20	9	BQ27
onberry Quad, G52	46	BB34
onberry Ter, G52	46	BB34
ookston Av, G52	46	BC33
ookston Ct, G52	46	BC33
ookston Dr, G52	46	BB33
ookston Dr, Pais. PA1	46	BB33
ookston Gdns, G52	46	BB33
ookston Gro, G52	46	BC33
ookston Pl, G52	46	BB33
ookston Quad, G52	46	BB33
ookston Rd, G52	46	BB34
ookston Rd, G53	60	BC37
osbie La, G20	21	BL21
osbie St, G20	21	BL21
oss, The, Pais. PA1	44	AU32
oss Arthurlie St, (Barr.) G78	73	AX42
ossbank Av, G42	65	BU36
ossbank Dr, G42	65	BT36
ossbank Rd, G42	65	BT36
ossbank Ter, G42	65	BT36
ossflat Cres, Pais. PA1	45	AW32
osshill Av, G42	65	BR36
osshill Rd, (Ruther.) G73	66	BX39
osslees Dr, (Thornlie.) G46	76	BH42
osslees Pk, (Thornlie.) G46	76	BH42
osslees Rd, (Thornlie.) G46	76	BH43
ossloan Rd, G51	48	BH30
ossloan Ter, G51	48	BH30
ossmill Av, (Barr.) G78	74	AZ41
ossmyloof Gdns, G41	64	BM36
oss St, G32	68	CE36
oss St, Pais. PA1	44	AS33
ossstobs Rd, G53	61	BC36
ossview Pl, (Baill.) G69	56	CM32
ossview Pl, (Baill.) G69	56	CM32
ovie Rd, G53	60	BC38
owflats Vw, (Udd.) G71	71	CS36
owhill Dr, G32	54	CG31
owhill Rd, (Bishop.) G64	23	BV21
owhill St, G22	22	BS23
ow La, G13	20	BH24
owlin Cres, G33	40	CD29
own Circ, G12	35	BL26
own Gdns, G12	35	BL26
ownhall Pl, G32	54	CE32
ownhall Rd, G32	54	CE32
ownpoint Rd, G40	51	BV32
own Rd N, G12	35	BK26
Crown Rd S, G12	35	BK26
Crown St, G5	14	BS32
Crown St, (Baill.) G69	55	CH34
Crown Ter, G12	35	BK26
Crow Rd, G11	34	BJ26
Crow Rd, G13	20	BH24
Crow Wd Rd, (Chry.) G69	27	CK22
Crowwood Roundabout, (Stepps) G33	27	CH22
Crow Wd Ter, (Chry.) G69	27	CK22
Croy Pl, G21	24	BY24
Croy Rd, G21	24	BY24
Cruachan Av, Pais. PA2	58	AU37
Cruachan Av, Renf. PA4	31	AY28
Cruachan Dr, (Barr.) G78	73	AY44
Cruachan Rd, (Ruther.) G73	81	BZ42
Cruachan St, (Thornlie.) G46	76	BH41
Cruachan Way, (Barr.) G78	73	AY43
Cruden St, G51	48	BH31
Crum Av, (Thornlie.) G46	76	BH42
Crusader Av, G13	19	BF20
Cubie St, G40	51	BV32
Cuilhill Rd, (Baill.) G69	57	CP30
Cuillins, The, (Udd.) G71	70	CN36
Cuillins Rd, (Ruther.) G73	81	BZ42
Cuillin Way, (Barr.) G78	73	AY43
Culbin Dr, G13	18	BB21
Cullen Pl, (Udd.) G71	71	CO37
Cullen St, G32	53	CC33
Culloden St, G31	38	BX29
Culrain Gdns, G32	53	CC32
Culrain St, G32	53	CC32
Culross La, G32	54	CE33
Culross St, G32	54	CE33
Cults St, G51	48	BH31
Culzean Cres, (Baill.) G69	55	CJ33
Culzean Dr, G32	54	CF33
Cumberland Pl, G5	51	BS33
Cumberland Pl, Coat. ML5	57	CS33
Cumberland St, G5	14	BR32
Cumbernauld Rd, G31	52	BX30
Cumbernauld Rd, G33	39	BZ28
Cumbernauld Rd, (Chry.)	27	CJ22
Cumbrae Pl, Pais. PA2	44	AU38
Cumbrae Rd, Renf. PA4	32	AZ28
Cumbrae St, G33	39	CC29
Cumlodden Dr, G20	21	BL22
Cumming Dr, G42	64	BR37
Cumnock Dr, (Barr.) G78	74	AZ44
Cumnock Rd, G33	25	CA23
Cunard Ct, Clyde. G81	17	AX21
Cunard St, Clyde. G81	17	AX21
Cunningham Dr, (Giff.) G46	77	BN42
Cunningham Rd, G52	32	BB29
Cunningham Rd, (Ruther.) G73	66	BY36
Curfew Rd, G13	19	BF20
Curle St, G14	33	BF27
Curling Cres, G44	65	BS38
Currie Pl, G20	22	BP23
Currie St, G20	21	BN23
Curtis Av, G44	65	BU38
Curtis Av, (Ruther.) G73	65	BS37
Curzon St, G20	21	BN23
Cut, The, (Udd.) G71	84	CP40
Cuthbertson St, G42	64	BO35
Cuthbert St, (Udd.) G71	71	CR38
Cuthelton Dr, G31	53	CA33
Cuthelton St, G31	53	BZ33
Cuthelton Ter, G31	53	BZ33
Cypress Av, (Udd.) G71	71	CR37
Cypress St, G22	23	BT24
Cypress Way, (Camb.) G72	83	CH41
Cyprus Av, (Elder.) PA5	45	AR35
Cyril St, Pais. PA1	45	AW33

D

Daer Av, Renf. PA4	32	BA28
Dairsie Gdns, (Bishop.) G64	24	BZ21
Dairsie St, G44	78	BP41
Daisy St, G42	64	BR36
Dakota Way, Renf. PA4	32	AZ28
Dalbeth Pl, G32	67	CB35
Dalbeth Rd, G32	67	CB35
Dalcraig Cres, (Blan.) G72	84	CL43
Dalcross St, G11	35	BL27
Daldowie Av, G32	54	CF34
Daldowie Rd, (Udd.) G71	69	CJ35
Dale Path, G40	51	BV33
Dale St, G40	51	BV33
Daleview Av, G12	21	BK23
Dale Way, (Ruther.) G73	80	BX41
Dalfoil Ct, Pais. PA1	46	BB33
Dalgarroch Av, Clyde. G81	18	BA21
Dalhousie La, G3	9	BQ28
Dalhousie St, G3	9	BQ28
Dalilea Dr, G34	42	CM28
Dalilea Pl, G34	42	CM28
Dalintober St, G5	13	BQ32
Dalkeith Av, G41	49	BK33
Dalmahoy St, G32	53	CA30
Dalmally St, G20	36	BP26
Dalmarnock Br, G40	66	BX35
Dalmarnock Br, (Ruther.) G73	66	BX35
Dalmarnock Ct, G40	52	BX34
Dalmarnock Dr, G40	51	BV33
Dalmarnock Rd, G40	51	BV33
Dalmarnock Rd, (Ruther.) G73	66	BX35
Dalmarnock Rd Trd Est, (Ruther.) G73	66	BX36
Dalmary Dr, Pais. PA1	45	AX31
Dalmellington Dr, G53	61	BC37
Dalmellington Rd, G53	60	BC37
Dalmeny Av, (Giff.) G46	77	BL42
Dalmeny Dr, (Barr.) G78	73	AW43
Dalmeny St, G5	65	BU35
Dalnair St, G3	35	BL28
Dalness St, G32	53	CC34
Dalreoch Av, (Baill.) G69	56	CL32
Dalriada St, G40	52	BY33
Dalry Rd, (Udd.) G71	71	CR38
Dalry St, G32	54	CD33
Dalserf Ct, G31	52	BX32
Dalserf Cres, (Giff.) G46	77	BK44
Dalserf Gdns, G31	52	BX32
Dalserf St, G31	52	BX32
Dalsholm Av, G20	20	BK21
Dalsholm Ind Est, G20	21	BK22
Dalsholm Rd, G20	20	BK22
Dalswinton Path, G34	42	CM29
Dalswinton St, G34	42	CL29
Dalton Av, Clyde. G81	18	BA20
Dalton St, G31	53	CA32
Dalveen Ct, (Barr.) G78	73	AY44
Dalveen Dr, (Udd.) G71	70	CN37
Dalveen St, G32	53	CC32
Dalveen Way, (Ruther.) G73	80	BY42
Dalwhinnie Av, (Blan.) G72	84	CL43
Daly Gdns, (Blan.) G72	84	CN44
Dalziel Dr, G41	49	BL34
Dalziel Quad, G41	49	BL34
Dalziel Rd, G52	32	BB29
Damshot Cres, G53	61	BF36
Damshot Rd, G53	61	BF38
Danby Rd, (Baill.) G69	55	CH33
Danes Av, G14	33	BE25
Danes Cres, G14	19	BD24

Street	Page	Grid
Danes Dr, G14	19	BD24
Dargarvel Av, G41	38	BK33
Darleith St, G32	53	CB32
Darnaway Av, G33	40	CF27
Darnaway Dr, G33	40	CF27
Darnaway St, G33	40	CF27
Darnick St, G21	38	BX26
Darnley Gdns, G41	63	BN35
Darnley Ind Est, G53	75	BD41
Darnley Mains Rd, G53	75	BE42
Darnley Rd, G41	63	BN35
Darnley Rd, (Barr.) G78	74	AZ42
Darnley St, G41	64	BP35
Dartford St, G22	36	BR26
Darvel Cres, Pais. PA1	46	AZ32
Davaar Dr, Pais. PA2	58	AU38
Davaar Rd, Renf. PA4	32	AZ28
Davaar St, G40	52	BX33
Dava St, G51	48	BJ30
David Pl, (Baill.) G69	55	CH33
David Pl, Pais. PA3	45	AX30
Davidson Pl, G32	54	CE31
Davidson St, G40	66	BW35
Davidson St, Clyde. G81	18	BA21
David St, G40	52	BW32
David Way, Pais. PA3	45	AX30
Davieland Rd, (Giff.) G46	76	BJ44
Daviot St, G51	47	BF31
Dawson Pl, G4	36	BR26
Dawson Rd, G4	36	BR26
Deaconsbank Av, (Thornlie.) G46	75	BF44
Deaconsbank Cres, (Thornlie.) G46	75	BF44
Deaconsbank Gro, (Thornlie.) G46	76	BG44
Deaconsbank Pl, (Thornlie.) G46	75	BF44
Dealston Rd, (Barr.) G78	73	AX41
Deanbrae St, (Udd.) G71	71	CP39
Dean Cres, (Chry.) G69	28	CM20
Deanfield Quad, G52	46	BB31
Dean Pk Dr, (Camb.) G72	82	CF41
Dean Pk Rd, Renf. PA4	32	BA27
Deans Av, (Camb.) G72	82	CF42
Deanside Rd, G52	32	BC29
Deanston Av, (Barr.) G78	73	AX44
Deanston Dr, G41	63	BM37
Deanston Gdns, (Barr.) G78	73	AX44
Deanston Pk, (Barr.) G78	73	AX44
Dean St, Clyde. G81	18	AY20
Deanwood Av, G44	78	BP42
Deanwood Rd, G44	78	BP42
Dechmont Av, (Camb.) G72	82	CF42
Dechmont Cotts, (Camb.) G72	83	CH42
Dechmont Gdns, (Blan.) G72	84	CL44
Dechmont Pl, (Camb.) G72	82	CF42
Dechmont St, G31	52	BY32
Dechmont Vw, (Udd.) G71	71	CQ38
Dee Av, Renf. PA4	32	BA26
Dee St, G33	38	BZ28
Delny Pl, G33	55	CG30
Delvin Rd, G44	64	BQ39
Denbeck St, G32	53	CB32
Denbrae St, G32	53	CB32
Dene Wk, (Bishop.) G64	24	BY21
Denewood Av, Pais. PA2	58	AT37
Denham St, G22	36	BR26
Denholm Dr, (Giff.) G46	77	BL44
Denmark St, G22	36	BS25
Denmilne Gdns, G34	56	CL30
Denmilne Path, G34	56	CL30
Denmilne Pl, G34	56	CL30
Denmilne Rd, (Baill.) G69	56	CM30
Denmilne St, G34	56	CL30
Derby St, G3	8	BN29
Derby Ter La, G3	8	BN28
Derwent Dr, Coat. ML5	43	CS27
Derwent St, G22	36	BR25
Despard Av, G32	54	CF33
Despard Gdns, G32	54	CG33
Deveron Av, (Giff.) G46	77	BM43
Deveron St, G33	38	BZ28
Deveron St, Coat. ML5	43	CS28
Devol Cres, G53	61	BD37
Devondale Av, (Blan.) G72	84	CM44
Devon Pl, G41	50	BR33
Devonshire Gdns, G12	35	BK25
Devonshire Ter, G12	35	BK25
Devonshire Ter La, G12	35	BK25
Devon St, G5	50	BR33
Dewar Cl, (Udd.) G71	71	CQ36
Diana Av, G13	19	BD21
Dick St, G20	36	BP26
Dilwara Av, G14	34	BG27
Dinard Dr, (Giff.) G46	77	BL41
Dinart St, G33	38	BZ28
Dinduff St, G34	42	CL28
Dinmont Rd, G41	63	BM36
Dinwiddie St, G21	38	BY27
Dirleton Dr, G41	63	BN37
Dirleton Pl, G41	63	BN37
Dixon Av, G42	64	BR36
Dixon Rd, G42	64	BR36
Dixons Blazes Ind Est, G5	50	BS34
Dixon St, G1	14	BR31
Dixon St, Pais. PA1	45	AV33
Dobbies Ln, G4	11	BT29
Dobbies Ln Pl, G4	10	BU29
Dochart Av, Renf. PA4	32	BA28
Dochart St, G33	39	CA27
Dock St, Clyde. G81	18	AZ22
Dodhill Pl, G13	19	BD23
Dodside Gdns, G32	54	CE33
Dodside Pl, G32	54	CE33
Dodside St, G32	54	CE33
Dolan St, (Baill.) G69	55	CK32
Dollar Ter, G20	21	BL21
Dolphin Rd, G41	63	BM35
Donaldson Grn, (Udd.) G71	71	CR37
Donaldswood Pk, Pais. PA2	58	AS37
Donaldswood Rd, Pais. PA2	58	AS37
Donald Way, (Udd.) G71	71	CQ38
Don Av, Renf. PA4	32	BA27
Doncaster St, G20	36	BQ25
Donnies Brae, (Neil.) G78	73	AV44
Don St, G33	38	BZ29
Doonfoot Rd, G43	63	BM39
Dora St, G40	51	BV34
Dorchester Av, G12	20	BJ23
Dorchester Ct, G12	20	BJ23
Dorchester Pl, G12	20	BJ23
Dorlin Rd, G33	27	CG24
Dormanside Rd, G53	47	BD34
Dornal Av, G13	18	BA22
Dornford Av, G32	68	CF35
Dornford Rd, G32	68	CF35
Dornie Dr, G32	68	CD37
Dornie Dr, (Thornlie.) G46	76	BG42
Dornoch Av, (Giff.) G46	77	BL44
Dornoch Pl, (Chry.) G69	28	CM20
Dornoch St, G40	51	BV32
Dorset St, G3	9	BP29
Dosk Av, G13	18	BA21
Dosk Pl, G13	18	BB21
Dougalston Rd, G23	21	BN20
Douglas Av, G32	68	CD37
Douglas Av, (Giff.) G46	77	BL44
Douglas Av, (Ruther.) G73	80	BY41
Douglas Cres, (Udd.) G71	71	CR38
Douglas Dr, G15	18	BE20
Douglas Dr, (Baill.) G69	55	CH33
Douglas Dr, (Both.) G71	85	CQ43
Douglas Dr, (Camb.) G72	81	CB40
Douglas Gdns, (Giff.) G46	77	BL44
Douglas Gdns, (Udd.) G71	84	CF40
Douglas Gate, (Camb.) G72	81	CE40
Douglas La, G2	9	BQ30
Douglas Rd, Renf. PA4	31	AW30
Douglas St, G2	9	BQ30
Douglas St, (Udd.) G71	71	CR39
Douglas St, Pais. PA1	44	AS32
Dougray Pl, (Barr.) G78	73	AY43
Dougrie Dr, G45	79	BT43
Dougrie Gdns, G45	79	BT44
Dougrie Pl, G45	79	BU43
Dougrie Rd, G45	79	BT44
Dougrie St, G45	79	BU43
Dougrie Ter, G45	79	BT43
Doune Gdns, G20	35	BN26
Doune Gdns La, G20	35	BN26
Doune Quad, G20	35	BN26
Dovecot, G43	63	BM38
Dovecothall St, (Barr.) G78	74	AZ42
Dover St, G3	8	BN30
Dowanhill St, G11	35	BL27
Dowanhill St, G12	35	BL26
Dowanside Rd, G12	35	BL26
Downcraig Dr, G45	79	BS43
Downcraig Gro, G45	79	BS44
Downcraig Rd, G45	79	BS44
Downcraig Ter, G45	79	BS43
Downfield Gdns, (Both.) G71	84	CN44
Downfield St, G32	53	CA34
Downiebrae Rd, (Ruther.) G73	66	BX37
Downie Cl, (Udd.) G71	71	CR37
Downs St, G21	37	BV25
Dowrie Cres, G53	61	BD36
Drakemire Av, G45	79	BS43
Drakemire Dr, G44	78	BR43
Drakemire Dr, G45	78	BR43
Drake St, G40	15	BU32
Dreghorn St, G31	52	BX31
Drimnin Rd, G33	27	CH23
Drive Rd, G51	34	BG30
Drochil St, G34	41	CH28
Drumbeg Dr, G53	61	BC39
Drumbottle Rd, G21	24	CA24
Drumcavel Rd, (Muir.) G69	28	CN23
Drumclog Gdns, G33	25	CB23
Drumcross Rd, G53	61	BE36
Drumcross Rd, G53	61	BE36
Drumhead La, G32	67	CB35
Drumhead Pl, G32	67	CB35
Drumhead Rd, G32	67	CB35
Drumilaw Rd, (Ruther.) G73	80	BV40
Drumilaw Way, (Ruther.) G73	80	BV40
Drumlaken St, G23	21	BL20
Drumlanrig Av, G34	42	CL29
Drumlanrig Pl, G34	42	CL29
Drumlochy Rd, G33	39	CD28
Drummond Av, (Ruther.) G73	65	BV37
Drummond Dr, Pais. PA1	46	AA33
Drummover Dr, G31	34	BJ30
Drumoyne Av, G51	34	BG30
Drumoyne Circ, G51	48	BG31
Drumoyne Dr, G51	48	BG30
Drumoyne Pl, G51	48	BG31
Drumoyne Quad, G51	48	BG31
Drumoyne Rd, G51	48	BG31

Name	Page	Grid
umoyne Sq, G51	48	BG30
umpark St, (Thornlie.) G46	76	BH41
umpark St, Coat. ML5	57	CR33
umpellier Av, (Baill.) G69	55	CK34
umpellier St, Coat. ML5	57	CS30
umpellier Pl, (Baill.) G69	55	CK33
umpellier Rd, (Baill.) G69	55	CJ34
umreoch Dr, G33	39	BZ27
umreoch Dr, G42	65	BU37
umreoch Pl, G42	65	BU37
umsack Av, (Chry.) G69	27	CK21
umsargard Rd, (Ruther.) G73	80	BZ40
ms Cres, Pais. PA3	44	AS31
mshaw Dr, G32	68	CE37
hard Rd, G53	47	BC34
ry St, G2	14	BR30
ad St, (Thornlie.) G46	76	BG40
burgh Av, (Ruther.) G73	66	BX38
burn Av, G52	47	BC32
gate, G4	15	BU30
grange Rd, G33	40	CE27
t St, G52	48	BG32
noch Pl, G22	22	BR22
sdale St, G14	18	BB24
art St, G20	21	BL21
obs Rd, (Barr.) G78	74	BA42
oton Path, G34	41	CK28
oton St, G34	41	CK28
hall Pl, G14	18	BA23
chess Pl, (Ruther.) G73	66	BY37
chess Rd, (Ruther.) G73	66	BY36
chray Dr, Pais. PA1	46	BB33
chray La, G33	38	BZ28
chray St, G33	38	BZ28
shope St, G33	40	CF27
dley Dr, G12	34	BJ26
dley Dr, Coat. ML5	43	CS27
dley La, G12	34	BJ26
fus Pl, G32	68	CE37
fus St, G34	41	CH28
fus Ter, G32	68	CE37
sdale Rd, G32	68	CE37
kes Gate, (Both.) G71	84	CN41
kes Rd, (Baill.) G69	57	CP32
kes Rd, (Camb.) G72	67	CA39
kes Rd, (Ruther.) G73	80	BY40
ke St, G4	15	BU30
ke St, G31	52	BW30
ke St, Pais. PA2	58	AU35
sie Rd, G21	24	BY23
mbarton Rd, G11	33	BJ27
mbarton Rd, G14	34	BG27
mbreck Av, G41	48	BJ33
mbreck Ct, G41	48	BJ34
mbreck Pl, G41	48	BJ34
mbreck Rd, G41	48	BK34
mbreck Sq, G41	48	BJ33
hagoil Gdns, G45	79	BU43
hagoil Pl, G45	79	BU44
hagoil St, G45	79	BU43
hagoil St, G45	79	BU43
hagoil Ter, G45	79	BU44
halistair Dr, G33	26	CD24
han Pl, G33	55	CG30
hard Rd, (Ruther.) G73	66	BX38
hard St, G20	36	BP25
haskin St, G11	35	BL28
har Av, (Ruther.) G73	66	BY39
beith Pl, G20	21	BM24
blane St, G4	10	BR28
ncan Av, G14	33	BE26
acansby Rd, G33	54	CF31
chattan St, G31	51	BV30
Dunchattan St, G31	51	BV30
Dunchurch Rd, Pais. PA1	46	AZ32
Dunclutha Dr, (Both.) G71	85	CQ44
Dunclutha St, G40	66	BX35
Duncombe St, G20	21	BM22
Duncruin Dr, (Bishop.) G64	23	BU20
Duncruin St, G20	21	BM22
Duncryne Av, G32	54	CF33
Duncryne Gdns, G32	54	CF33
Duncryne Pl, (Bishop.) G64	23	BU21
Dundashill, G4	10	BR27
Dundas La, G1	10	BS29
Dundas St, G1	10	BS29
Dundee Dr, G52	47	BD33
Dundee Path, G52	47	BE34
Dundonald Rd, G12	35	BL25
Dundonald Rd, Pais. PA3	45	AW30
Dundrennan Rd, G42	64	BP38
Dunearn Pl, Pais. PA2	45	AW34
Dunearn St, G4	9	BP27
Dunedin Ter, Clyde. G81	17	AY21
Dunellan St, G52	48	BG32
Dungeonhill Rd, G34	42	CM29
Dunglass Av, G14	18	BE25
Dunira St, G32	53	CB34
Dunivaig St, G33	54	CG29
Dunkeld Av, (Ruther.) G73	66	BX38
Dunkeld St, G31	52	BY33
Dunlop Cres, (Both.) G71	85	CQ44
Dunlop Gro, (Udd.) G71	71	CQ36
Dunlop St, G1	10	BS31
Dunlop St, (Camb.) G72	68	CG39
Dunmore St, Clyde. G81	17	AY21
Dunnachie Dr, Coat. ML5	57	CR33
Dunnichen Gdns, (Bishop.) G64	24	BZ20
Dunnottar St, G33	40	CD27
Dunn St, G40	52	BW33
Dunn St, Pais. PA1	45	AW32
Dunolly St, G21	38	BW28
Dunphail Dr, G34	42	CM29
Dunphail Rd, G34	42	CM29
Dunragit St, G31	52	BY30
Dunrobin St, G31	52	BX31
Dunrod St, G32	53	CD33
Dunside Dr, G53	61	BC39
Dunskaith Pl, G34	42	CM30
Dunskaith St, G34	42	CM29
Dunsmuir St, G51	48	BK30
Dunsyre Pl, G23	21	BN20
Dunsyre St, G33	39	CA29
Duntarvie Av, G34	42	CL29
Duntarvie Cl, G34	42	CL29
Duntarvie Cres, G34	42	CL29
Duntarvie Dr, G34	41	CK29
Duntarvie Gdns, G34	42	CL29
Duntarvie Gro, G34	42	CL29
Duntarvie Pl, G34	41	CK29
Duntarvie Rd, G34	41	CK29
Dunterlie Av, G13	18	BA21
Dunterlie Ct, (Barr.) G78	73	AY42
Duntreath Av, G13	18	BA21
Duntreath Av, G15	18	BB20
Duntreath Dr, G15	18	BB20
Duntreath Gdns, G15	18	BB20
Duntreath Gro, G15	18	BB20
Duntroon St, G31	38	BX29
Dunure Dr, (Ruther.) G73	79	BV40
Dunure St, G20	21	BM22
Dunvegan Av, (Udd.) G71	71	CM37
Dunwan Av, G13	18	BB22
Dunwan Pl, G13	18	BB22
Durham St, G41	12	BM32
Durno Path, G33	54	CG30
Duror St, G32	53	CC31
Durris Gdns, G32	54	CF34
Durward Av, G41	63	BM36
Durward Ct, G41	63	BM36
Duthie Pk Gdns, G13	19	BF23
Duthie Pk Pl, G13	19	BF22
Duthil St, G51	47	BF31
Dyce La, G11	34	BJ27
Dykebar Av, G13	19	BC23
Dykebar Cres, Pais. PA2	59	AX35
Dykehead La, G33	54	CF30
Dykehead Rd, (Baill.) G69	57	CP32
Dykehead St, G33	54	CF30
Dykemuir St, G21	38	BW25
Dyke Pl, G13	19	BC21
Dyke Rd, G13	18	BC22
Dyke Rd, G14	18	BB23
Dyke St, (Baill.) G69	56	CL32
Dyke St, Coat. ML5	57	CR33

E

Name	Page	Grid
Eaglesham Pl, G51	12	BN31
Eagle St, G4	10	BS27
Earlbank Av, G14	33	BE25
Earl Haig Rd, G52	46	BB30
Earl La, G14	33	BE26
Earl Pl, G14	33	BE26
Earlscourt, (Mood.) G69	29	CP20
Earls Gate, (Both.) G71	84	CN42
Earlspark Av, G43	64	BP38
Earlston Av, G21	37	BV28
Earlston Pl, G21	11	BU28
Earl St, G14	33	BE26
Earlybraes Dr, G32	54	CG31
Earlybraes Gdns, G33	54	CF31
Earnock St, G33	38	BZ25
Earnside St, G32	54	CD32
Earn St, G33	39	CA28
Easdale Dr, G32	53	CC33
East Av, (Udd.) G71	71	CS39
East Av, Renf. PA4	32	AZ26
Eastbank Dr, G32	54	CE32
Eastbank Pl, G32	54	CE32
Eastbank Ri, G32	54	CE32
East Barns St, Clyde. G81	18	AZ21
East Buchanan St, Pais. PA1	44	AV32
Eastburn Cres, G21	24	BX23
Eastburn Rd, G21	24	BX24
East Campbell St, G1	15	BU31
Eastcote Av, G14	34	BG26
Eastcroft, (Ruther.) G73	66	BX37
Eastcroft Ter, G21	38	BW25
Easter Av, (Udd.) G71	70	CN39
Eastercraigs, G31	38	BX29
Easterhill Pl, G32	53	CB34
Easterhill St, G32	53	CB34
Easterhouse Quad, G34	56	CL30
Easterhouse Rd, G34	42	CL29
Easterhouse Rd, (Baill.) G69	55	CK32
Easterhouse Township Centre, G34	41	CJ29
Easter Ms, (Udd.) G71	70	CN39
Easter Queenslie Rd, G33	41	CG29
Eastfield Av, (Camb.) G72	67	CA39
Eastfield Rd, G21	37	BU25
Eastgate, (Gart.) G69	29	CQ24
East Greenlees Av, (Camb.) G72	82	CE42
East Greenlees Cres, (Camb.) G72	82	CD42
East Greenlees Dr, (Camb.) G72	82	CE42
East Greenlees Gro, (Camb.) G72	81	CC42
East Greenlees Rd, (Camb.) G72	81	CC42
Easthall Pl, G33	55	CH30

Street	Page	Grid
East Kilbride Rd, (Ruther.) G73	80	BY40
East La, Pais. PA1	45	AW33
Eastmuir St, G32	54	CD32
East Queenslie Ind Est, G33	40	CG29
East Springfield Ter, (Bishop.) G64	24	BX21
Eastvale Pl, G3	35	BL29
East Wellington St, G31	52	BZ32
East Whitby St, G31	52	BY33
Eastwood Av, G41	63	BM37
Eastwood Av, (Giff.) G46	77	BL43
Eastwood Cres, (Thornlie.) G46	76	BH41
Eastwoodmains Rd, (Giff.) G46	77	BL44
Eastwoodmains Rd, (Clark.) G76	77	BL44
Eastwood Pk, (Giff.) G46	77	BJ43
Eastwood Pk, (Thornlie.) G46	76	BJ43
Eastwood Vw, (Camb.) G72	68	CG39
Eckford St, G32	53	CC33
Eday St, G22	23	BT23
Edderton Pl, G34	55	CJ30
Edderton Way, G34	55	CJ30
Eddlewood Ct, G33	55	CH30
Eddlewood Pl, G33	55	CH30
Eddlewood Rd, G33	55	CH30
Eden La, G33	38	BZ28
Eden Pk, (Both.) G71	84	CP43
Eden Pl, (Camb.) G72	82	CF40
Eden Pl, Renf. PA4	32	BA27
Eden St, G33	38	BZ28
Edenwood St, G31	53	CA32
Edgam Dr, G52	48	BE32
Edgefauld Av, G21	37	BV26
Edgefauld Dr, G21	37	BV25
Edgefauld Pl, G21	23	BV24
Edgefauld Rd, G21	37	BV25
Edgehill La, G11	34	BJ25
Edgehill Rd, G11	34	BH25
Edgemont St, G41	63	BN37
Edinbeg Av, G42	65	BU37
Edinbeg Pl, G42	65	BU37
Edinburgh Rd, G33	53	BZ30
Edinburgh Rd, (Baill.) G69	55	CH31
Edington St, G4	10	BR27
Edison St, G52	32	BA29
Edmiston Dr, G51	48	BH31
Edrom Ct, G32	53	CB32
Edrom St, G32	53	CB32
Edward Av, Renf. PA4	32	BA25
Edward St, (Baill.) G69	57	CP32
Edward St, Clyde. G81	18	AZ22
Edwin St, G51	12	BM32
Edzell Ct, G14	33	BF27
Edzell Gdns, (Bishop.) G64	24	BY21
Edzell Pl, G14	33	BF26
Edzell St, G14	33	BF27
Egidia Av, (Giff.) G46	77	BL43
Egilsay Cres, G22	22	BS21
Egilsay Pl, G22	22	BS21
Egilsay St, G22	22	BS21
Egilsay Ter, G22	22	BS21
Eglinton Ct, G5	14	BR32
Eglinton Dr, (Giff.) G46	77	BL43
Eglinton St, G5	14	BR32
Eighth St, (Udd.) G71	70	CN36
Eildon Dr, (Barr.) G78	73	AY44
Elcho St, G40	51	BV31
Elder Cres, (Camb.) G72	83	CG41
Elder Gro, (Udd.) G71	71	CR38
Elder Gro Av, G51	47	BF30
Elder Gro Ct, G51	47	BF30
Elder Gro Pl, G51	47	BF30
Elderpark Gro, G51	48	BH30
Elderpark St, G51	48	BH30
Elderslie St, G3	9	BP28
Elder St, G51	34	BH29
Eldon Gdns, (Bishop.) G64	23	BU20
Eldon St, G3	8	BN27
Elibank St, G33	39	CC28
Elie St, G11	35	BL27
Elizabethan Way, Renf. PA4	31	AY28
Elizabeth Cres, (Thornlie.) G46	76	BJ42
Elizabeth St, G51	49	BL32
Ellangowan Rd, G41	63	BL37
Ellesmere St, G22	36	BQ25
Elliot Av, (Giff.) G46	77	BL43
Elliot Dr, (Giff.) G46	77	BL42
Elliot Pl, G3	8	BN29
Elliot St, G3	12	BN30
Ellisland Cres, (Ruther.) G73	79	BV40
Ellisland Rd, G43	63	BM39
Ellismuir Pl, (Baill.) G69	56	CL33
Ellismuir Rd, (Baill.) G69	56	CL33
Ellismuir Way, (Udd.) G71	71	CQ36
Elliston Av, G53	75	BE40
Elliston Cres, G53	75	BE40
Elliston Dr, G53	75	BE40
Ellon Way, Pais. PA3	45	AV30
Elm Av, Renf. PA4	31	AY25
Elm Bk, (Bishop.) G64	24	BX20
Elmbank Av, (Udd.) G71	71	CR38
Elmbank Cres, G2	9	BQ29
Elmbank St, G2	9	BQ29
Elmbank St La, G2	9	BQ29
Elm Dr, (Camb.) G72	82	CE40
Elmfoot St, G5	65	BT35
Elmira Rd, (Muir.) G69	28	CL22
Elmore Av, G44	78	BR40
Elmore La, G44	78	BR40
Elm Rd, (Ruther.) G73	80	BX41
Elm Rd, Pais. PA2	59	AW36
Elmslie Ct, (Baill.) G69	56	CL33
Elm St, G14	33	BF26
Elmtree Gdns, G45	79	BV41
Elmvale Row, G21	23	BU24
Elmvale St, G21	23	BU24
Elm Way, (Camb.) G72	83	CG41
Elmwood Av, G11	34	BH25
Elmwood Ct, (Both.) G71	85	CQ43
Elmwood La, G11	34	BH25
Elphinstone Pl, G51	49	BL30
Elrig Rd, G44	78	BP40
Elvan St, G32	53	CB32
Elvan Dr, G13	19	BD23
Emerson Rd, (Bishop.) G64	24	BW20
Emerson St, G20	22	BQ23
Endfield Av, G12	21	BK23
Endrick Dr, Pais. PA1	45	AX31
Endrick St, G21	37	BT26
Ensay St, G22	23	BT22
Enterkin St, G32	53	CB33
Eriboll Pl, G22	22	BR22
Eriboll St, G22	22	BR22
Ericht Rd, G43	77	BL40
Eriska Av, G14	19	BC24
Erradale St, G22	22	BQ22
Errogie St, G34	55	CK29
Errol Gdns, G5	50	BS33
Erskine Av, G41	49	BK33
Erskine Sq, G52	46	BB30
Ervie St, G34	56	CL30
Esk Av, Renf. PA4	32	BA27
Eskbank St, G32	53	CC31
Eskbank Toll, (Giff.) G46	77	BK44
Eskdale Dr, (Ruther.) G73	66	BZ38
Eskdale St, G42		BR36
Esk St, G14	18	BB24
Esmond St, G3	35	BL28
Espedair St, Pais. PA2	44	AU…
Essenden Av, G14	34	BG…
Essex Dr, G14	34	BG…
Essex La, G14	33	BF…
Esslemont Av, G14	19	BD…
Estate Quad, G32	68	CE…
Estate Rd, G32	68	CE…
Etive Cres, (Bishop.) G64	24	BX…
Etive Dr, (Giff.) G46	77	BM…
Etive St, G32	53	CC…
Eton La, G12	8	BN…
Ettrick Cres, (Ruther.) G73	66	BY…
Ettrick Pl, G43		BM…
Evan Cres, (Giff.) G46	77	BM…
Evan Dr, (Giff.) G46	77	BM…
Evanton Dr, (Thornlie.) G46	76	BG…
Evanton Pl, (Thornlie.) G46	76	BG…
Everard Ct, G21	23	BL…
Everard Dr, G21	23	BL…
Everard Pl, G21	23	BL…
Everard Quad, G21	23	BL…
Everglades, The, (Chry.) G69	27	CH…
Eversley St, G32	53	CC…
Everton Rd, G53	61	BE…
Ewing Pl, G31	52	BY…
Ewing St, (Ruther.) G73	66	BW…
Exeter Dr, G11	34	BJ…
Eynort St, G22	22	BQ…

F

Street	Page	Grid
Fagan Ct, (Blan.) G72	84	CN…
Fairbairn Cres, (Thornlie.) G46	76	BJ…
Fairbairn St, G40	52	BW…
Fairburn St, G32	53	CB…
Fairfax Av, G44	78	BS…
Fairfield Dr, Renf. PA4	32	AZ…
Fairfield Pl, (Both.) G71	85	CR…
Fairfield St, G51	34	BH…
Fairhaven Rd, G23	21	BN…
Fairhill Av, G53	61	BE…
Fairholm St, G32	53	CB…
Fairley St, G51	49	BK…
Fairlie Pk Dr, G11	34	BJ…
Fairway Av, Pais. PA2	58	AT…
Fairyknowe Gdns, (Both.) G71	85	CR…
Falcon Ter, G20	21	BL…
Falcon Ter La, G20	21	BL…
Falfield St, G5	50	BQ…
Falkland Cres, (Bishop.) G64	24	BZ…
Falkland La, G12	35	BK…
Falkland St, G12	34	BK…
Falloch Rd, G42	64	BQ…
Fallside Av, (Udd.) G71	71	CS…
Fallside Rd, (Both.) G71	85	CQ…
Falside Av, Pais. PA2	58	AU…
Falside Rd, G32	68	CD…
Falside Rd, Pais. PA2	58	AU…
Fara St, G23	22	BP…
Farie St, (Ruther.) G73	65	BV…
Farm Ct, (Both.) G71	85	CP…
Farme Castle Ct, (Ruther.) G73	66	BW…
Farme Castle Est, (Ruther.) G73	66	BW…
Farme Cross, (Ruther.) G73	66	BX…
Farmeloan Ind Est, (Ruther.) G73	66	BX…
Farmeloan Rd, (Ruther.) G73	66	BX…
Farmington Av, G32	54	CH…
Farmington Gdns, G32	54	CH…
Farmington Gate, G32	54	CH…
Farmington Gro, G32	54	CH…

Street	Page	Grid
rm Rd, G41	48	BK32
rm Rd, (Blan.) G72	84	CM44
rne Dr, G44	78	BR41
rnell St, G4	10	BK27
skin Cres, G53	60	BB38
skin Pl, G53	60	BB38
skin Rd, G53	60	BB38
stnet St, G33	39	CC29
ulds, (Baill.) G69	51	BT34
ulds Gdns, (Baill.) G69	56	CL32
uldshead Rd, Renf. PA4	31	AY26
uldspark Cres, (Baill.) G69	56	CL31
arnmore Rd, G20	21	BM23
lton Pl, G13	18	BB22
ndoch St, G32	53	CC33
nella St, G32	54	CD32
nnsbank Av, (Ruther.) G73	80	BZ42
nwick Dr, (Barr.) G78	74	AZ44
nwick Rd, (Giff.) G46	77	BK44
reneze Av, (Barr.) G78	73	AX42
reneze Av, Renf. PA4	31	AW29
reneze Cres, G13	18	BC22
reneze Dr, Pais. PA2	58	AX36
reneze Gro, (Barr.) G78	73	AX41
reneze Rd, (Neil.) G78	72	AU44
rgus Dr, G20	35	BN25
rgus La, G20	35	BP25
rguson Av, Renf. PA4	32	AZ26
rguson St, Renf. PA4	32	AZ25
rnan St, G32	53	CB32
rn Av, (Bishop.) G64	24	BX21
rnbank Av, (Camb.) G72	82	CE41
rnbank St, G21	23	BU24
rnbank St, G22	23	BU24
rnbrae Av, (Ruther.) G73	80	BY42
rnbrae Way, (Ruther.) G73	80	BX42
rncroft Dr, G44	79	BT40
rndale Ct, G21	21	BM21
rndale Dr, G21	21	BM20
rndale Gdns, G23	21	BM21
rndale Pl, G23	21	BM21
rn Dr, (Barr.) G78	73	AX41
rness Oval, G21	24	BY22
rness Pl, G21	24	BY22
rness Rd, G21	24	BY23
rngrove Av, G12	21	BK23
rnhill Av, (Both.) G71	85	CQ43
rnhill Rd, (Ruther.) G73	80	BW41
rnie Gdns, G20	21	BN22
rn La, G13	20	BH24
rnleigh Rd, G43	77	BM40
rry Rd, G3	35	BK28
rry Rd, (Both.) G71	85	CQ43
rry Rd, (Udd.) G71	70	CN39
rry Rd, Renf. PA4	32	AZ25
rsit Ct, G43	63	BL39
rsit St, G43	63	BL39
etlar Dr, G44	78	BS40
ttercairn Gdns, (Bishop.) G64	24	BY20
ttes St, G33	39	CB29
dra St, G33	39	CB29
elden Pl, G40	52	BW32
elden St, G40	52	BW32
edhead Dr, G43	76	BJ40
edhead Sq, G43	76	BJ40
fe Av, G52	47	BD33
fe Cres, (Both.) G71	85	CQ44
fe Way, (Bishop.) G64	24	BY20
fth Av, G12	20	BH24
fth Av, (Stepps) G33	26	CD24
fth Av, Renf. PA4	31	AY27
fty Pitches Pl, G51	47	BD30
Fifty Pitches Rd, G51	47	BD30
Fifty Pitches Way, G52	33	BD29
Finart Dr, Pais. PA2	59	AX36
Finch Dr, G13	18	BC21
Findhorn St, G33	38	BZ29
Findochty St, G33	40	CG28
Fingal St, G20	21	BM22
Fingask St, G32	54	CE33
Finglas Av, Pais. PA2	59	AX36
Finglen Pl, G53	75	BD41
Fingleton Av, (Barr.) G78	74	AZ44
Finhaven St, G32	53	CA34
Finlarig St, G34	56	CL30
Finlas St, G22	37	BT25
Finlay Dr, G31	52	BW30
Finnart Sq, G40	51	BV34
Finnart St, G40	51	BV34
Finnieston Quay, G3	12	BN30
Finnieston Sq, G3	8	BN30
Finnieston St, G3	12	BN30
Finsbay St, G51	48	AU37
Fintry Av, Pais. PA2	58	AU37
Fintry Cres, (Bishop.) G64	24	BX21
Fintry Cres, (Barr.) G78	73	AY44
Fintry Dr, G44	64	BS38
Firbank Ter, (Barr.) G78	74	BA44
Fir Ct, (Camb.) G72	83	CG41
Firdon Cres, G15	19	BC20
Fir Gro, (Udd.) G71	71	CR38
Firhill Rd, G20	36	BQ25
Firhill St, G20	36	BQ25
Firpark Pl, (Bishop.) G64	24	BX21
Firpark Rd, (Bishop.) G64	24	BX21
Firpark St, G31	37	BV29
Firpark Ter, G31	51	BV30
Fir Pl, (Baill.) G69	55	CJ34
Fir Pl, (Camb.) G72	82	CE39
First Av, (Millerston) G33	26	CD24
First Av, G44	78	BR43
First Av, (Kirk.) G66	26	CF20
First Av, (Udd.) G71	70	CN37
First Av, Renf. PA4	31	AY27
First Gdns, G41	48	BJ33
First St, (Udd.) G71	70	CP37
Firwood Dr, G44	64	BS39
Fisher Ct, G31	51	BV30
Fishers Rd, Renf. PA4	17	AY23
Fishescoates Av, (Ruther.) G73	80	BY40
Fishescoates Gdns, (Ruther.) G73	80	BY40
Fitzalan Dr, Pais. PA3	45	AW31
Fitzalan Rd, Renf. PA4	31	AW29
Fitzroy La, G3	8	BN29
Flax Rd, (Udd.) G71	85	CQ40
Fleet Av, Renf. PA4	32	BA28
Fleet St, G32	54	CD33
Fleming Av, (Chry.) G69	28	CL22
Fleming Av, Clyde. G81	18	AZ20
Fleming St, G31	52	BX31
Fleming St, Pais. PA3	44	AU30
Fleming Ind Est, (Camb.) G72		
Flemington Rd, (Camb.) G72	83	CH44
Flemington St, G21	37	BV26
Fleurs Av, G41	49	BK33
Fleurs Rd, G41	48	BK33
Florence Dr, (Giff.) G46	77	BL43
Florence Gdns, (Ruther.) G73	80	BY41
Florence St, G5	14	BS32
Florida Av, G42	64	BR37
Florida Cres, G42	64	BR37
Florida Dr, G42	64	BQ37
Florida Gdns, (Baill.) G69	55	CJ32
Florida Sq, G42	64	BR37
Florida St, G42	64	BR37
Florish Rd, Ersk. PA8	16	AT21
Flures Av, Ersk. PA8	16	AU21
Flures Cres, Ersk. PA8	16	AU21
Flures Dr, Ersk. PA8	16	AU21
Flures Pl, Ersk. PA8	16	AU21
Fochabers Dr, G52	47	BE31
Fogo Pl, G20	21	BM23
Foinaven Dr, (Thornlie.) G46	62	BH39
Foinaven Gdns, (Thornlie.) G46	62	BJ39
Foinaven Way, (Thornlie.) G46	76	BJ40
Forbes Dr, G40	51	BV32
Forbes Pl, Pais. PA1	44	AU33
Forbes St, G40	51	BV31
Fordneuk St, G40	52	BW32
Fordoun St, G34	42	CM29
Ford Rd, G12	35	BM26
Fordyce St, G11	35	BK27
Foremount Ter La, G12	35	BK26
Forest Dr, (Both.) G71	85	CQ42
Foresthall Cres, G21	38	BW26
Foresthall Dr, G21	38	BW26
Forest Pl, Pais. PA2	58	AU35
Fore St, G14	33	BE26
Forfar Av, G52	47	BD33
Forfar Cres, (Bishop.) G64	24	BY21
Forgan Gdns, (Bishop.) G64	24	BZ21
Forge Pl, G21	38	BX27
Forge Retail Pk, G31	52	BX31
Forge Shop Cen, The, G31	52	BY32
Forge St, G21	38	BX27
Forglen St, G34	41	CK28
Formby Dr, G23	21	BM20
Forres Av, (Giff.) G46	77	BL42
Forres Gate, (Giff.) G46	77	BM43
Forrestfield St, G21	38	BW28
Forrest Gate, (Udd.) G71	71	CR36
Forrest St, G40	52	BW32
Fortevoit Av, (Baill.) G69	56	CL32
Fortevoit Pl, (Baill.) G69	56	CL32
Forth St, G41	50	BP34
Forth, Clyde. G81	17	AY20
Forties Ct, (Thornlie.) G46	76	BH40
Forties Cres, (Thornlie.) G46	76	BJ40
Forties Gdns, (Thornlie.) G46	76	BJ40
Forties Way, (Thornlie.) G46	76	BJ40
Fortingall Av, G12	21	BL23
Fortingall Pl, G12	21	BL23
Fortrose St, G11	34	BK27
Fotheringay La, G41	63	BM35
Fotheringay Rd, G41	63	BM35
Foulis La, G13	20	BH23
Foulis St, G13	20	BH23
Foundry La, (Barr.) G78	73	AY43
Foundry St, G21	37	BV25
Fountain Dr, (Inch.) Renf. PA4	16	AS24
Fountainwell Av, G21	37	BT26
Fountainwell Dr, G21	11	BT27
Fountainwell Pl, G21	11	BT27
Fountainwell Rd, G21	11	BT27
Fountainwell Sq, G21	11	BU27
Fountainwell Ter, G21	11	BU27
Fourth Av, G33	26	CD24
Fourth Av, (Kirk.) G66	26	CF20
Fourth Av, Renf. PA4	31	AY27
Fourth Gdns, G41	48	BJ33
Fourth St, (Udd.) G71	70	CP36
Foxbar Dr, G13	19	BD23
Foxglove Pl, G53	75	BD42
Foxhills Pl, G23	21	BN20
Foxley St, G32	68	CE36

Street	Page	Grid
Fox St, G1	14	BR31
Foyers Ter, G21	38	BW25
Francis St, G5	50	BO33
Frankfield Rd, G33	26	CG24
Frankfield St, G33	39	BZ27
Frankfort St, G41	63	BN36
Franklin St, G40	51	BV34
Fraser Av, (Ruther.) G73	66	BY38
Fraser St, (Camb.) G72	67	CA39
Frazer St, G40	52	BW32
Freeland Cres, G53	61	BD39
Freeland Dr, G53	61	BD39
Freeland Dr, (Inch.) Renf. PA4	16	AS23
French St, G40	51	BV34
French St, Renf. PA4	31	AX27
Freuchie St, G34	55	CK30
Friarscourt Av, G13	19	BF21
Friarscourt Rd, (Chry.) G69	27	CK20
Friarton Rd, G43	64	BP39
Friendship Way, Renf. PA4	32	AZ28
Fruin Pl, G22	37	BS25
Fruin Rd, G15	18	BB20
Fruin St, G22	37	BS25
Fulbar Av, Renf. PA4	31	AY25
Fulbar La, Renf. PA4	32	AZ25
Fulbar Rd, G51	47	BE30
Fulbar St, Renf. PA4	32	AZ25
Fullarton Av, G32	67	CC35
Fullarton Dr, G32	67	CC36
Fullarton La, G32	67	CC36
Fullarton Rd, G32	67	CB37
Fullerton St, Pais. PA3	44	AT30
Fullerton Ter, Pais. PA3	44	AU30
Fulmar Ct, (Bishop.) G64	23	BV21
Fulton St, G13	19	BF22
Fulwood Av, G13	18	BB22
Fulwood Pl, G13	18	BB22
Fyvie Av, G43	76	BK40

G

Street	Page	Grid
Gadie Av, Renf. PA4	32	BA27
Gadie St, G33	38	BZ29
Gadloch St, G22	22	BS23
Gadsburn Ct, G21	24	BY23
Gadshill St, G21	37	BV27
Gailes Pk, (Both.) G71	84	CP43
Gailes St, G40	52	BX33
Gainside Rd, (Glenb.) Coat. ML5	29	CS23
Gairbraid Av, G20	21	BL23
Gairbraid Ct, G20	21	BL23
Gairbraid Pl, G20	21	BM23
Gairbraid Ter, (Baill.) G69	57	CQ32
Gala Av, Renf. PA4	32	BA27
Gala St, G33	39	CA27
Galdenoch St, G33	40	CD27
Gallan Av, G23	21	BN20
Galloway Dr, (Ruther.) G73	80	BX42
Galloway St, G21	23	BV23
Gallowflat St, (Ruther.) G73	66	BX37
Gallowgate, G1	15	BT31
Gallowgate, G4	15	BU31
Gallowgate, G31	52	BW31
Gallowgate, G40	15	BW31
Gallowhill Rd, Pais. PA3	45	AW31
Galston St, G53	60	BB39
Gamrie Gdns, G53	61	BC38
Gamrie Rd, G53	60	BC38
Gannochy Dr, (Bishop.) G64	24	BY20
Gantock Cres, G33	40	CD29
Gardenside Av, G32	68	CD37
Gardenside Av, (Udd.) G71	70	CN39
Gardenside Cres, G32	68	CD37
Gardenside Gro, G32	68	CD37
Gardenside Pl, G32	68	CD37
Gardenside St, (Udd.) G71	70	CN39
Gardner Gro, (Udd.) G71	71	CO37
Gardner St, G11	35	BK27
Garfield Av, G31	53	BW31
Garforth Rd, (Baill.) G69	55	CH33
Gargrave Av, (Baill.) G69	55	CH33
Garion Dr, G13	19	BD23
Garlieston Rd, G33	55	CH31
Garmouth Ct, G51	34	BJ29
Garmouth St, G51	34	BH29
Garnet St, G3	9	BQ28
Garnet St, G3	9	BQ28
Garnie Av, Ersk. PA8	16	AT20
Garnie Cres, Ersk. PA8	16	AT20
Garnieland Rd, Ersk. PA8	16	AT20
Garnie La, Ersk. PA8	16	AT21
Garnie Oval, Ersk. PA8	16	AT20
Garnie Pl, Ersk. PA8	16	AT20
Garnkirk La, G33	27	CG24
Garnock St, G21	37	BV27
Garrioch Cres, G20	21	BM24
Garrioch Dr, G20	21	BL23
Garriochmill Rd, G20	35	BN25
Garrioch Quad, G20	21	BM24
Garrioch Rd, G20	35	BM25
Garrowhill Dr, (Baill.) G69	55	CH33
Garry Av, G44	64	BD38
Garry St, G44	64	BD38
Garscadden Rd, G15	18	BC20
Garscadden Rd S, G13	18	BC21
Garscube Cross, G4	10	BR27
Garscube Rd, G4	36	BQ26
Garscube Rd, G20	36	BQ26
Gartartan Rd, Pais. PA1	46	BB32
Gartcloss Rd, Coat. ML5	43	CS27
Gartcosh Rd, (Gart.) G69	43	CQ29
Gartcraig Pl, G33	39	CB28
Gartcraig Rd, G33	39	CA29
Gartferry St, G21	37	BV25
Garthland Dr, G31	37	BW30
Garthland La, Pais. PA1	45	AV32
Gartliston Ter, (Baill.) G69	57	CQ32
Gartloch Cotts, (Gart.) G69	42	CN26
Gartloch Cotts, (Muir.) G69	27	CK24
Gartloch Rd, G33	39	CB27
Gartloch Rd, G34	40	CE28
Gartloch Rd, (Gart.) G69	42	CL26
Gartmore Gdns, (Udd.) G71	70	CN37
Gartmore Rd, Pais. PA1	45	AX33
Gartmore Ter, (Camb.) G72	81	CA42
Gartness Dr, G31	53	BX30
Gartocher Dr, G32	54	CE32
Gartocher Rd, G32	54	CE32
Gartocher Ter, G32	54	CE32
Gartons Rd, G21	24	BY24
Garturk St, G42	51	BR36
Garvald St, G40	52	BX34
Garve Av, G44	78	BQ41
Garvel Cres, G33	55	CG31
Garvel Rd, G33	55	CG31
Garvock Dr, G43	76	BJ40
Gaskin Path, G33	26	CG24
Gask Pl, G13	18	BB21
Gatehouse St, G32	54	CD32
Gateside Av, (Camb.) G72	82	CF40
Gateside Cres, (Barr.) G78	73	AW44
Gateside Rd, (Barr.) G78	72	AV44
Gateside St, G31	52	BX31
Gauldry Av, G52	47	BE34
Gauze St, Pais. PA1	44	AU32
Gavinton St, G44	78	BP40
Gayne Dr, (Glenb.) Coat. ML5	29	CS23
Gear Ter, G40	66	BX…
Geddes Rd, G21	24	BY…
Gelston St, G32	54	CD…
Generals Gate, (Udd.) G71	70	CN…
General Terminus Quay, G51	13	BP…
George Gray St, (Ruther.) G73	66	BY…
George La, Pais. PA1	44	AU…
George Mann Ter, (Ruther.) G73	80	BW…
George Pl, Pais. PA1	44	AU…
George Reith Av, G12	20	BH…
George Sq, G2	14	BS…
George St, G1	14	BS…
George St, (Baill.) G69	55	CK…
George St, (Barr.) G78	73	AX…
George St, Pais. PA1	44	AT…
Gertrude Pl, (Barr.) G78	73	AW…
Gibson Rd, Renf. PA4	31	AY…
Gibson St, G12	8	BN…
Gibson St, G40	15	BU…
Giffnock Pk Av, (Giff.) G46	77	BL…
Gifford Dr, G52	47	BC…
Gilbertfield Pl, G33	40	CD…
Gilbertfield Rd, (Camb.) G72	82	CE…
Gilbertfield St, G33	40	CD…
Gilbert St, G3	35	BL…
Gilhill St, G20	21	BM…
Gila St, (Camb.) G72	67	CA…
Gillies La, (Baill.) G69	56	CL…
Gilmanton St, G32	53	CC…
Gilmour Cres, (Ruther.) G73	65	BV…
Gilmour Pl, G5	51	BS…
Gilmour St, Pais. PA1	44	AU…
Girdons Way, (Udd.) G71	70	CN…
Girthon St, G32	54	CE…
Girvan St, G33	38	BZ…
Gladney Av, G13	18	BA…
Gladsmuir Rd, G52	47	BD…
Gladstone Av, (Barr.) G78	73	AX…
Gladstone St, G4	9	BQ…
Glaive Rd, G13	19	BF…
Glamis Rd, G31	52	BZ…
Glanderston Ct, G13	19	BC…
Glanderston Dr, G13	19	BC…
Glasgow Airport, (Abbots.) Pais. PA3	30	AT…
Glasgow & Edinburgh Rd, (Baill.) G69	57	CP…
Glasgow Br, G1	14	BR…
Glasgow Br, G5	14	BR…
Glasgow Business Pk, (Baill.) G69	55	CK…
Glasgow Cross, G1	15	BT…
Glasgow E Investment Pk, G32	67	CB…
Glasgow Grn, G1	15	BT…
Glasgow Grn, G40	15	BT…
Glasgow Rd, G53	74	AZ…
Glasgow Rd, (Baill.) G69	55	CH…
Glasgow Rd, (Udd.) G71	70	CN…
Glasgow Rd, (Blan.) G72	84	CL…
Glasgow Rd, (Camb.) G72	67	CA…
Glasgow Rd, (Turnlaw) G72	81	CB…
Glasgow Rd, (Ruther.) G73	65	BV…
Glasgow Rd, (Barr.) G78	72	AW…
Glasgow Rd, Clyde. G81	17	AX…
Glasgow Rd, Coat. ML5	57	CS…
Glasgow Rd, Pais. PA1	45	AW…
Glasgow Rd, Renf. PA4	32	BA…
Glasgow St, G12	35	BN…
Glassel Rd, G34	42	CM…
Glasserton Pl, G43	78	BP…
Glasserton Rd, G43	78	BP…
Glassford St, G1	14	BS…

audhall Av, (Gart.) G69	28	CN22
ebe, The, (Both.) G71	85	CR43
ebe Av, (Both.) G71	85	CR43
ebe Ct, G4	11	BT29
ebe Hollow, (Both.) G71	85	CR43
ebe Pl, (Camb.) G72	82	CD40
ebe Pl, (Ruther.) G73	65	BV37
ebe St, G4	11	BT29
ebe St, Renf. PA4	32	AZ26
ebe Wynd, (Both.) G71	85	CR43
eddoch Rd, G52	46	BA31
enacre Cres, (Udd.) G71	70	CN37
enacre Gdns, G51	79	BT42
enacre Gro, G45	79	BU41
enacre St, G45	79	BT42
en Affric Av, G53	75	BE41
enalmond St, G32	53	CC33
enapp Av, Pais. PA2	59	AX36
enapp Rd, Pais. PA2	59	AX36
enapp St, G41	50	BP34
enarklet Cres, Pais. PA2	59	AX36
enarklet Dr, Pais. PA2	59	AW36
enartney Rd, (Chry.) G69	28	CL20
enashdale Way, Pais. PA2	59	AW36
en Av, G32	54	CD31
enavon Rd, G20	21	BM22
enbank Dr, (Thornlie.) G46	76	BH43
enbarr St, G21	37	BV28
enbrittle Dr, Pais. PA2	59	AW36
enbrittle Pl, Pais. PA2	59	AW36
enbrittle Way, Pais. PA2	59	AW36
enbuck Av, G33	25	CB33
enbuck St, G33	25	CB33
enburn Av, (Baill.) G69	56	CL32
enburn Av, (Camb.) G72	81	BZ40
enburn Cres, (Udd.) G71	71	CT36
enburn Cres, Pais. PA2	58	AT38
enburn Rd, (Glenb.) Coat. ML5	29	CS23
enburn Pl, G34	55	CH30
enburn Rd, (Giff.) G46	77	BK44
encairn Dr, G20	21	BN22
encairn Dr, G41	63	BM35
encairn Dr, (Ruther.) G73	65	BV37
encairn Gdns, G41	63	BM35
encairn Gdns, (Camb.) G72	82	CF40
encairn La, G41	64	BP35
encairn Rd, Pais. PA3	31	AW29
encally Av, Pais. PA2	59	AX36
enclora Dr, Pais. PA2	59	AW36
encloy St, G20	21	BL22
en Clunie Dr, G53	75	BE41
encoe Pl, G13	20	BG22
encoe Rd, (Ruther.) G73	80	BZ42
encoe St, G13	20	BH22
en Cona Dr, G53	75	BE41
encorse Rd, Pais. PA2	58	AS35
encorse St, G32	53	CA30
en Cres, G13	18	BA22
encroft Av, (Udd.) G71	70	CN37
encroft Rd, G44	79	BT40
endale Cres, (Bishop.) G64	24	BY21
endale Dr, (Bishop.) G64	24	BY21
endale Pl, G31	52	BX31
endale Pl, (Bishop.) G64	24	BY21
endale St, G31	52	BX31
endaruel Rd, (Ruther.) G73	81	CA43
endarvel Gdns, G22	37	BT25
endee Gdns, Renf. PA4	32	AZ27
endee Rd, Renf. PA4	32	AZ27
en Dene Way, G53	75	BE41
Glendevon Sq, G33	40	CD27
Glen Dewar Pl, G53	75	BE41
Glendinning Rd, G13	20	BG20
Glendore St, G14	34	BG27
Glenduffhill Rd, (Baill.) G69	55	CH32
Gleneagles La N, G14	33	BE25
Gleneagles La S, G14	33	BE25
Gleneagles Pk, (Both.) G71	84	CP43
Glenelg Quad, G34	42	CM28
Glen Esk Cres, G53	75	BE41
Glen Esk Dr, G53	75	BE41
Glen Etive Pl, (Ruther.) G73	81	CA43
Glenfarg Rd, (Ruther.) G73	80	BX41
Glenfarg St, G20	9	BQ27
Glenfield Av, Pais. PA2	58	AT38
Glenfield Cres, Pais. PA2	58	AT39
Glenfield Gdns, Pais. PA2	58	AT39
Glenfield Gra, Pais. PA2	58	AU39
Glenfield Gro, Pais. PA2	58	AT39
Glenfield Rd, Pais. PA2	58	AS38
Glenfinnan Dr, G20	21	BM23
Glenfinnan Dr, G20	21	BM23
Glenfruin Cres, Pais. PA2	59	AX36
Glengarry Dr, G52	47	BE32
Glengavel Cres, G33	25	CB23
Glen Gavin Way, Pais. PA2	59	AX36
Glenhead Cres, G22	23	BS23
Glenhead St, G22	23	BS23
Gleniffer Av, G13	18	BC23
Gleniffer Dr, (Barr.) G78	73	AW40
Gleniffer Rd, Renf. PA4	31	AX29
Glenisla St, G31	53	CB34
Glen Kyle Dr, G53	75	BE41
Glen La, Pais. PA3	44	AU32
Glenlee Cres, G52	46	BB34
Glenlora Dr, G53	60	BC38
Glenlora Ter, G53	61	BD38
Glen Loy Pl, G53	75	BE41
Glenluce Dr, G32	54	CF34
Glenlui Av, (Ruther.) G73	80	BX40
Glen Luss Pl, G53	75	BE41
Glen Lyon Pl, (Ruther.) G73	80	BX42
Glenmavis St, G4	10	BR28
Glenmore Av, G42	65	BU37
Glen Moriston Rd, G53	75	BE41
Glenmuir Dr, G53	75	BD40
Glen Nevis Pl, (Ruther.) G73	80	BY43
Glen Ogle St, G32	54	CF33
Glen Orchy Dr, G53	75	BE41
Glen Orchy Gro, G53	75	BF41
Glen Orchy Way, G53	75	BE42
Glenpark Av, (Thornlie.) G46	76	BH43
Glenpark Rd, G31	52	BX31
Glenpark St, G31	52	BX31
Glenpark Ter, (Camb.) G72	67	CA38
Glenraith Rd, G33	40	CD26
Glenraith Sq, G33	40	CD26
Glenraith Wk, G33	40	CD26
Glen Rd, G32	54	CD30
Glen Sax Dr, Renf. PA4	32	BA28
Glenshee Ct, G31	53	BZ34
Glenshee Gdns, G31	53	CA34
Glenshee St, G31	53	BZ33
Glenshiel Av, Pais. PA2	59	AW36
Glenshira Av, Pais. PA2	59	AW36
Glenside Av, G53	60	BD35
Glenside Dr, (Ruther.) G73	67	BZ38
Glenspean St, G43	63	BL39
Glen St, (Camb.) G72	82	CF41
Glen St, (Barr.) G78	73	AY42
Glen St, Pais. PA3	44	AT32
Glentanar Pl, G22	22	BR21
Glentanar Rd, G22	22	BR21
Glentarbert Rd, (Ruther.) G73	80	BZ42
Glentrool Gdns, G22	37	BS25
Glenturret St, G32	53	CC33
Glentyan Dr, G53	60	BC38
Glentyan Pl, G53	60	BC38
Glenview Pl, (Blan.) G72	84	CM44
Glenville Av, (Giff.) G46	77	BK42
Glenwood Business Pk, G45	79	BU42
Glenwood Dr, (Thornlie.) G46	76	BH43
Glenwood Path, G45	79	BU42
Glenwood Pl, G45	79	BU42
Gloucester Av, (Ruther.) G73	80	BZ40
Gloucester St, G5	13	BQ32
Gockston Rd, Pais. PA3	44	AT30
Gogar Pl, G33	39	CA29
Gogar St, G33	39	CA29
Goldberry Av, G14	19	BD24
Goldie Rd, (Udd.) G71	85	CQ41
Golf Ct, G44	77	BN43
Golf Dr, G15	18	BB20
Golf Dr, Pais. PA1	45	AY33
Golfhill Dr, G31	38	BW29
Golf Rd, (Ruther.) G73	80	BX41
Golfview Dr, Coat. ML5	57	CS31
Golfview Pl, Coat. ML5	57	CS30
Golspie St, G51	34	BJ29
Goosedubbs, G1	14	BS31
Gopher Av, (Udd.) G71	71	CR37
Gorbals Cross, G5	14	BS32
Gorbals St, G5	50	BR33
Gordon Av, G44	77	BN43
Gordon Av, G52	32	BA29
Gordon Av, (Baill.) G69	55	CH32
Gordon Dr, G44	77	BN42
Gordon Rd, G44	77	BN42
Gordon St, G1	14	BR30
Gordon St, Pais. PA1	44	AU33
Gordon Ter, (Blan.) G72	84	CL43
Gorebridge St, G32	53	CA30
Gorget Av, G13	19	BE20
Gorget Pl, G13	19	BE20
Gorget Quad, G13	19	BD20
Gorse Dr, (Barr.) G78	73	AX41
Gorse Pl, (Udd.) G71	71	CR37
Gorsewood, (Bishop.) G64	23	BU20
Gorstan St, G23	21	BM21
Gosford La, G14	33	BC25
Goudie St, Pais. PA3	44	AS30
Gough St, G33	38	BZ29
Gourlay St, G21	37	BT26
Govan Cross Shop Cen, G51	34	BJ29
Govanhill St, G42	64	BR35
Govan Rd, G51	49	BL31
Gowanlea Av, G15	18	BC20
Gowanlea Dr, (Giff.) G46	77	BM41
Gowanlea Ter, (Udd.) G71	71	CR38
Gower St, G41	49	BL33
Gower St, G51	49	BL33
Gower Ter, G41	49	BL32
Grace Av, (Baill.) G69	56	CP32
Grace St, G3	13	BP30
Graffham Av, (Giff.) G46	77	BM42
Grafton Pl, G1	10	BS29
Graham Av, (Camb.) G72	82	CF40
Graham Sq, G31	51	BV31
Grahamston Ct, Pais. PA2	59	AY37
Grahamston Cres, Pais. PA2	59	AY37
Grahamston Pk, (Barr.) G78	73	AX40

Street	Page	Ref
Grahamston Pl, Pais. PA2	59	AY37
Grahamston Rd, (Barr.) G78	59	AX39
Grahamston Rd, Pais. PA2	59	AX39
Graham St, (Barr.) G78	73	AX42
Graham Ter, (Bishop.) G64	24	BX22
Graignestock St, G40	15	BU32
Grainger Rd, (Bishop.) G64	24	BZ20
Grampian Av, Pais. PA2	58	AT37
Grampian Cres, G32	54	CD33
Grampian Pl, G32	54	CD33
Grampian Rd, G32	54	CD33
Grampian Way, (Barr.) G78	73	AY44
Granby La, G12	35	BM26
Grandtully Dr, G12	21	BL23
Grange Rd, G42	64	BQ37
Gran St, Clyde. G81	18	BA21
Grantlea Gro, G32	54	CF33
Grantlea Ter, G32	54	CF33
Grantley Gdns, G41	63	BM37
Grantley St, G41	63	BM37
Granton St, G5	65	BU35
Grants Av, Pais. PA2	58	AS36
Grants Cres, Pais. PA2	58	AT37
Grants Pl, Pais. PA2	58	AS37
Grant St, G3	9	BP28
Grants Way, Pais. PA2	58	AS36
Granville St, G3	9	BP29
Gray's Rd, (Udd.) G71		CR40
Gray St, G3	8	BN28
Great Dovehill, G1	15	BT31
Great George St, G12	35	BM26
Great Hamilton St, Pais. PA2	58	AU35
Great Western Retail Pk, G15	18	BB20
Great Western Rd, G4	35	BN26
Great Western Rd, G12	35	BK25
Great Western Rd, G13	18	BB20
Great Western Rd, G15	18	BB20
Great Western Ter, G12	35	BL25
Great Western Ter La, G12	35	BL25
Green, The, G40	15	BU32
Greenacres Ct, G53	75	BE41
Greenacres Dr, G53	75	BE41
Greenacres Way, G53	75	BE41
Greenan Av, G42	65	BU38
Greenbank Dr, Pais. PA2	58	AT38
Greenbank St, (Ruther.) G73	66	BW37
Greendyke St, G1	15	BT31
Greenend Pl, G32	54	CE30
Greenfield Av, G32	54	CD31
Greenfield Pl, G32	54	CD31
Greenfield Rd, G32	54	CE30
Greenfield St, G51	48	BH30
Greengairs Av, G51	33	BF29
Greenhead Rd, (Inch.) Renf. PA4	16	AS31
Greenhead St, G40	51	BU33
Greenhill, (Bishop.) G64		BY21
Greenhill Av, (Giff.) G46	77	BK44
Greenhill Av, (Gart.) G69	28	CN22
Greenhill Business Pk, Pais. PA3	44	AS31
Greenhill Ct, (Ruther.) G73	66	BW37
Greenhill Rd, (Ruther.) G73	66	BW37
Greenhill Rd, Pais. PA3	44	AS31
Greenhill St, (Ruther.) G73	66	BW38
Greenholm Av, (Udd.) G71	70	CN38
Greenholme St, G44	64	BQ39
Greenknowe Rd, G43	62	BK39
Greenlaw Av, Pais. PA1	45	AW32
Greenlaw Cres, Pais. PA1	45	AW31
Greenlaw Dr, Pais. PA1	45	AW32
Greenlaw Gdns, Pais. PA1	45	AW31
Greenlaw Rd, G14	18	AZ23
Greenlea Rd, (Chry.) G69	27	CK21
Greenlea St, G13	20	BG23
Greenlees Gdns, (Camb.) G72	81	CB42
Greenlees Pk, (Camb.) G72	81	CC42
Greenlees Rd, (Camb.) G72	80	CC40
Greenloan Av, G51	33	BF29
Greenmount, G22	22	BQ22
Greenock Av, G44	78	BR40
Greenock Rd, Pais. PA3		AS29
Green Pl, (Both.) G71	85	CR43
Greenrig, (Udd.) G71	70	CP39
Greenrig St, G33	39	BZ26
Greenrig St, (Udd.) G71	70	CP39
Green Rd, (Ruther.) G73	66	BW37
Greenshields Rd, (Baill.) G69	55	CK32
Greenside Cres, G33	39	CA26
Greenside St, G33	39	CA26
Green St, G40	15	BU32
Green St, (Both.) G71	85	CR43
Greentree Dr, (Baill.) G69	55	CH34
Greenview St, G43	63	BL37
Greenwood Av, (Camb.) G72	68	CG39
Greenwood Quad, Clyde. G81	18	AZ20
Grenville Dr, (Camb.) G72	81	CB41
Gretna St, G40	52	BX33
Greyfriars Rd, (Udd.) G71	70	CL37
Greyfriars St, G32	53	CB30
Greystone Av, (Ruther.) G73	66	BY39
Greywood St, G13	20	BG22
Grierson St, G33	38	BZ29
Grieve Cft, (Both.) G71	85	CP44
Griqua Ter, (Both.) G71	85	CR43
Grosvenor Cres, G12	35	BM26
Grosvenor La, G12	35	BM26
Grosvenor Ter, G12	35	BM26
Groveburn Av, (Thornlie.) G46	76	BJ41
Grovepark Ct, G20	9	BQ27
Grovepark Gdns, G20	9	BQ27
Grovepark Pl, G20	36	BQ26
Grovepark St, G20	36	BQ26
Grudie St, G34	41	CJ29
Gryffe Av, Renf. PA4	17	AX24
Gryffe St, G44	80	BQ38
Guildford St, G33	40	CE28
Gullane St, G11	35	BK28
Guthrie Dr, (Udd.) G71	71	CQ36
Guthrie St, G20	21	BM23

H

Street	Page	Ref
Haberlea Av, G53	78	BE42
Haddow Gro, (Udd.) G71	71	CQ37
Haggs Rd, G41	63	BL36
Haggswood Av, G41	63	BL35
Haghill Rd, G31	52	BY31
Haig Dr, (Baill.) G69	55	CH33
Haig St, G21	37	BV25
Hailes Av, G32	54	CF32
Haining, The, Renf. PA4	32	AZ27
Haining Rd, Renf. PA4	32	AZ26
Hairst St, Renf. PA4	32	AZ25
Halbert St, G41	63	BN36
Haldane St, G14	33	BF26
Hallbrae St, G33	39	CA27
Halley Dr, G13	18	BA22
Halley Pl, G13	18	BA23
Halley Sq, G13	18	BA23
Halley St, G13	18	BA22
Hallhill Cres, G33	54	CG...
Hallhill Rd, G32	54	CE...
Hallhill Rd, G33	54	CG...
Halliburton Rd, G34	55	CH...
Halliburton Ter, G34	55	CJ...
Halldale Cres, Renf. PA4	32	BB...
Hallrule Dr, G52	47	BE30
Hallside Av, (Camb.) G72	82	CG...
Hallside Boul, (Camb.) G72	83	CH...
Hallside Cres, (Camb.) G72	82	CG...
Hallside Dr, (Camb.) G72	82	CG...
Hallside Pl, G5	51	BS...
Hallside Rd, (Camb.) G72	83	CH...
Hall St, Clyde. G81	17	AW...
Hallydown Dr, G13	19	BE...
Halton Gdns, (Baill.) G69	55	CH...
Hamilton Av, G41	49	BM...
Hamilton Ct, Pais. PA2	58	AU...
Hamilton Cres, (Camb.) G72	82	CE...
Hamilton Cres, Renf. PA4	18	AZ...
Hamilton Dr, G12	35	BM...
Hamilton Dr, (Giff.) G46	77	BM...
Hamilton Dr, (Both.) G71	85	CR...
Hamilton Dr, (Camb.) G72	81	CE...
Hamiltonhill Rd, G22	36	BR...
Hamilton Pk Av, G12	35	BN...
Hamilton Rd, G32	68	CF...
Hamilton Rd, (Both.) G71	85	CR...
Hamilton Rd, (Udd.) G71	69	C...
Hamilton Rd, (Camb.) G72	82	CD...
Hamilton Rd, (Ruther.) G73	66	BX...
Hamilton St, G42	65	BX...
Hamilton St, Clyde. G81	18	AZ...
Hamilton St, Pais. PA3	44	AV...
Hamilton Ter, Clyde. G81	18	AZ...
Hamilton Vw, (Udd.) G71	71	CC...
Hampden Dr, G42	64	BP...
Hampden La, G42	64	BP...
Hampden Pk, G42	64	BP...
Hampden Ter, G42	64	BP...
Handel Pl, G5	50	BS...
Hanginshaw Pl, G42	64	BS...
Hanover Ct, G1	10	BS...
Hanover Gdns, Pais. PA1	44	AS...
Hanover St, G1	14	BS...
Hanson Pk, G31	37	BV...
Hanson St, G31	37	BV...
Hapland Av, G53	61	BE...
Hapland Rd, G53	61	BE...
Harbour La, Pais. PA3	44	AU...
Harbour Rd, Pais. PA3	44	AU...
Harbury Pl, G14	18	BB...
Harcourt Dr, G31	38	BX...
Hardgate Dr, G51	33	BE...
Hardgate Gdns, G51	33	BE...
Hardgate Pl, G51	33	BE...
Hardgate Rd, G51	33	BE...
Hardie Av, (Ruther.) G73	66	BY...
Hardridge Av, G52	61	B...
Hardridge Pl, G52	61	BC...
Hardridge Rd, G52	61	B...
Harefield Dr, G14	19	BD...
Harelaw Av, G44	78	BP...
Harelaw Av, (Barr.) G78	74	A...
Harelaw Cres, Pais. PA2	58	AS...
Harfield Dr, G32	54	C...
Harfield Gdns, G32	54	C...
Harhill St, G51	48	B...
Harland St, G14	33	B...
Harley St, G51	49	B...
Harmetray St, G22	23	B...
Harmony Ct, G52	48	B...
Harmony Pl, G51	48	B...
Harmony Row, G51	48	B...
Harmsworth St, G11	34	B...
Harport St, (Thornlie.) G46	76	BC...

Name	Page	Grid
rriet Pl, G43	63	BK39
rriet St, (Ruther.) G73	66	BW37
rris Rd, G23	21	BM30
rtfield Ter, Pais. PA2	59	AV35
rtstone St, G53	47	BC31
rtstone Rd, G53	61	BD38
rtstone Ter, G53	61	BD38
rt St, G31	53	CA32
rvey St, G4	10	BS27
rvie St, G51	12	BM31
rwood St, G32	53	CA30
stie St, G3	8	BM28
tfield Dr, G12	20	BH24
thaway Dr, (Giff.) G46	77	BK43
thaway La, G20	21	BN24
thaway St, G20	21	BN24
thersage Av, (Baill.) G69	55	CK32
thersage Dr, (Baill.) G69	55	CK32
thersage Gdns, (Baill.) G69	55	CK32
tton Dr, G52	47	BC33
tton Gdns, G52	46	BB33
tton Path, G52	47	BC33
ughburn Pl, G53	61	BD38
ughburn Rd, G53	61	BD38
ugh Rd, G3	8	BM29
velock La, G11	35	BJ27
velock St, G11	35	BL27
wick St, G13	18	BA22
wkhead Av, Pais. PA2	59	AX35
wkhead Rd, Pais. PA1	45	AX33
wkhead Rd, Pais. PA2	59	AY36
wthorn Av, (Bishop.) G64		
wthorn Av, Ersk. PA8	16	AU21
wthorn Cres, Ersk. PA8	16	AU21
wthorn Gdns, (Camb.) G72	83	CG41
wthorn Quad, G22	23	BS24
wthorn Rd, (Bishop.) G64	16	AU21
wthorn St, G22	22	BS24
wthorn Ter, (Udd.) G71	71	CR38
wthorn Wk, (Camb.) G72	81	BZ40
wthorn Way, Ersk. PA8	16	AU21
yburn Av, G11	34	BJ26
yburn Gate, G11	34	BK27
yburn La, G11	34	BJ26
yburn St, G11	34	BK28
yfield Ct, G5	51	BT33
yfield St, G5	51	BT33
ylynn St, G14	34	BG27
ymarket St, G32	53	CA30
yston Cres, G22	22	BR24
yston St, G22	22	BR24
ywood St, G22	22	BR23
zel Av, G44	78	BP41
zel Dene, (Bishop.) G64	24	BX20
zelden Gdns, G44	77	BN41
zelden Pk, G44	77	BN41
zellea Dr, (Giff.) G46	77	BM41
zel Ter, (Udd.) G71	71	CR38
zelwood Gdns, (Ruther.) G73	80	BY41
zelwood Rd, G41	49	BN34
zlitt St, G20	22	BR23
ath Av, (Bishop.) G64	24	BX21
athcliff Av, (Blan.) G72	84	CL44
ather Av, (Barr.) G78	73	AW40
atherbrae, (Bishop.) G64	23	BU20
atheryknowe Rd, (Baill.) G69	42	CN29
athfield St, G33	40	CE29
athside Rd, (Giff.) G46	77	BM42
Heathwood Dr, (Thornlie.) G46	76	BJ42
Hector Rd, G41	63	BM37
Helensburgh Dr, G13	19	BF23
Helenslea, (Camb.) G72	82	CF41
Helen St, G51	48	BJ30
Helen St, G52	48	BH32
Helenvale Ct, G31	52	BZ33
Helenvale St, G31	52	BY33
Helmsdale Av, (Blan.) G72	84	CL42
Helmsdale Ct, (Camb.) G72	82	CF40
Hemlock St, G13	20	BG22
Henderson Av, (Camb.) G72	68	CG39
Henderson St, G20	36	BP26
Henderson St, Clyde. G81	18	BA21
Henderson St, Pais. PA1	44	AT32
Henrietta St, G14	33	BE26
Henry St, (Barr.) G78	73	AX42
Hepburn Rd, G52	47	BD30
Herald Av, G13	19	BF20
Herbertson Gro, (Blan.) G72	84	CL44
Herbertson St, G5	14	BR32
Herbert St, G20	36	BP26
Hercules Way, Renf. PA4	32	AZ28
Herma St, G23	21	BN21
Hermiston Av, G32	54	CD31
Hermiston Pl, G32	54	CE31
Hermiston Rd, G32	54	CD30
Hermitage Av, G13	19	BE22
Heron Av, G40	51	BV33
Herries Rd, G41	63	BL35
Herriet St, G41	50	BP34
Hertford Av, G12	20	BK23
Hexham Gdns, G41	63	BM36
Heys St, (Barr.) G78	73	AY43
Hickman St, G42	64	BR36
Hickman Ter, G42	64	BS35
Hickory Cres, (Udd.) G71	71	CS36
Hickory St, G22	23	BU24
Highburgh Dr, (Ruther.) G73	80	BX40
Highburgh Rd, G12	35	BL26
High Calside, Pais. PA2	44	AT34
High Craighall Rd, G4	10	BR27
Highcroft Av, G44	79	BT40
Highfield Av, Pais. PA2	58	AS38
Highfield Cres, Pais. PA2	58	AT38
Highfield Dr, G12	21	BK23
Highfield Dr, (Ruther.) G73	80	BY42
Highfield Pl, G12	21	BK23
Highland La, G51	35	BL29
Highland Mair, Renf. PA4	31	AS34
High Parksail, Ersk. PA8	16	AS21
High Rd, (Castlehead) Pais. PA2	44	AS34
High St, G1	15	BT31
High St, G4	15	BT31
High St, (Ruther.) G73	66	BW37
High St, Pais. PA1	44	AT33
Hilary Av, (Baill.) G69	55	CH32
Hilda Cres, G33	39	CA25
Hillary Av, (Ruther.) G73	67	BZ39
Hillbrae St, G51	47	BF31
Hillcrest, (Chry.) G69	28	CM21
Hillcrest Av, G32	68	CD30
Hillcrest Av, G44	77	BN41
Hillcrest Rd, G32	68	CE37
Hillcrest Rd, (Udd.) G71	71	CQ38
Hillcrest Ter, (Both.) G71	85	CR42
Hillcroft Ter, (Bishop.) G64	23	BV21
Hillend Rd, G22	21	BQ22
Hillend Rd, (Ruther.) G73	80	BX40
Hillfoot Av, (Ruther.) G73	66	BW38
Hillfoot Gdns, (Udd.) G71	70	CN37
Hillfoot St, G31	52	BW30
Hillhead Av, (Ruther.) G73	80	BX41
Hillhead Pl, (Ruther.) G73	80	BX41
Hillhead Rd, G21	24	BZ22
Hillhead St, G12	8	BM27
Hillhouse St, G21	38	BW25
Hillington Gdns, G52	47	BE33
Hillington Ind Est, G52	32	BB29
Hillington Pk Circ, G52	47	BE32
Hillington Quad, G52	47	BC32
Hillington Rd, G52	32	BB27
Hillington Rd S, G52	47	BC32
Hillington Shop Cen, (Hillington Ind. Est.) G52	32	BB29
Hillington Ter, G52	47	BC32
Hillkirk St, G21	37	BU25
Hillpark Av, Pais. PA2	58	AT36
Hillpark Dr, G43	63	BL39
Hill Path, G52	46	BC32
Hill Pl, G52	46	BC32
Hillsborough Rd, (Baill.) G69	55	CH32
Hillside Ct, (Thornlie.) G46	76	BH42
Hillside Dr, (Barr.) G78	73	AW42
Hillside Gro, (Barr.) G78	73	AW42
Hillside Quad, G43	77	BK40
Hillside Rd, G43	77	BK40
Hillside Rd, (Barr.) G78	73	AW42
Hillside Rd, Pais. PA2	59	AW35
Hill St, G3	9	BQ28
Hill St, G14	18	BC24
Hillsview, (Chry.) G69	28	CL21
Hillview Cres, G22	22	BR21
Hillview Cres, (Udd.) G71	70	CN37
Hillview Dr, (Blan.) G72	84	CM43
Hillview Gdns, (Bishop.) G64	24	BZ21
Hillview St, G32	53	CB32
Hilton Gdns, G13	20	BH22
Hilton Ter, G13	20	BG22
Hilton Ter, (Camb.) G72	81	CA42
Hinshaw St, G20	36	BQ26
Hinshelwood Dr, G51	48	BJ31
Hirsel Pl, (Both.) G71	85	CR42
Hobart St, G22	36	BR25
Hobden St, G21	38	BW26
Hoddam Av, G45	79	BV42
Hoddam Ter, G45	80	BW42
Hogarth Av, G32	52	BZ30
Hogarth Cres, G32	53	BZ30
Hogarth Dr, G32	53	BZ30
Hogarth Gdns, G32	52	BZ30
Hogganfield Ct, G33	39	BZ27
Hogganfield St, G33	39	BZ27
Holeburn La, G43	63	BL39
Holeburn Rd, G43	63	BL39
Holehouse Dr, G13	18	BC23
Holland St, G2	9	BQ29
Hollinwell Rd, G23	21	BM31
Hollowglen Rd, G32	54	CD31
Hollybank Pl, (Camb.) G72	82	CD41
Hollybank St, G21	38	BW28
Hollybrook St, G42	64	BS35
Hollybush Rd, G52	46	BB32
Holly Dr, G21	38	BW26
Holm Av, (Udd.) G71	70	CN39
Holm Av, Pais. PA2	58	AV35
Holmbank Av, G41	63	BM38
Holmbrae Av, (Udd.) G71	71	CP38
Holmbrae Rd, (Udd.) G71	70	CP38
Holmbyre Ct, G45	78	BR44
Holmbyre Rd, G45	78	BS44
Holmbyre Ter, G45	78	BS43
Holmes Av, Renf. PA4	31	AY28
Holmfauldhead Dr, G51	34	BG29

Street	Page	Grid
Holmfauld Rd, G51	34	BG28
Holmhead Cres, G44	64	BO39
Holmhead Pl, G44	64	BO39
Holmhead Rd, G44	78	BQ40
Holmhill Av, (Camb.) G72	81	CC41
Holmhill Dr, (Camb.) G72	81	CB42
Holmhills Gdns, (Camb.) G72	81	CB41
Holmhills Gro, (Camb.) G72	81	CB41
Holmhills Pl, (Camb.) G72	81	CB41
Holmhills Rd, (Camb.) G72	81	CB42
Holmhills Ter, (Camb.) G72	81	CB41
Holmlea Rd, G44	64	BO38
Holms Pl, (Gart.) G69	28	CN22
Holm St, G2	13	BO30
Holmwood Av, (Udd.) G71	70	CP38
Holmwood Gdns, (Udd.) G71	70	CP39
Holmwood Gro, G44	78	BQ41
Holyrood Cres, G20	9	BP27
Holyrood Quad, G20	9	BP27
Holywell St, G31	52	BX32
Homeston Av, (Both.) G71	85	CQ42
Honeybog Rd, G52	46	BA30
Hopefield Av, G12	21	BL24
Hopehill Gdns, G20	36	BO26
Hopehill Rd, G20	36	BQ26
Hopeman Av, (Thornlie.) G46	76	BG41
Hopeman Dr, (Thornlie.) G46	76	BG41
Hopeman Rd, (Thornlie.) G46	76	BG41
Hopeman St, (Thornlie.) G46	76	BG41
Hope St, G2	14	BR30
Hopetoun St, G20	38	BW26
Hornal Rd, (Udd.) G71	85	CP41
Hornbeam Rd, (Udd.) G71	71	CR37
Horndean Cres, G33	47	CF29
Hornshill Fm Rd, (Stepps) G33	27	CG29
Hornshill St, G21	38	BW25
Horselethill Rd, G12	35	BL25
Hospital St, G5	14	BS32
Hotspur St, G20	21	BN24
Houldsworth St, G3	8	BN29
Househillmuir Cres, G53	61	BE39
Househillmuir Pl, G53	61	BE38
Househillmuir Rd, G53	60	BD39
Househillwood Cres, G53	61	BD38
Househillwood Rd, G53	61	BD39
Housel Av, G13	19	BD23
Houston Pl, G5	13	BP31
Houston St, G5	13	BP32
Houston St, Renf. PA4	32	AZ25
Howard St, G1	14	BR31
Howard St, Pais. PA1	45	AW32
Howat St, G51	34	BJ29
Howe Gdns, (Udd.) G71	71	CD38
Howford Rd, G52	47	BD33
Howieshill Av, (Camb.) G72	82	CD40
Howieshill Rd, (Camb.) G72	82	CE40
Howth Dr, G13	20	BH21
Howth Ter, G13	20	BH21
Hoxley Pl, G20	22	BP23
Hoylake Pk, (Both.) G71	84	CP43
Hoylake Pl, G23	21	BN20
Hozier Cres, (Udd.) G71	71	CP37
Hozier Pl, (Both.) G71	85	CR42
Hughenden Dr, G12	35	BK25
Hughenden Gdns, G12	34	BJ25
Hughenden La, G12	34	BK25
Hughenden Rd, G12	35	BK25
Hugh Murray Gro, (Camb.) G72	82	CE40
Hugo St, G20	22	BP24
Hume Dr, (Both.) G71	85	CQ42
Hume Dr, (Udd.) G71	70	CN38
Hume St, Clyde. G81	17	AX20
Hunterfield Dr, (Camb.) G72	81	CA40
Hunterhill Av, Pais. PA2	44	AV34
Hunterhill Rd, Pais. PA2	44	AV34
Hunter Rd, (Ruther.) G73	66	BY36
Huntershill Rd, (Bishop.) G64	24	BW21
Huntershill Way, (Bishop.) G64	23	BV22
Hunter St, G4	15	BU31
Hunter St, Pais. PA1	44	AU32
Huntingdon Rd, G21	11	BU27
Huntingdon Sq, G21	11	BU27
Huntingtower Rd, (Baill.) G69	55	CH33
Huntly Rd, G52	32	BB29
Huntly Av, (Giff.) G46	77	BM43
Huntly Ct, (Bishop.) G64	24	BW21
Huntly Dr, (Camb.) G72	82	CD41
Huntly Gdns, G12	35	BL26
Huntly Rd, G12	35	BL26
Huntly Ter, Pais. PA2	59	AW36
Hurlethill Ct, G53	60	BB38
Hurlet Rd, G53	59	AY37
Hurlet Rd, Pais. PA2	59	AY37
Hurlford Av, G13	18	BB22
Hurly Hawkin, (Bishop.) G64	24	BZ21
Hutcheson Rd, (Thornlie.) G46	76	BJ43
Hutcheson St, G1	14	BS30
Hutchinson Pl, (Camb.) G72	82	CG42
Hutchinsontown Ct, G5	51	BS33
Hutton Dr, G51	34	BG29
Hydepark St, G3	13	BP30
Hyndal Av, G53	61	BD36
Hyndland Av, G11	35	BK27
Hyndland Rd, G12	35	BL26
Hyndland St, G11	35	BL27
Hyndlee Dr, G52	47	BE32
Ian Smith Ct, Clyde. G81	18	AZ21
Ibroxholm Av, G51	49	BK32
Ibroxholm Oval, G51	49	BK32
Ibrox Ind Est, G51	49	BL31
Ibrox Ter, G51	49	BL31
Ibrox Ter La, G51	49	BK31
Ilay Av, (Bears.) G61	20	BH21
Ilay Ct, (Bears.) G61	20	BJ21
Ilay Rd, (Bears.) G61	20	BJ21
Inchbrae Rd, G52	47	BE33
Inchholm St, G11	34	BG27
Inchinnan Business Pk, (Inch.) Renf. PA4	30	AS25
Inchinnan Dr, (Inch.) Renf. PA4	30	AS25
Inchinnan Rd, Pais. PA3	44	AU30
Inchinnan Rd, Renf. PA4	31	AX25
Inchkeith Pl, G32	54	CD30
Inchlee St, G14	34	BG27
Inchmurrin Dr, (Ruther.) G73	80	BZ43
Inchmurrin Gdns, (Ruther.) G73	81	BZ43
Inchmurrin Pl, (Ruther.) G73	80	BZ43
Inchnock Av, (Gart.) G69	29	CP...
Inchoch St, G33	40	CG...
Incle St, Pais. PA1	44	AV...
India Dr, (Inch.) Renf. PA4	16	AS...
India St, G2	9	BC...
Inga St, G20	21	BN...
Ingerbreck Av, (Ruther.) G73	80	BZ...
Ingleby Dr, G31	52	BW...
Inglefield St, G42	64	BP...
Ingleneuk Av, G33	26	CD...
Inglestone Av, (Thornlie.) G46	76	BJ...
Inglis St, G31	52	BW...
Ingram St, G1	14	BS...
Inishail Rd, G33	40	CE...
Inkerman Rd, G52	46	BB...
Innellan Gdns, G20	21	BK...
Innellan Pl, G20	20	BK...
Innerwick Pl, G52	47	BD...
Inverclyde Gdns, (Ruther.) G73	81	BZ...
Inveresk Quad, G32	53	CC...
Inveresk St, G32	53	CC...
Inverewe Av, (Thornlie.) G46	75	BF...
Inverewe Dr, (Thornlie.) G46	75	BF...
Inverewe Gdns, (Thornlie.) G46	75	BF...
Inverewe Pl, (Thornlie.) G46	75	BF...
Invergarry Av, (Thornlie.) G46	75	BF...
Invergarry Ct, (Thornlie.) G46	76	BG...
Invergarry Dr, (Thornlie.) G46	75	BF...
Invergarry Gdns, (Thornlie.) G46	75	BF...
Invergarry Gro, (Thornlie.) G46	75	BF...
Invergarry Quad, (Thornlie.) G46	76	BG...
Invergarry Vw, (Thornlie.) G46	76	BG...
Invergordon Av, G43	64	BH...
Invergyle Dr, G52	47	BD...
Inverlair Av, G43	64	BH...
Inverlair Av, G44	64	BH...
Inverleith St, G32	52	BZ...
Inverlochy St, G33	40	CF...
Inverness St, G51	48	BF...
Inver Rd, G33	54	CG...
Invershiel Rd, G23	21	BM...
Invershin Dr, G20	21	BM...
Inverurie St, G21	37	BT...
Inzievar Ter, G32	68	CD...
Iona Cres, Pais. PA2	58	AT...
Iona Rd, (Ruther.) G73	81	CA...
Iona Rd, Renf. PA4	31	AY...
Iona St, G51	48	BK...
Iona Way, (Stepps) G33	40	CF...
Iris Av, G45	80	BW...
Irongray St, G31	52	BX...
Irvine St, G40	52	BX...
Iser La, G41	64	BP...
Islay Av, (Ruther.) G73	81	CA...
Islay Cres, Pais. PA2	58	AT...
Ivanhoe Rd, G13	19	BF...
Ivybank Av, (Camb.) G72	82	CE...
Ivy Rd, (Udd.) G71	71	CS...

J

Jackson Dr, G33	27	CH...
Jacks Rd, (Udd.) G71	85	CO...
Jagger Gdns, (Baill.) G69	55	CH...

Street	Page	Ref
maica St, G1	14	BR31
mes Dunlop Gdns, (Bishop.) G64	24	BX22
mes Gray St, G41	63	BN36
mes Morrison St, G1	15	BT31
mes Nisbet St, G21	11	BU29
mes St, G40	51	BU33
mes Watt St, G2	13	BQ30
mieson Ct, G42	64	BR35
mieson St, G42	64	BR35
nebank Av, (Camb.) G72	82	CE41
nefield St, G31	52	BX32
ne Pl, G5	51	BS33
ne Rae Gdns, Clyde. G81	18	AZ21
rdine Ter, (Gart.) G69	29	CF24
dburgh Av, (Ruther.) G73	66	BX38
nny Lind Ct, G46	76	BG43
nny's Well Ct, Pais. PA2	59	AX35
nny's Well Rd, Pais. PA2	59	AX35
viston Rd, G33	40	CE27
ssie St, G42	65	BT35
celyn Sq, G1	14	BS31
nn Brown Pl, (Chry.) G69	28	CL21
nn Hendry Rd, (Udd.) G71	85	CO31
nn Knox St, G4	15	BU30
nn Knox St, Clyde. G81	17	AY21
nn Marshall St, (Bishop.) G64	23	BU22
nsburn Rd, G53	61	BD39
nsburn Rd, G53	61	BD39
nn Smith Gate, (Barr.) G78	73	AY41
nnson Av, (Camb.) G72	81	CC40
nnston Av, Clyde. G81	18	AZ21
nnstone Av, G52	47	BD31
nnstone Dr, (Ruther.) G73	66	BW38
nnston Rd, (Gart.) G69	29	CQ23
nnston St, Pais. PA1	44	AW33
nn St, G1	14	BS30
nn St, (Barr.) G78	73	AX42
ppa St, G33	53	CA30
rdanhill Cres, G13	19	BF24
rdanhill Dr, G13	19	BE24
rdanhill La, G13	20	BG24
rdan St, G14	33	BJ27
rdanvale Av, G14	33	BF27
witt Av, Clyde. G81	18	AZ20
bilee Ct, G52	46	BB30
ian Av, G12	35	BL25
ian La, G12	35	BL25
niper Pl, G32	55	CH33
niper Ter, G32	55	CG33
ra Av, Renf. PA4	32	AX28
ra Ct, G52	48	BG32
ra Dr, (Blan.) G72	84	CL42
ra Rd, Pais. PA2	58	AT38
ra St, G52	48	BH32
ra Wynd, (Glenb.) Coat. ML5	29	CS23
m Dr, G53	61	BE39
trine Av, (Bishop.) G64	24	BX20
rine Pl, (Camb.) G72	67	CC39
vstone Rd, G15	19	BC20
re St, G21	37	BV25
al Av, G15	19	BC21
al Cres, G15	19	BC21
al Dr, G15	18	BC21
al Pl, G15	19	BC21
Kearn Av, G15	19	BD20
Kearn Pl, G15	19	BD20
Keats Pk, (Both.) G71	85	CR42
Keir Hardie Ct, (Bishop.) G64	24	BW20
Keir St, G41	50	BP34
Keirs Wk, (Camb.) G72	67	CC39
Keith Av, (Giff.) G46	77	BM42
Keith Ct, G11	35	BL28
Keith St, G11	35	BL27
Kelbourne St, G20	35	BN25
Kelburn Gdns, (Baill.) G69	55	CJ34
Kelburne Gdns, Pais. PA1	45	AW32
Kelburne Oval, Pais. PA1	45	AW32
Kelhead Av, G52	46	BB32
Kelhead Dr, G52	46	BB32
Kelhead Path, G52	46	BB32
Kelhead Pl, G52	46	BB32
Kellas St, G51	48	BJ30
Kelso Av, (Ruther.) G73	66	BX38
Kelso Pl, G14	18	BA23
Kelso St, G13	18	BA21
Kelso St, G14	18	BA23
Kelton St, G32	54	CD33
Kelvin Av, G52	32	BB29
Kelvin Ct, G12	20	BH23
Kelvindale Gdns, G20	21	BL23
Kelvindale Pl, G20	21	BK23
Kelvindale Rd, G12	21	BM23
Kelvin Dr, G20	35	BM25
Kelvin Dr, (Barr.) G78	74	AZ44
Kelvingrove St, G3	8	BN29
Kelvinhaugh Gate, G3	8	BM29
Kelvinhaugh Pl, G3	8	BN29
Kelvinhaugh St, G3	35	BL29
Kelvinside Av, G20	35	BN25
Kelvinside Dr, G20	36	BP25
Kelvinside Gdns, G20	35	BN25
Kelvinside Gdns E, G20	36	BP25
Kelvinside Gdns La, G20	35	BN25
Kelvinside Ter S, G20	35	BN26
Kelvinside Ter W, G20	35	BN26
Kelvin Way, G3	8	BM28
Kelvin Way, (Both.) G71	85	CQ42
Kemp Av, Pais. PA3	31	AW28
Kempock St, G31	52	BY33
Kempsthorn Cres, G53	61	BC36
Kempsthorn Pl, G53	61	BD36
Kempsthorn Rd, G53	60	BC36
Kemp St, G21	37	BU25
Kendal Av, (Giff.) G46	77	BL42
Kendal Dr, G12	20	BJ23
Kenilworth Av, G41	63	BM37
Kenmar Gdns, (Udd.) G71	70	CN37
Kenmore St, G32	53	CC32
Kenmuir Av, G32	54	CG34
Kenmuirhill Gdns, G32	68	CF35
Kenmuirhill Gate, G32	68	CF35
Kenmuirhill Rd, G32	68	CF35
Kenmuir Rd, G32	68	CE37
Kenmuir St, Coat. ML5	57	CR33
Kenmure Av, (Bishop.) G64	23	BU20
Kenmure Cres, (Bishop.) G64	23	BV20
Kenmure Dr, (Bishop.) G64	23	BV20
Kenmure Gdns, (Bishop.) G64	23	BU20
Kenmure La, (Bishop.) G64	23	BV20
Kenmure St, G41	64	BP35
Kenmure Way, (Ruther.) G73	80	BX42
Kennedar Dr, G51	34	BG29
Kennedy Ct, (Giff.) G46	77	BL41
Kennedy Path, G4	11	BT29
Kennedy St, G4	11	BT28
Kennet St, G21	38	BW28
Kennishead Av, (Thornlie.) G46	76	BG40
Kennishead Pl, (Thornlie.) G46	76	BG40
Kennishead Rd, G43	76	BH40
Kennishead Rd, (Thornlie.) G46	76	BG40
Kennishead Rd, G53	75	BD41
Kennisholm Av, (Thornlie.) G46	76	BG40
Kennisholm Pl, (Thornlie.) G46	76	BG40
Kennoway Dr, G11	34	BH27
Kennyhill Sq, G31	38	BX30
Kensington Dr, (Giff.) G46	77	BM44
Kensington Gate La, G12	35	BL25
Kensington Rd, G12	35	BL25
Kentallen Rd, G33	54	CG31
Kent Dr, (Ruther.) G73	81	BZ40
Kentigern Ter, (Bishop.) G64	24	BW21
Kent Rd, G3	8	BN29
Kent St, G40	15	BU31
Keppel Dr, G44	65	BU38
Keppochhill Dr, G21	37	BT26
Keppochhill Pl, G21	11	BT27
Keppochhill Rd, G21	37	BT27
Keppochhill Rd, G22	36	BS26
Keppochhill Way, G21	11	BT27
Keppoch St, G21	37	BT26
Kerr Dr, G40	51	BV32
Kerrera Pl, G33	54	CF31
Kerrera Rd, G33	54	CF31
Kerr Gdns, (Udd.) G71	71	CQ37
Kerr Pl, G40	51	BV32
Kerr St, G40	51	BV32
Kerr St, (Barr.) G78	73	AW43
Kerr St, Pais. PA3	44	AT32
Kerrycroy Av, G42	65	BT38
Kerrycroy St, G42	65	BT37
Kerrydale St, G40	52	BX33
Kerrylamont Av, G42	65	BU38
Kersland Av, G12	35	BM26
Kersland St, G12	35	BM26
Kessock Dr, G22	36	BR26
Kessock Pl, G22	36	BR26
Kestrel Rd, G13	19	BE23
Kew Gdns, (Udd.) G71	71	CR38
Kew La, G12	35	BM26
Kew Ter, G12	35	BM26
Kidston Pl, G5	50	BS33
Kidston Ter, G5	50	BS33
Kilbeg Ter, (Thornlie.) G46	75	BF42
Kilberry St, G21	38	BW28
Kilbirnie Pl, G5	50	BQ33
Kilbirnie St, G5	50	BQ33
Kilbride St, G5	65	BT35
Kilbride Vw, (Udd.) G71	71	CQ38
Kilburn Gro, (Blan.) G72	84	CM44
Kilburn Pl, G13	19	BD23
Kilchattan Dr, G44	65	BS38
Kilchoan Rd, G33	40	CE27
Kildale Way, (Ruther.) G73	66	BV37
Kildary Av, G44	78	BQ40
Kildary Rd, G44	78	BQ40
Kildermorie Rd, G34	41	CH29
Kildonan Dr, G11	34	BJ27
Kildrostan St, G41	64	BP35
Kilearn Rd, Pais. PA3	45	AX30
Kilearn Way, Pais. PA3	45	AX30
Kilfinan St, G22	22	BR22

Name	Page	Ref
Kilgarth St, Coat. ML5	57	CR33
Kilkerran Dr, G33	25	CB23
Killearn Dr, Pais. PA1	46	BB33
Killearn St, G22	36	BR25
Killermont Meadows, (Both.) G71	84	CN43
Killermont St, G2	10	BS29
Killiegrew Rd, G41	63	BM35
Killin St, G32	54	CD34
Killoch Dr, G13	18	BC22
Killoch Dr, (Barr.) G78	74	AZ44
Kilmailing Rd, G44	78	BR40
Kilmany Dr, G32	53	CB32
Kilmany Gdns, G32	53	CB32
Kilmarnock Rd, G41	63	BM39
Kilmarnock Rd, G43	63	BM39
Kilmarin Pl, (Thornlie.) G46	76	BG41
Kilmarin Pl, (Udd.) G71	71	CQ36
Kilmaurs Dr, (Giff.) G46	77	BN42
Kilmaurs St, G51	48	BH31
Kilmorie Dr, (Ruther.) G73	65	BU38
Kilmory Av, (Udd.) G71	71	CQ38
Kilmuir Cres, (Thornlie.) G46	75	BF41
Kilmuir Dr, (Thornlie.) G46	76	BG41
Kilmuir Rd, (Thornlie.) G46	76	BG41
Kilmuir Rd, (Udd.) G71	71	CP36
Kilmun St, G20	21	BM22
Kilncroft La, Pais. PA2	58	AU35
Kilnside Rd, Pais. PA1	45	AV32
Kiloran St, (Thornlie.) G46	76	BH41
Kilpatrick Cres, Pais. PA2	58	AT36
Kilpatrick Dr, Renf. PA4	31	AX29
Kilpatrick Way, (Udd.) G71	71	CQ37
Kiltearn Rd, G33	55	CH30
Kilvaxter Dr, (Thornlie.) G46	76	BG41
Kilwynet Way, Pais. PA3	45	AW30
Kinalty Rd, G44	78	BQ40
Kinarvie Cres, G53	60	BB38
Kinarvie Gdns, G53	60	BB38
Kinarvie Pl, G53	60	BB38
Kinarvie Rd, G53	60	BB38
Kinarvie Ter, G53	60	BB38
Kinbuck St, G22	37	BT25
Kincaid Gdns, (Camb.) G72	67	CC38
Kincardine Dr, (Bishop.) G64	24	BX21
Kincardine Sq, G33	40	CF27
Kincath Av, (Ruther.) G73	80	BZ42
Kincraig St, G51	47	BF31
Kinellan Rd, (Bears.) G61	39	BH20
Kinellar Dr, G14	18	BC23
Kingarth La, G42	64	BQ35
Kingarth St, G42	64	BQ35
King Edward Rd, G13	20	BH24
Kingfisher Dr, G13	18	BB22
Kingfisher Gdns, G13	18	BC22
King George V Br, G1	14	BR31
King George V Br, G5	14	BR31
King George V Dock, G51	33	BD27
King George V Gdns, Renf. PA4	32	BA27
King George Pk Av, Renf. PA4	32	BA28
Kinghorn Dr, G44	64	BS39
King Pl, (Baill.) G69	57	CQ32
Kingsacre Rd, G44	65	BT38
Kingsacre Rd, (Ruther.) G73	65	BU38
Kingsbarns Dr, G44	64	BR38
Kingsborough Gdns, G12	35	BK26
Kingsborough La, G12	35	BK26
Kingsborough La E, G12	35	BK26
Kingsbrae Av, G44	64	BS38
King's Br, G5	51	BT33
King's Br, G40	51	BT33
Kingsbridge Cres, G44	65	BT39
Kingsbridge Dr, G44	65	BT39
Kingsbridge Dr, (Ruther.) G73	65	BU39
Kingsbridge Pk Gdns, G44	65	BT39
Kingsburgh Dr, Pais. PA1	45	AX31
Kingsburn Dr, (Ruther.) G73	66	BW39
Kingsburn Gro, (Ruther.) G73	66	BW39
Kingscliffe Av, G44	65	BS39
Kingscourt Av, G44	65	BT38
Kings Cres, (Camb.) G72	82	CD40
Kings Cross, G31	51	BV30
Kingsdale Av, G44	65	BS38
King's Dr, G40	51	BU33
Kingsdyke Av, G44	65	BS38
Kingsford Av, G44	77	BN41
Kingsheath Av, (Ruther.) G73	65	BU39
Kingshill Dr, G44	65	BS39
Kingshouse Av, G44	65	BS38
Kingshurst Av, G44	65	BS38
Kings Inch Dr, G51	33	BD28
Kings Inch Pl, Renf. PA4	33	BB27
Kings Inch Rd, G51	32	BA25
Kings Inch Rd, Renf. PA4	32	BA25
Kingsknowe Dr, (Ruther.) G73	65	BU39
Kingsland Cres, G52	47	BD31
Kingsland Dr, G52	47	BD31
Kingsley Av, G42	64	BR36
Kingsley Ct, (Udd.) G71	71	CQ38
Kingslynn Dr, G44	65	BT39
King's Pk Av, G44	65	BS39
King's Pk Av, (Ruther.) G73	65	BU39
King's Pk Rd, G44	64	BR38
Kings Pl, G22	22	BR22
Kingston Av, (Udd.) G71	71	CQ37
Kingston Br, G3	13	BQ31
Kingston Br, G5	13	BQ31
Kingston Ind Est, G5	13	BP32
Kingston St, G5	13	BQ31
King St, G1	14	BS31
King St, (Ruther.) G73	66	BX37
King St, Clyde. G81	18	AZ21
King St, Pais. PA1	44	AS32
King St, Vw. (Ruther.) G73	66	BV38
Kingsway, G14	19	BC24
Kingsway Ct, G14	19	BD24
Kingswood Dr, G44	65	BS39
Kingussie Dr, G44	65	BS39
Kiniver Dr, G15	19	BC20
Kinloch Av, (Camb.) G72	82	CD41
Kinloch Rd, Renf. PA4	31	AX28
Kinloch St, G40	52	BY33
Kinmount Av, G44	64	BR38
Kinnaird Pl, (Bishop.) G64	24	BX21
Kinnear Rd, G40	52	BX34
Kinnell Av, G52	61	BE34
Kinnell Cres, G52	47	BE34
Kinnell Sq, G52	47	BE34
Kinning Pk Ind Est, G5	13	BP32
Kinning St, G5	13	BQ32
Kinpurnie Rd, Pais. PA1	46	AZ32
Kinross Av, G52	47	BD33
Kinsail Dr, G52	46	BB31
Kinstone Av, G14	18	BC24
Kintillo Dr, G13	19	BD23
Kintore Rd, G43	64	BP39
Kintra St, G51	48	BK30
Kintyre St, G21	38	BW28
Kippen St, G22	23	BT23
Kippford St, G32	54	CE33
Kirkaig Av, Renf. PA4	32	BB28
Kirkbean Av, (Ruther.) G73	80	BW41
Kirkburn Av, (Camb.) G72	81	CC40
Kirkcaldy Rd, G41	63	BM36
Kirkconnel Av, G13	18	BB23
Kirkconnel Dr, (Ruther.) G73	79	BV40
Kirkdale Dr, G52	48	BG33
Kirkfield Rd, (Both.) G71	85	CQ42
Kirkhill Av, (Camb.) G72	81	CC41
Kirkhill Dr, G20	21	BN24
Kirkhill Gdns, (Camb.) G72	81	CC41
Kirkhill Gro, (Camb.) G72	81	CC41
Kirkhill Pl, (Gart.) G69	29	CP25
Kirkhill Rd, (Udd.) G71	70	CN38
Kirkhill Ter, (Camb.) G72	81	CC41
Kirkinner Rd, G32	54	CF33
Kirkintilloch Rd, (Bishop.) G64	23	BV19
Kirklandneuk Rd, Renf. PA4	31	AX25
Kirklands Cres, (Both.) G71	85	CQ42
Kirkland St, G20	36	BP26
Kirklee Circ, G12	35	BL26
Kirklee Gdns, G12	21	BL25
Kirklee Gdns La, G12	35	BM26
Kirklee Gate, G12	35	BM26
Kirklee Pl, G12	35	BM26
Kirklee Quad, G12	35	BM26
Kirklee Rd, G12	35	BL26
Kirklee Ter, G12	35	BL26
Kirklee Ter La, G12	35	BL26
Kirkliston St, G32	53	CB31
Kirk Ms, (Camb.) G72	81	CC40
Kirkmuir Dr, (Ruther.) G73	80	BX43
Kirknewton St, G32	53	CC32
Kirkoswald Rd, G43	63	BM39
Kirkpatrick St, G33	27	CG25
Kirkpatrick St, G40	52	BW32
Kirk Pl, (Udd.) G71	84	CN40
Kirkriggs Av, (Ruther.) G73	80	BX41
Kirkriggs Gdns, (Ruther.) G73	80	BX41
Kirkton Av, G13	18	BC23
Kirkton Av, (Barr.) G78	73	AX44
Kirkton Cres, G13	18	BC23
Kirkton Rd, (Camb.) G72	82	CD40
Kirktonside, (Barr.) G78	73	AX44
Kirkview Gdns, (Udd.) G71	70	CN38
Kirkville Pl, G15	19	BD20
Kirkwall Av, (Blan.) G72	84	CL42
Kirkwell Rd, G44	78	BR40
Kirkwood Av, (Stepps) G33	27	CH24
Kirkwood Av, Clyde. G81	18	AZ21
Kirkwood Rd, (Udd.) G71	71	CC37
Kirkwood St, G51	49	BL31
Kirkwood St, (Ruther.) G73	66	BW37
Kirn St, G20	21	BL22
Kirriemuir Av, G52	47	BE33
Kirriemuir Pl, G52	47	BE33
Kirriemuir Rd, (Bishop.) G64	24	BY20
Kirtle Dr, Renf. PA4	32	BA28
Kishorn Pl, G33	40	CE26
Knapdale St, G22	22	BC22
Knightsbridge St, G13	19	BF23
Knightscliffe Av, G13	19	BF22
Knights Gate, (Both.) G71	84	CN41
Knightswood Cross, G13	19	BF22
Knightswood Rd, G13	19	BF22
Knightswood Ter, (Blan.) G72	84	CN43
Knockburnie Rd, (Both.) G71	85	CQ42
Knockhall St, G33	40	CF27
Knockhill Dr, G44	64	BR38

Street	Page	Grid
ckhill Rd, Renf. PA4	31	AW28
ockside Av, Pais. PA2	58	AT38
ock Way, Pais. PA1	45	AW32
owehead Dr, (Udd.) G71	70	CN39
owehead Gdns, (Udd.) G71	49	BN34
owehead Ter, G41	49	BN34
owe Rd, (Chry.) G69	28	CL21
owe Rd, Pais. PA3	45	AX30
owetap St, G20	21	BN22
eakin Rd, (Thornlie.) G46	75	BF42
eakin Ter, (Thornlie.) G46	75	BF42
e Ct, (Camb.) G72	67	CC39
e Dr, (Giff.) G46	77	BK42
epark Rd, (Udd.) G71	70	CM39
epark Cres, (Udd.) G71	70	CM38
epark Dr, (Udd.) G71	70	CM38
erhea Rd, (Thornlie.) G46	75	BF42
e Sq, (Ruther.) G73	79	BV40
e St, G4	10	BS28
Belle Allee, G3	8	BN28
Belle Pl, G3	8	BN28
urnum Rd, G41	49	BL33
Crosse Ter, G12	35	BM26
y St, Pais. PA1	45	AW32
le Ter, G52	47	BC33
hope Pl, G13	18	BA21
dyacres, (Inch.) Renf. PA4	16	AT23
yacres Way, (Inch.) Renf. PA4	16	AT23
ybank St, G52	48	BG33
yburn St, Pais. PA1	45	AW33
yphill Dr, (Baill.) G69	55	CJ33
y Isle Cres, (Udd.) G71	70	CN39
y Jane Gdns, (Both.) G71	84	CN41
ykirk Cres, G52	47	BD31
ykirk Cres, Pais. PA2	45	AV34
ykirk Dr, G52	47	BD31
y La, Pais. PA1	44	AT33
ymuir Cres, G53	61	BE35
ywell St, G4	15	BU30
gan Rd, G43	77	BN40
gan Rd, (Bishop.) G64	24	BX20
gan Ter, Renf. PA4	31	AX25
dlaw Gdns, (Udd.) G71	71	CP36
dlaw St, G5	13	BQ32
hlands Rd, (Both.) G71	85	CR43
hmuir St, (Udd.) G71	85	CP40
hpark Harbour, Pais. PA3	44	AU30
hpark Vw, Pais. PA3	44	AU30
d Gro, (Udd.) G71	71	CQ37
d Pl, G40	51	BV33
ds Gate, (Udd.) G71	84	CM40
g Dr, (Blan.) G72	68	CL43
herton Dr, G52	47	BD31
hhill Quad, G41	12	BM32
hhill St, G41	12	BM32
hb St, G22	22	BR23
ington Rd, G52	47	BD33
lash Cres, G33	40	CD29
lash Sq, G33	40	CE29
mmoor Av, G46	87	BE33
mmuir Ct, Pais. PA2	58	AU37
mmuir Rd, Pais. PA3	58	AT37
aont Rd, G21	24	BX23
rk St, G1	13	BT31
caster Cres, G12	35	BL25
Lancaster Cres La, G12	35	BL25
Lancaster Ter, G12	35	BL25
Lancefield Quay, G3	12	BN30
Lancefield St, G3	13	BP30
Landemer Dr, (Ruther.) G73	65	BV39
Landressy Pl, G40	51	BU33
Landressy St, G40	51	BV33
Lanfine Rd, Pais. PA1	45	AX32
Langa St, G20	21	BN22
Lang Av, Renf. PA4	31	AY28
Langbar Cres, G33	54	CG30
Langbar Gdns, G33	55	CH30
Langcraigs Dr, Pais. PA2	58	AS39
Langcraigs Ter, Pais. PA2	58	AS39
Langcroft Dr, (Camb.) G72	82	CE41
Langcroft Pl, G51	47	BE30
Langcroft Rd, G51	47	BE30
Langdale Av, G33	39	CA26
Langdale St, G33	39	CA26
Langford Dr, G53	75	BC42
Langford Pl, G53	75	BD42
Langhaul Pl, G53	60	BB36
Langhaul Rd, G53	60	BB36
Langlands Av, G51	33	BF29
Langlands Dr, G51	47	BF30
Langlands Rd, G51	47	BF30
Langlea Av, (Camb.) G72	81	BZ41
Langlea Ct, (Camb.) G72	81	CA41
Langlea Gdns, (Camb.) G72	81	CA40
Langlea Gro, (Camb.) G72	81	CA41
Langlea Rd, (Camb.) G72	81	CA41
Langlea Way, (Camb.) G72	81	CA40
Langley Av, G13	19	BD21
Langlook Rd, G53	60	BB36
Langmuirhead Rd, (Kirk.) G66	25	CC21
Langmuir Rd, (Baill.) G69	57	CO32
Langmuir Way, (Baill.) G69	57	CO32
Langness Rd, G33	40	CD29
Langrig Rd, G21	38	BW25
Langshot St, G51	12	BN30
Langside Av, G41	63	BM36
Langside Av, (Udd.) G71	71	CS39
Langside Ct, (Both.) G71	85	CR44
Langside Dr, G43	77	BN40
Langside Gdns, G42	64	BO38
Langside La, G42	64	BO36
Langside Pl, G41	64	BP37
Langside Rd, G42	64	BO36
Langside Rd, (Both.) G71	85	CR44
Langside St, G51	46	BB32
Langstile Pl, G52	46	BB32
Langstile Rd, G52	46	BB32
Lang St, Pais. PA1	45	AW33
Langton Cres, G53	61	BE37
Langton Cres, (Barr.) G78	74	AZ44
Langton Gdns, (Baill.) G69	55	CH33
Langton Rd, G53	61	BE37
Langtree Av, (Giff.) G46	76	BJ44
Lanrig Pl, (Chry.) G69	28	CL21
Lanrig Rd, (Chry.) G69	28	CL21
Lansbury Gdns, Pais. PA3	44	AT30
Lansdowne Cres, G20	9	BP27
Lansdowne Cres La, G20	9	BP27
Lanton Dr, G52	47	BD31
Lanton Rd, G43	77	BN40
Lappin St, Clyde. G81	18	AZ21
Larbert St, G4	28	BR28
Larch Av, (Bishop.) G64	24	BX21
Larchfield Av, G14	33	BD25
Larchfield Pl, (Ruther.) G73	80	BY41
Larchfield Pl, G14	33	BD25
Larchfield Rd, (Bears.) G61	20	BH20
Larchgrove Av, G32	54	CE31
Larchgrove Rd, G32	54	CE30
Larch Gro, G41	49	BK32
Largie Rd, G43	78	BP40
Largo Pl, G51	48	BG30
Largs St, G31	52	BX30
Larkin Gdns, Pais. PA3	44	AT30
Lasswade St, G14	18	BA23
Latherton Dr, G20	21	BM24
Latimer Gdns, G52	47	BC33
Laudedale La, G12	34	BK26
Lauderdale Gdns, G12	34	BK26
Lauder Dr, (Ruther.) G73	66	BZ39
Lauder Gdns, (Blan.) G72	84	CL43
Laundry La, G33	26	CE24
Laurelbank Rd, (Chry.) G69	27	CK22
Laurel Av, (Udd.) G71	70	CP37
Laurel Pk Cl, G13	19	BE24
Laurel Pk Gdns, G13	19	BE24
Laurel Pl, G11	34	BJ26
Laurel St, G11	34	BJ27
Laurel Wk, (Ruther.) G73	80	BY42
Laurel Way, (Barr.) G78	73	AX42
Laurie Ct, (Udd.) G71	71	CQ38
Laurieston Pl, G5	50	BR33
Laurieston Way, (Ruther.) G73	80	BX41
Laverockhall St, G21	37	BV26
Laverock Av, (Chry.) G69	28	CP20
Lawers Rd, G43	76	BK40
Lawers Rd, Renf. PA4	31	AX28
Lawmoor Av, G5	51	BS34
Lawmoor Pl, G5	65	BS35
Lawmoor Rd, G5	51	BS34
Lawmoor St, G5	51	BS34
Lawn St, Pais. PA1	44	AV32
Lawrence Av, (Giff.) G46	76	BL44
Lawrence St, G11	35	BL27
Lawrie St, G11	35	BK27
Law St, G40	52	BW32
Laxford Av, G44	78	BQ41
Leabank Av, Pais. PA2	58	AU37
Leadburn Rd, G21	38	BY25
Leadburn St, G32	53	CA30
Leader St, G33	39	BZ28
Leander Cres, Renf. PA4	32	BA27
Leckie St, G43	63	BL37
Ledaig Pl, G31	52	BY30
Ledaig St, G31	52	BY30
Ledard Rd, G42	64	BP37
Ledgowan Pl, G20	21	BM21
Ledi Rd, G43	77	BL40
Lednock Rd, (Stepps) G33	26	CE24
Lednock Rd, G52	47	BC32
Lee Av, G33	39	CA28
Leebank Dr, G44	88	BP44
Lee Cres, (Bishop.) G64	24	BW21
Leefield Dr, G44	78	BP43
Leehill Rd, G21	23	BU22
Leeside Rd, G21	23	BU22
Leesland, (Udd.) G71	71	CO37
Leewood Dr, G44	78	BO43
Leggatston Dr, G53	75	BE42
Leggatston Rd, G53	75	BE43
Leglen Wd Cres, G21	25	BZ23
Leglen Wd Dr, G21	25	BZ23
Leglen Wd Pl, G21	25	BZ23
Leglen Wd Rd, G21	25	BZ23
Leicester Av, G12	21	BK24
Leighton St, G20	21	BN23
Leithland Av, G53	61	BD36
Leithland Rd, G53	61	BD36
Leith St, G33	39	BZ29
Lendel Pl, G51	12	BM32
Lenihall Dr, G45	79	BU43
Lenihall Ter, G45	79	BU43
Lennox Av, G14	33	BE26
Lennox Cres, (Bishop.) G64	23	BV21

Street	Pg	Ref
Lennox Gdns, G14	33	BF25
Lennox La E, G14	33	BF26
Lennox Ter, Pais. PA3	31	AW29
Lentran St, G34	56	CM30
Leny St, G20	36	BP25
Lenzie Pl, G21	23	BV23
Lenzie Rd, (Stepps) G33	26	CF23
Lenzie St, G21	23	BV24
Lenzie Ter, G21	23	BV24
Lenzie Way, G21	23	BV23
Leslie Rd, G41	49	BN34
Leslie St, G41	50	BP34
Lesmuir Dr, G14	18	BB24
Lesmuir Pl, G14	18	BB23
Letham Ct, G43	77	BN40
Letham Dr, G43	77	BN40
Letham Dr, (Bishop.) G64	24	BY21
Lethamhill Cres, G33	39	CB28
Lethamhill Pl, G33	39	CA28
Lethamhill Rd, G33	39	CA28
Letham Oval, (Bishop.) G64	24	BZ21
Letherby Dr, G42	64	BR38
Letherby Dr, G44	64	BR38
Lethington Av, G41	63	BN37
Lethington Pl, G41	63	BN37
Letterfearn Dr, G23	21	BN20
Letterickhills Cres, (Camb.) G72	82	CG42
Lettoch St, G51	48	BJ30
Leven Av, (Bishop.) G64	24	BX20
Leven Sq, Renf. PA4	31	AX25
Leven St, G41	50	BP34
Levern Br Ct, G53	60	BB38
Levern Br Gro, G53	60	BB38
Levern Br Pl, G53	60	BB39
Levern Br Rd, G53	60	BB39
Levern Br Way, G53	60	BB39
Levern Cres, (Barr.) G78	73	AX44
Leverndale Cres, G53	60	BB36
Leverndale Ind Cen, G53	60	BB37
Leverndale Rd, G53	60	BB36
Levern Gdns, (Barr.) G78	73	AX42
Levernside Av, (Barr.) G78	73	AW43
Levernside Cres, G53	60	BD36
Levernside Rd, G53	61	BE36
Lewis Av, Renf. PA4	32	AZ28
Lewiston Rd, G23	21	BM20
Leyden Ct, G20	21	BN24
Leyden Gdns, G20	21	BN24
Leyden St, G20	21	BN24
Leys, The, (Bishop.) G64	24	BW20
Liberton St, G33	39	BZ29
Liberty Av, (Baill.) G69	57	CQ32
Libo Av, G53	61	BF36
Library Gdns, (Camb.) G72	67	CB39
Liddells Ct, (Bishop.) G64	24	BW21
Liddell St, G32	68	CE36
Liddesdale Pl, G22	22	BU21
Liddesdale Rd, G22	22	BS22
Liddesdale Sq, G22	22	BU22
Liddesdale Ter, G22	22	BU22
Liddoch Way, (Ruther.) G73	65	BV37
Liff Gdns, (Bishop.) G64	24	BZ21
Liff Pl, G34	42	CL28
Lightburn Pl, G32	54	CD30
Lightburn Rd, G31	52	CF41
Lightburn Rd, (Camb.) G72	82	CF41
Lilac Cres, (Udd.) G71	71	CR39
Lilac Gdns, (Bishop.) G64	24	BX21
Lilac Wynd, (Camb.) G72	83	CG41
Lilybank Av, (Muir.) G69	28	CL22
Lilybank Av, (Camb.) G72	82	CF41
Lilybank Gdns, G12	8	BM27
Lilybank Gdns La, G12	8	BM27
Lily St, G40	52	BX34
Limecraigs Av, Pais. PA2	58	AS38
Limecraigs Cres, Pais. PA2	58	AS38
Limeside Av, (Ruther.) G73	66	BX38
Limeside Gdns, (Ruther.) G73	66	BY38
Lime St, G14	33	BF26
Limetree Av, (Udd.) G71	71	CR37
Limetree Quad, (Udd.) G71	71	CS37
Linacre Dr, G32	54	CE32
Linacre Gdns, G32	54	CF32
Linburn Pl, G52	46	BC31
Linburn Rd, G52	46	BA30
Lincoln Av, G13	19	BE22
Lincoln Av, (Udd.) G71	71	CP36
Lincuan Av, (Giff.) G46	78	BL44
Lindams, (Udd.) G71	85	CP40
Linden Pl, G13	20	BH22
Linden St, G13	20	BH22
Lindores Av, (Ruther.) G73	66	BX38
Lindrick Dr, G23	21	BN21
Lindsaybeg Ct, (Chry.) G69	27	CL21
Lindsay Dr, G12	21	BK23
Lindsay Pl, G12	21	BK23
Linfern Rd, G12	35	BL26
Links Rd, G32	54	CF34
Links Rd, G44	78	BS41
Linlithgow Gdns, G32	54	CF32
Linn Cres, Pais. PA2	58	AS38
Linndale Dr, G51	78	BS44
Linndale Gdns, G51	78	BS44
Linndale Rd, G51	78	BS44
Linndale Rd, G51	79	BS44
Linn Dr, G44	78	BP42
Linnet Pl, G13	18	BB22
Linnhead Dr, G53	61	BD39
Linnhead Pl, G14	33	BD25
Linnhe Av, G44	78	BQ41
Linnhe Av, (Bishop.) G64	24	BX20
Linnhe Dr, (Barr.) G78	73	AX40
Linnhe Pl, (Blan.) G72	84	CL43
Linn Pk, G44	78	BR42
Linnpark Av, G44	78	BP43
Linnpark Ct, G44	78	BP43
Linn Pk Ind Est, G45	78	BR43
Linn Valley Vw, G45	79	BT42
Linnwell Cres, Pais. PA2	58	AT37
Linnwood Ct, G44	78	BQ40
Linside Av, Pais. PA1	45	AW33
Linthaugh Rd, G53	61	BC35
Linthouse Bldgs, G51	34	BG29
Linthouse Rd, G51	34	BG28
Lintlaw, (Blan.) G72	84	CM44
Lintlaw Dr, G52	47	BD31
Linton St, G33	39	CA29
Lismore Av, Renf. PA4	32	AZ28
Lismore Dr, Pais. PA2	58	AT38
Lismore Rd, G12	20	BK24
Lister Rd, G52	46	BC30
Lister St, G4	11	BT28
Lithgow Pl, Pais. PA2	49	AW35
Little Dovehill, G1	15	BT31
Littlehill Cres, G53	61	BC37
Littlemill Dr, G53	61	BC37
Littlemill Gdns, G53	61	BC37
Littleton St, G23	21	BM20
Livingstone Av, G52	32	BC29
Livingstone Cres, (Blan.) G72	84	CM44
Livingstone St, Clyde. G81	17	AY20
Lloyd Av, G32	67	CC35
Lloyd St, G31	38	BW29
Lloyd St, (Ruther.) G73	66	BX36
Loanbank Quad, G51	48	BH30
Loancroft Av, (Baill.) G69	56	CL34
Loancroft Gdns, (Udd.) G71	84	CN40
Loancroft Gate, (Udd.) G71	84	CN
Loancroft Pl, (Baill.) G69	55	CK
Loanend Cotts, (Camb.) G72	83	CH
Loanfoot Av, G13	19	BC
Loanhead Av, Renf. PA4	32	AZ
Loanhead St, G32	53	CE
Lobnitz Av, Renf. PA4	32	AZ
Lochaber Dr, (Ruther.) G73	80	BZ
Loch Achray St, G32	54	CE
Lochaline Dr, G44	78	BQ
Lochalsh Pl, (Blan.) G72	83	CH
Lochar Cres, G53	61	BI
Lochay St, G32	54	CE
Lochbrae Dr, (Ruther.) G73	80	BZ
Lochbridge Rd, G34	55	C
Lochburn Cres, G20	21	BN
Lochburn Pas, G20	21	BN
Lochburn Rd, G20	21	BN
Lochdochart Rd, G34	56	C
Lochearnhead Rd, G33	26	CD
Lochend Av, (Gart.) G69	28	Cl
Lochend Dr, G34	41	CH
Lochend Rd, G34	42	CM
Lochend Rd, (Gart.) G69	29	C
Lochfield Cres, Pais. PA2	58	A
Lochfield Dr, Pais. PA2	59	AW
Lochfield Gdns, G34	42	C
Lochfield Rd, Pais. PA2	58	A
Lochgilp St, G20	21	B
Lochgreen Pl, Coat. ML5	43	C
Lochgreen St, G33	39	B
Lochiel La, (Ruther.) G73	81	B
Lochiel Rd, (Thornlie.) G46	76	B
Lochinver Dr, G44	78	B
Loch Katrine St, G32	54	C
Loch Laidon St, G32	54	C
Lochlea Rd, G43	63	B
Lochlea Rd, (Ruther.) G73	79	B
Lochleven La, G42	64	B
Lochleven Rd, G42	64	B
Lochlibo Av, G13	18	B
Lochlibo Cres, (Barr.) G78	73	A
Lochlibo Ter, (Barr.) G78	73	A
Lochmaben Rd, G52	46	B
Lochmaddy Av, G44	78	B
Lochore Av, Pais. PA3	45	A
Loch Rd, (Stepps) G33	26	C
Lochside, (Gart.) G69	29	C
Lochsloy Ct, G22	37	B
Lochview Cotts, (Gart.) G69	42	C
Lochview Cres, G33	39	C
Lochview Dr, G33	39	C
Lochview Gdns, G33	39	C
Lochview Pl, G33	39	C
Lochview Rd, Coat. ML5	43	C
Lochview Ter, (Gart.) G69	28	C
Loch Voil St, G32	54	C
Lochwood St, G33	39	C
Lochy Av, Renf. PA4	32	B
Lochy Gdns, (Bishop.) G64	24	B
Lockerbie Av, G43	64	B
Lockhart Av, (Camb.) G72	68	C
Lockhart Dr, (Camb.) G72	68	C
Lockhart St, G21	38	B
Locksley Av, G13	19	B
Logan Dr, Pais. PA3	44	A
Logan St, G5	51	B
Loganswell Dr, (Thornlie.) G46	76	B
Loganswell Gdns, (Thornlie.) G46	76	B
Loganswell Pl, (Thornlie.) G46	76	B
Loganswell Rd, (Thornlie.) G46	76	B

Lom-Man 113

max St, G33	38	BZ29
mond Av, Renf. PA4	31	AX28
mond Cres, Pais. PA2	58	AT37
mond Dr, (Both.) G71	85	CR42
mond Dr, (Barr.) G78	73	AX41
mond Pl, (Stepps) G33	40	CG25
mond Rd, (Udd.) G71	71	CP36
nond St, G22	22	BR24
ndon Rd, G1	15	BT31
ndon Rd, G31	52	BX33
ndon Rd, G32	67	CA35
ndon Rd, G40	15	BU32
ndon St, Renf. PA4	18	AZ24
ndon Way, G1	15	BT31
nend, Pais. PA1	44	AV33
ngay Pl, G22	23	BS21
ngay St, G22	23	BS21
ngcroft Dr, Renf. PA4	31	AY25
ngden St, Clyde. G81	18	AZ21
ngford St, G33	39	BZ29
nglee, (Baill.) G69	55	CK33
ng Row, (Baill.) G69	56	CL31
ngstone Rd, G33	40	CD29
nmay Rd, G33	40	CF29
nsdale Av, (Giff.) G46	77	BL42
a Dr, G52	48	BG33
etto Pl, G33	39	CB29
etto St, G33	39	CB29
n Av, (Chry.) G69	28	CM21
ne Rd, G52	32	BB29
ne St, G51	12	BM31
ne Ter, (Camb.) G72	81	CB42
skin Dr, G22	22	BS22
ssie Cres, Renf. PA4	32	BB27
ssie St, G33	39	BZ28
hian Cres, Pais. PA2	58	AT36
hian St, G52	32	BA29
uden Hill Rd, G33	25	CA23
udon Rd, G33	26	CD24
unsdale Pl, G14	33	BD25
urdes Av, G52	47	BF33
urdes Ct, G52	47	BF33
vat Pl, G52	46	BA30
vat Pl, (Ruther.) G73	81	BZ41
ve St, Pais. PA3	44	AU30
v Cres, Clyde. G81	18	AZ21
wer Bourtree Dr, (Ruther.) G73	80	BY41
wer Millgate, (Udd.) G71	70	CP39
wndes St, (Barr.) G78	73	AY43
v Parksail, Ersk. PA8	16	AS21
w Rd, (Castlehead) Pais. PA2	44	AS34
yne Dr, Renf. PA4	32	BB27
ath St, G51	34	BJ29
bas Av, G42	65	BT38
bas Pl, G42	65	BT38
onaig Rd, G43	63	BN39
kingsford Av, (Inch.) Renf. PA4	16	AT22
kingsford Dr, (Inch.) Renf. PA4	16	AS22
kingsford Rd, (Inch.) Renf. PA4	16	AS22
y Brae, (Udd.) G71	70	CN37
fness Gdns, G32	68	CD35
gar Dr, G52	48	BG33
gar Pl, G44	79	BU40
giebank Pl, (Baill.) G69	57	CQ33
ng Rd, G52	48	BG32
na Gdns, G51	47	BE30
nloch St, G21	38	BW25
nsden St, G3	8	BM29
an Dr, (Bishop.) G64	24	BY21
an Pl, G51	48	BG30
carty Pl, G32	53	CC34
carty St, G32	53	CC34
derston Cl, G53	61	BD39
Lunderston Dr, G53	61	BC38
Lunderston Gdns, G53	61	BD39
Lundie Gdns, (Bishop.) G64	24	BZ21
Lundie St, G32	53	CA34
Lusshill Ter, (Udd.) G71	69	CK35
Luss Rd, G51	48	BH30
Lybster Cres, (Ruther.) G73	81	BZ42
Lyle Pl, Pais. PA2	59	AV35
Lylesland Ct, Pais. PA2	58	AU35
Lymburn St, G3	8	BM28
Lyndale Pl, G20	21	BM21
Lyndale Rd, G20	21	BM21
Lyndhurst Gdns, G20	36	BP26
Lyndhurst Gdns La, G20	35	BN25
Lynedoch Cres, G3	9	BP28
Lynedoch Cres La, G3	9	BP28
Lynedoch Pl, G3	9	BP28
Lynedoch St, G3	9	BP28
Lynedoch Ter, G3	9	BP28
Lyne Dr, G23	21	BN20
Lynnhurst, (Udd.) G71	71	CP38
Lynton Av, (Giff.) G46	76	BJ44
Lyoncross Av, (Barr.) G78	74	AZ43
Lyoncross Rd, G53	61	BD35
Lytham Dr, G23	21	BN20
Lytham Meadows, (Both.) G71	84	CN43

M

McAlpine St, G2	13	BQ30
Macarthur Wynd, (Camb.) G72	82	CE40
McAslin Ct, G4	11	BT29
McAslin St, G4	11	BU29
Macbeth Pl, G31	52	BZ33
Macbeth St, G31	52	BZ33
McCallum Av, (Ruther.) G73	66	BX38
Maccallum Dr, (Camb.) G72	82	CE40
McCloy Gdns, G53	60	BB39
McClue Av, Renf. PA4	31	AX25
McClue Rd, Renf. PA4	31	AY25
McCracken Av, Renf. PA4	31	AX27
McCracken Dr, (Udd.) G71	71	CS37
McCreery St, Clyde. G81	18	AZ21
McCulloch Av, (Udd.) G71	71	CS39
McCulloch St, G41	50	BP33
McDonald Cres, Clyde. G81	18	AZ21
Macdougall Dr, (Camb.) G72	82	CE40
Macdougall St, G43	63	BL38
Macdowall St, Pais. PA3	44	AT31
Macduff Pl, G31	52	BZ33
Macduff St, G31	52	BZ33
Mace Rd, G13	19	BE20
Macfarlane Cres, (Camb.) G72	82	CE40
McFarlane St, G4	15	BU31
McFarlane St, Pais. PA3	44	AS30
McGown St, Pais. PA3	44	AT31
McGregor Av, Renf. PA4	31	AX27
McGregor St, G51	48	BH31
McGregor St, Clyde. G81	18	AZ21
Machrie Dr, G45	79	BV41
Machrie Rd, G45	79	BV41
Machrie St, G45	79	BV41
McIntosh Ct, G31	51	BV30
McIntosh St, G31	51	BV30
McIntyre Pl, Pais. PA2	58	AU35
McIntyre St, G3	13	BP30
McIver St, (Camb.) G72	68	CG39
Mackean St, Pais. PA3	44	AS31
McKechnie St, G51	34	BJ29
Mackeith St, G40	51	BV33
McKenzie St, Pais. PA3	44	AS32
McKerrell St, Pais. PA1	45	AW32
Mackinlay St, G5	50	BR33
McLaren Av, Renf. PA4	31	AY28
McLaren Cres, G20	21	BN22
McLaren Gdns, G20	21	BN22
Maclean Sq, G51	12	BM31
Maclean St, G51	12	BM31
Maclean St, Clyde. G81	18	BA21
Maclellan St, G41	49	BL32
McLennan St, G42	64	BQ37
Macleod St, G4	11	BU29
Macleod Way, (Camb.) G72	82	CE40
Macmillan Gdns, (Udd.) G71	71	CQ37
McNair St, G32	53	CC32
McNeil Av, Clyde. G81	18	BA20
McNeil Gdns, G5	51	BT33
McNeil St, G5	51	BT33
McPhail St, G40	51	BU33
McPhater St, G4	10	BR28
McPherson Dr, (Both.) G71	85	CR42
Madison Av, G44	78	BR40
Madras Pl, G40	51	BV34
Madras St, G40	51	BV34
Mafeking St, G51	49	BK31
Magnolia Dr, (Camb.) G72	83	CH42
Magnolia Pl, (Udd.) G71	71	CS37
Magnus Cres, G44	78	BR41
Mahon Ct, (Mood.) G69	28	CP20
Maidland Rd, G53	61	BE37
Mainhill Av, (Baill.) G69	56	CM32
Mainhill Dr, (Baill.) G69	56	CL32
Mainhill Pl, (Baill.) G69	56	CL32
Mainhill Rd, (Baill.) G69	56	CP32
Main Rd, (Castlehead) Pais. PA2	44	AT33
Mains Av, (Giff.) G46	77	BK44
Mainscroft, Ersk. PA8	16	AS20
Mains Dr, Ersk. PA8	16	AS20
Mains River, Ersk. PA8	16	AS20
Main St, G40	51	BV34
Main St, (Thornlie.) G46	76	BH42
Main St, (Baill.) G69	56	CL33
Main St, (Chry.) G69	28	CL21
Main St, (Both.) G71	85	CQ43
Main St, (Udd.) G71	70	CP39
Main St, (Camb.) G72	67	CC39
Main St, (Ruther.) G73	66	BW37
Main St, (Barr.) G78	73	AX43
Mains Wd, Ersk. PA8	16	AT20
Mair St, G51	12	BN31
Maitland Pl, Renf. PA4	31	AX27
Maitland St, G4	10	BR28
Malin Pl, G33	39	CB29
Mallaig Rd, G51	47	BF30
Malloch St, G20	21	BN24
Malta Ter, G5	50	BR33
Maltbarns St, G20	36	BQ26
Malvern Ct, G31	52	BW31
Malvern Way, Pais. PA3	30	AT29
Mamore Pl, G43	63	BL39
Mamore St, G43	63	BL39
Manchester Dr, G12	20	BJ23
Mannering Ct, G41	63	BL37
Mannering Rd, G41	63	BL37
Manor Rd, G14	34	BG25
Manor Rd, G15	18	BB20
Manor Rd, (Gart.) G69	29	CP24
Manor Way, (Ruther.) G73	80	BY41
Manresa Pl, G4	10	BR27
Manse Av, (Both.) G71	85	CQ43
Manse Brae, G44	64	BR39
Manse Brae, (Camb.) G72	83	CJ40
Manse Ct, (Barr.) G78	74	AZ42

Street	Page	Grid
Mansfield Av, (Camb.) G72	81	CC41
Manse Gdns, G32	54	CF33
Mansel St, G21	23	BV24
Manse Rd, G32	54	CF33
Manse Rd, (Baill.) G69	56	CN31
Manse St, Renf. PA4	32	AZ25
Mansewood Rd, G43	63	BK39
Mansfield Dr, (Udd.) G71	71	CP39
Mansfield Rd, G52	46	BB30
Mansfield St, G11	35	BL27
Mansion Ct, (Camb.) G72	67	CC39
Mansionhouse Av, G32	68	CE37
Mansionhouse Dr, G32	54	CE31
Mansionhouse Gdns, G41	63	BN38
Mansionhouse Gro, G32	54	CG34
Mansionhouse Rd, G32	54	CG33
Mansionhouse Rd, G41	63	BN38
Mansionhouse Rd, Pais. PA1	45	AW32
Mansion St, G22	53	BS24
Mansion St, (Camb.) G72	67	CC39
Maple Cres, (Camb.) G72	33	CH42
Maple Rd, G41	49	BK34
Marchbank Gdns, Pais. PA1	46	AZ33
Marchfield Av, Pais. PA3	30	AT29
March St, G41	49	BP35
Maree Dr, G52	48	BG33
Maree Gdns, (Bishop.) G64	24	BX20
Marfield St, G32	53	CA30
Mar Gdns, (Ruther.) G73	80	BZ41
Marguerite Gdns, (Both.) G71	85	CR43
Marine Cres, G51	12	BN31
Marine Gdns, G51	13	BP31
Mariscat Rd, G41	63	BN35
Marjory Dr, Pais. PA3	45	AW30
Marjory Rd, Renf. PA4	31	AW28
Markdow Av, G53	60	BC36
Market Rd, (Udd.) G71	71	CS38
Market St, (Udd.) G71	71	CS38
Marlach Pl, G53	60	BC36
Marlborough Av, G11	34	BH26
Marlborough La N, G11	34	BH26
Marlborough La S, G11	34	BH26
Marldon La, G11	34	BH26
Marlow St, G41	49	BN33
Marne St, G31	52	BX30
Marnock Ter, Pais. PA2	45	AW34
Marquis Gate, (Udd.) G71	24	CN40
Marshall's La, Pais. PA1	44	AU33
Martha St, G1	35	BS29
Martin Cres, (Baill.) G69	56	CL32
Martin St, G40	51	BV34
Mart St, G1	14	BS31
Martyrs Pl, (Bishop.) G64	24	BW21
Marwick St, G31	52	BX30
Maryhill Rd, G20	38	BP26
Maryhill Shop Cen, G20	21	BN24
Maryland Dr, G52	48	BG33
Maryland Gdns, G52	48	BG32
Mary Sq, (Baill.) G69	57	CP32
Maryston Pl, G33	39	BZ27
Maryston St, G33	39	BZ27
Mary St, G4	10	BR27
Mary St, Pais. PA2	44	AU35
Maryville Av, (Giff.) G46	77	BL43
Maryville Gdns, (Giff.) G46	77	BL43
Maryville Vw, (Udd.) G71	70	CM36
Marywood Sq, G41	49	BP35
Masterton St, G21	37	BS26
Masterton Way, (Udd.) G71	71	CR36
Mathieson Rd, (Ruther.) G73	66	BY36
Mathieson St, Pais. PA1	45	AX32
Matilda Rd, G41	49	BN34
Mauchline St, G5	50	BQ33
Maukinfauld Ct, G32	53	BZ34
Maukinfauld Gdns, G31	53	CA33
Maukinfauld Rd, G32	53	CA34
Mauldslie St, G40	52	BX33
Maule Dr, G11	34	BJ27
Mavis Bank Gdns, G64	23	BV21
Mavisbank Gdns, G51	12	BN31
Mavisbank Ter, Pais. PA1	45	AV34
Maxton Av, (Barr.) G78	73	AW42
Maxton Gro, (Barr.) G78	73	AW43
Maxton Ter, (Camb.) G72	81	CB42
Maxwell Av, G41	49	BN33
Maxwell Av, (Baill.) G69	55	CJ33
Maxwell Dr, G41	49	BL33
Maxwell Dr, (Baill.) G69	55	CJ32
Maxwell Gdns, G41	49	BM33
Maxwell Gro, G41	49	BM33
Maxwell Oval, G41	50	BP33
Maxwell Pl, G41	50	BQ34
Maxwell Rd, G41	50	BP33
Maxwell St, G1	14	BS31
Maxwell St, (Baill.) G69	55	CK33
Maxwell St, Pais. PA3	44	AU32
Maxwell Ter, G41	49	BN33
Maxwelton Ct, Pais. PA1	45	AS33
Maxwelton St, Pais. PA1	44	AS34
Maxwelton Rd, G33	39	BZ27
Maybank La, G42	64	BQ36
Mayberry Cres, G32	54	CF32
Mayberry Gdns, G32	54	CF32
Mayberry Gro, G32	54	CF32
Maybole St, G53	60	BB39
Mayfield St, G20	22	BP23
May Rd, Pais. PA2	58	AU36
May Ter, G42	64	BR37
May Ter, (Giff.) G46	77	BL42
Meadowbank La, (Udd.) G71	70	CN39
Meadow La, (Both.) G71	85	CR43
Meadow La, Renf. PA4	18	AZ24
Meadowpark St, G31	52	BX30
Meadow Rd, G11	34	BJ27
Meadows Av, Ersk. PA8	16	AS20
Meadows Dr, Ersk. PA8	16	AS20
Meadowside Ind Est, Renf. PA4	18	AZ23
Meadowside Quay, G11	34	BG28
Meadowside St, G11	34	BJ28
Meadowside St, Renf. PA4	18	AZ24
Meadowwell St, G32	54	CD32
Medwin St, (Camb.) G72	82	CF40
Medwyn St, G14	37	BF26
Meek Pl, (Camb.) G72	82	CD40
Megan St, G40	51	BV33
Meikle Av, Renf. PA4	31	AY27
Meiklerig Cres, G53	61	BE35
Meikle Rd, G53	61	BE37
Meiklewood Rd, G51	47	BF31
Melbourne Ct, (Giff.) G46	77	BM42
Melbourne St, G31	51	BV31
Meldrum Gdns, G41	63	BM35
Meldrum St, Clyde. G81	18	AZ21
Melford Av, (Giff.) G46	77	BM43
Melfort Av, G41	48	BK33
Mellerstain Dr, G14	18	BA23
Melrose Av, (Ruther.) G73	66	BX38
Melrose Ct, (Ruther.) G73	66	BX38
Melrose Gdns, G20	36	BP26
Melrose Gdns, (Udd.) G71	71	CP36
Melrose Pl, (Blan.) G72		CL44
Melvaig Pl, G20	21	BM24
Melville St, G41	50	BP34
Memel St, G21	23	BU24
Memus Av, G52	48	BE33
Menock Rd, G44	64	BR39
Menteith Av, (Bishop.) G64	24	BX20
Menteith Dr, (Ruther.) G73	80	B...
Menteith Pl, (Ruther.) G73	80	B...
Menzies Dr, G21	24	BV...
Menzies Pl, G21	24	BV...
Menzies Rd, G21	24	BV...
Merchant La, G1	14	BS...
Merkland Rd, Coat. ML5	43	C...
Merkland St, G11	34	BJ...
Merlewood Av, (Both.) G71	85	C...
Merlinford Av, Renf. PA4	32	BA...
Merlinford Dr, Renf. PA4	32	BA...
Merlinford Way, Renf. PA4	32	BA...
Merlin Way, Pais. PA3	45	A...
Merrick Gdns, G51	48	BH...
Merrick Ter, (Udd.) G71	71	C...
Merrick Way, (Ruther.) G73	80	B...
Merryburn Av, (Giff.) G46	77	BN...
Merrycrest Av, (Giff.) G46	77	BN...
Merrycroft Av, (Giff.) G46	77	BN...
Merryland Pl, G51	49	B...
Merryland St, G51	49	B...
Merrylee Cres, (Giff.) G46	77	B...
Merrylee Pk Av, (Giff.) G46	77	BN...
Merrylee Pk La, (Giff.) G46	77	B...
Merrylee Pk Ms, (Giff.) G46	77	BN...
Merrylee Rd, G43	77	B...
Merrylee Rd, G44	77	B...
Merryton Av, (Giff.) G46	77	B...
Merryvale Av, (Giff.) G46	77	B...
Merryvale Pl, (Giff.) G46	77	B...
Merton Dr, G52	47	B...
Meryon Gdns, G32	68	C...
Methil St, G14	33	B...
Methuen Rd, Pais. PA3	31	A...
Methven St, G31	53	B...
Mews La, Pais. PA3	45	A...
Micklehouse Oval, (Baill.) G69	55	C...
Micklehouse Pl, (Baill.) G69	55	C...
Micklehouse Rd, (Baill.) G69	55	C...
Micklehouse Wynd, (Baill.) G69	55	C...
Mid Cotts, (Gart.) G69	42	C...
Midcroft Av, G44	79	B...
Middle Pk, Pais. PA2	58	A...
Middlesex Gdns, G41	12	B...
Middlesex St, G41	12	B...
Middleton St, G51	49	B...
Midland St, G1	14	B...
Midlem Dr, G52	47	B...
Midlem Oval, G52	47	B...
Midlock St, G51	49	B...
Midlothian Dr, G41	63	B...
Midton Cotts, (Mood.) G69	29	C...
Midton St, G21	37	B...
Midwharf St, G4	10	B...
Milan St, G41	50	B...
Milford St, G33	39	C...
Millands Av, (Blan.) G72	84	C...
Millarbank St, G21	37	B...
Millar Ter, (Ruther.) G73	66	B...
Millbeg Cres, G33	55	C...
Millbeg Pl, G33	55	C...
Millbrae Av, (Chry.) G69	28	C...
Millbrae Ct, G42	64	B...
Millbrae Cres, G42	63	B...
Millbrae Cres, Clyde. G81	18	A...
Millbrae Gdns, G42	64	B...
Millbrae Rd, G42	63	B...
Millbrix Av, G14	18	A...
Millburn Av, (Ruther.) G73	66	B...
Millburn Av, Clyde. G81	18	B...
Millburn Av, Renf. PA4	32	B...
Millburn Dr, Renf. PA4	32	B...
Millburn Rd, Renf. PA4	32	A...

Name	Page	Grid
Iburn St, G21	37	BV28
Iburn Way, Renf. PA4	32	BA26
I Ct, (Ruther.) G73	66	BW37
I Cres, G40	51	BV34
Icroft Rd, (Ruther.) G73	65	BV36
Iennium Ct, G34	42	CL29
Iennium Gdns, G34	56	CL30
Ier Cl, (Bishop.) G64	24	BY21
Ier Dr, (Bishop.) G64	25	BZ21
Ierfield Rd, G40	52	BX34
Ierfield Rd, G40	52	BX34
Ier Gdns, (Bishop.) G64	25	BZ21
Ier La, Clyde. G81	17	AX20
Ier Pl, (Bishop.) G64	25	BZ21
Iersneuk Cres, G33	25	CC24
Ierston St, G31	52	BW31
Ier St, G1	14	BS30
Ier St, (Baill.) G69	55	CK33
Ier St, Clyde. G81	17	AX20
Iholm Rd, G44	78	BH41
Ighgate, (Udd.) G71	71	CP37
Ighgate Av, (Udd.) G71	71	CP37
Ighgate Cl, (Udd.) G71	70	CP38
Ilhouse Cres, G20	21	BL22
Ilhouse Dr, G20	21	BK22
Ilport Av, G44	64	BS38
I Rd, (Both.) G71	85	CG44
I Rd, (Camb.) G72	82	CF40
I Rd, Clyde. G81	18	AZ22
Ilroad Dr, G40	15	BU31
Ilroad Gdns, G40	51	BV31
Ilroad St, G40	15	BU31
Ilstream Ct, Pais. PA1	45	AV33
I St, G40	51	BV34
I St, (Ruther.) G73	66	BW37
I St, Pais. PA1	44	AV33
Ilview, (Barr.) G78	74	AZ42
Ilview Pl, G53	75	BD41
Ilwood St, G41	63	BN37
Inbank St, G31	38	BW29
Incroft Pl, G33	39	CC28
Incroft Rd, G33	39	CC28
Iner La, G13	20	BG24
Iner Rd, G13	20	BG24
Inpark Gdns, G41	12	BM32
Inpark St, G41	38	BN32
Iovaig Av, G23	21	BM20
Iovaig St, G23	21	BM20
Irig Rd, (Ruther.) G73	65	BV38
Iton Av, (Camb.) G72	81	CA40
Iton Dr, (Bishop.) G64	23	BU22
Iton Gdns, (Udd.) G71	70	CN37
Iton St, G4	10	BS28
Iverton Rd, (Giff.) G46	76	BJ44
Inard Rd, G41	63	BN36
Ierva St, G3	8	BN29
Ierva Way, G3	8	BN29
Ingarry St, G20	35	BN25
Ingulay Cres, G22	23	BT21
Ingulay Pl, G22	23	BU21
Ingulay St, G22	23	BT21
Imoir Rd, G53	60	BB38
Instrol Rd, G13	19	BF20
Ito Av, (Ruther.) G73	80	BZ41
Ito Cres, G52	48	BH32
Ito St, G52	48	BH32
Ieton St, G22	24	BR24
Ierlees Dr, G12	35	BL25
Ierlees La, G12	35	BL25
Ichell Av, (Camb.) G72	68	CG39
Ichell Av, Renf. PA4	31	AX27
Ichell St, (Ruther.) G73	66	BX39
Ichellhill Rd, G45	79	BX43
Ichell La, G1	14	BR30
Ichell St, G1	14	BR30
Ichell St, Coat. ML5	57	CR32
Ire Ct, G11	34	BH25
Ire Gate, G11	34	BH25
Mitre La, G14	33	BF25
Mitre La W, G14	33	BF25
Mitre Rd, G14	34	BH25
Mitre Rd, G14	34	BG25
Moat Av, G13	19	BE22
Mochrum Rd, G43	63	BN39
Moffat Pl, (Blan.) G72	84	CM44
Moffat St, G5	11	BT33
Moidart Av, Renf. PA4	31	AX25
Moidart Ct, (Barr.) G78	73	AX40
Moidart Cres, G52	48	BG32
Moidart Pl, G52	48	BG32
Moidart Rd, G52	48	BG32
Moir St, G1	15	BT31
Molendinar Cl, G33	39	CA27
Molendinar Gdns, G33	39	BZ27
Molendinar St, G1	15	BT31
Mollinsburn St, G21	37	BU26
Monach Rd, G33	40	CE29
Monar Dr, G22	36	BR26
Monart Pl, G20	22	BP24
Moncur St, G40	15	BU31
Moness Dr, G52	48	BG33
Monifieth Av, G52	47	BF34
Monikie Gdns, (Bishop.) G64	24	BZ20
Monkcastle Dr, (Camb.) G72	67	CC39
Monkland Vw Cres, (Baill.) G69	57	CP33
Monksbridge Av, G13	19	BE20
Monkscroft Av, G11	34	BJ26
Monmouth Av, G12	20	BJ23
Monreith Rd, G43	63	BN39
Monreith Rd E, G44	78	BQ40
Monroe Dr, (Udd.) G71	71	CP36
Monroe Pl, (Udd.) G71	71	CP36
Montague La, G12	35	BK25
Montague St, G4	9	BP27
Monteith Pl, G40	15	BU32
Monteith Row, G40	15	BU32
Montford Av, G44	65	BU38
Montford Av, (Ruther.) G73	65	BU38
Montfort Gate, (Barr.) G78	74	BA42
Montgarrie St, G51	47	BF31
Montgomery Av, Pais. PA3	31	AX29
Montgomery Dr, (Giff.) G46	77	BL44
Montgomery Rd, Pais. PA3	31	AW29
Montgomery St, G40	52	BW33
Montgomery St, (Camb.) G72	82	CG40
Montrave St, (Ruther.) G73	66	BY36
Montrave St, G52	47	BF32
Montrose Av, G52	68	CE36
Montrose Av, G32	82	BB29
Montrose Gdns, (Blan.) G72	84	CL43
Montrose St, G1	15	BT30
Montrose St, G4	11	BT30
Montrose Ter, (Bishop.) G64	24	BY22
Monument Dr, G33	25	CA24
Moodiesburn St, G33	39	BZ27
Moorburn Av, (Giff.) G46	76	BK42
Moorfoot Av, (Thornlie.) G46	76	BJ42
Moorfoot Av, Pais. PA2	48	AT36
Moorfoot St, G32	53	CA31
Moorhouse Av, G13	18	BB23
Moorhouse St, (Barr.) G78	73	AY43
Moorpark Av, G52	46	BB31
Moorpark Av, (Muir.) G69	27	CL22
Moorpark Dr, G52	46	BC31
Moorpark Pl, G52	46	BB31
Moorpark Sq, Renf. PA4	31	AX27
Morag Av, (Blan.) G72	84	CL44
Moraine Av, G15	19	BD20
Moraine Circ, G15	19	BC20
Moraine Dr, G15	19	BC20
Morar Dr, (Ruther.) G73	80	BX42
Morar Pl, Renf. PA4	31	AX25
Morar Rd, G52	48	BG32
Morar Ter, (Udd.) G71	71	CR38
Morar Ter, (Ruther.) G73	66	BZ42
Moravia Av, (Both.) G71	85	CQ42
Moray Ct, (Ruther.) G73	66	BW37
Moray Gdns, (Udd.) G71	70	CP37
Moray Gate, (Both.) G71	84	CN41
Moray Pl, G41	63	BN35
Moray Pl, (Bishop.) G64	24	BY20
Moray Pl, (Chry.) G69	28	CM21
Mordaunt St, G40	52	BW34
Moredun Cres, G32	54	CE30
Moredun St, G32	54	CE30
Morefield Rd, G51	47	BF30
Morgan Ms, G42	50	BR34
Morion Rd, G13	19	BF21
Morley St, G42	64	BQ38
Morningside St, G33	39	BZ29
Morrin St, G21	37	BU25
Morrison Ct, G2	14	BR30
Morrison St, G5	10	BR31
Morriston Cres, Renf. PA4	32	BB28
Morriston St, (Camb.) G72	67	CC39
Morton Gdns, G41	63	BL36
Morven Av, (Bishop.) G64	24	BY20
Morven Av, (Blan.) G72	84	CL44
Morven Av, Pais. PA2	58	AT37
Morven Gait, Ersk. PA8	16	AU21
Morven Gdns, (Udd.) G71	71	CP37
Morven La, (Blan.) G72	84	CL44
Morven Rd, (Camb.) G72	81	CB42
Morven St, G52	48	BG32
Morven Way, (Both.) G71	85	CR42
Mosesfield St, G21	23	BV24
Mosque Av, G5	14	BS32
Mossbank Av, G33	39	CB25
Mossbank Dr, G33	39	CB25
Moss, (Barr.) G78	73	AW40
Mossend La, G33	40	CF29
Mossend St, G33	54	CF30
Mossgiel Av, (Ruther.) G73	80	BW40
Mossgiel Gdns, (Udd.) G71	70	CN37
Mossgiel Pl, (Ruther.) G73	80	BW40
Mossgiel Rd, G43	63	BM38
Mossgiel Ter, (Blan.) G72	84	CL43
Moss Hts Av, G52	47	BF32
Mossland Rd, G52	32	BA29
Mosslands Rd, Pais. PA3	30	AT29
Mossneuk Dr, Pais. PA2	58	AS37
Mosspark Av, G52	48	BH34
Mosspark Boul, G52	48	BG33
Mosspark Dr, G52	47	BE33
Mosspark Oval, G52	48	BG34
Mosspark Sq, G52	48	BG34
Moss Path, (Baill.) G69	55	CH34
Moss Rd, G51	47	BE31
Moss Rd, (Muir.) G69	28	CL22
Moss-Side Rd, G41	63	BM36
Moss St, Pais. PA1	44	AU32
Mossvale Cres, G33	40	CE27
Mossvale La, Pais. PA3	44	AT31
Mossvale Path, G33	40	CE26
Mossvale Rd, G33	40	CD26
Mossvale Sq, G33	40	CE26
Mossvale Sq, Pais. PA3	44	AT31
Mossvale St, Pais. PA3	44	AT31
Mossvale Wk, G33	40	CE27
Mossview Quad, G52	47	BE32
Mossview Rd, G33	26	CG34
Mote Hill Rd, Pais. PA3	45	AW31

Moulin Circ, G52	47	BC33
Moulin Pl, G52	47	BC33
Moulin Rd, G52	47	BC33
Moulin Ter, G52	47	BC33
Mountainblue St, G31	53	BW32
Mount Annan Dr, G44	64	BR38
Mountgarrie Rd, G51	47	BF30
Mount Harriet Av, (Stepps) G33	26	CG23
Mount Harriet Dr, (Stepps) G33	26	CF23
Mount Lockhart, (Udd.) G71	69	CK35
Mount St, G20	36	BP26
Mount Stuart St, G41	63	BN37
Mount Vernon Av, G32	55	CD34
Mowbray Av, (Gart.) G69	29	CP24
Moyne Rd, G53	61	BC35
Muirbank Av, (Ruther.) G73	65	BV38
Muirbank Gdns, (Ruther.) G73	65	BV38
Muirbrae Rd, (Ruther.) G73	80	BX41
Muirburn Av, G44	78	BN41
Muirdrum Av, G52	47	BF34
Muirdykes Av, G52	46	BC32
Muirdykes Rd, G52	46	BC32
Muiredge Ct, (Udd.) G71	71	CP39
Muiredge Ter, (Baill.) G69	55	CK33
Muirend Av, G44	78	BP40
Muirend Rd, G44	77	BN41
Muirfield Cres, G23	21	BN20
Muirfield Meadows, (Both.) G71	84	CN43
Muirhead Ct, (Baill.) G69	56	CL33
Muirhead Gdns, (Baill.) G69	56	CL33
Muirhead Gate, (Udd.) G71	71	CR37
Muirhead Gro, (Baill.) G69	56	CL33
Muirhead Rd, (Baill.) G69	55	CK34
Muirhead Way, (Bishop.) G64	24	BZ20
Muirhill Av, G44	77	BN41
Muirhill Cres, G13	18	BC22
Muirkirk Dr, G13	20	BH22
Muirpark Av, Renf. PA4	31	AY27
Muirpark Dr, (Bishop.) G64	24	BW21
Muirpark St, G11	35	BK27
Muir Pk Ter, (Bishop.) G64	23	BV21
Muirshiel Av, G53	61	BE39
Muirshiel Cres, G53	61	BE39
Muirside Av, G32	54	CG34
Muirside Rd, (Baill.) G69	55	CK33
Muirside St, (Baill.) G69	55	CK33
Muirskeith Cres, G43	64	BP39
Muirskeith Pl, G43	64	BP39
Muirskeith Rd, G43	64	BP39
Muir St, (Bishop.) G64	24	BW20
Muir St, Renf. PA4	32	AZ25
Muir Ter, Pais. PA3	45	AW30
Muiryfauld Dr, G31	53	CA33
Mulben Cres, G53	60	BB38
Mulben Pl, G53	60	BB38
Mulben Ter, G53	60	BB38
Mulberry Rd, G43	77	BM40
Mulberry Rd, (Udd.) G71	71	CS36
Mulberry Wynd, (Camb.) G72	82	CH42
Mullardoch St, G23	21	BM20
Mull Av, Pais. PA2	58	AT38
Mull Av, Renf. PA4	31	AY28
Mull St, G21	38	BX27
Munlochy Rd, G51	47	BF30
Munro La, G13	20	BG24
Munro La E, G13	20	BG24
Munro Pl, G13	20	BG22
Munro Rd, G13	20	BG24
Murano St, G20	36	BP26
Muriel St, (Barr.) G78	73	AY42
Muriel St Ind Est, (Barr.) G78	73	AY41
Murray Business Area, Pais. PA3	44	AT31
Murrayfield Dr, (Bears.) G61	20	BG20
Murrayfield St, G32	53	CA30
Murray Path, (Udd.) G71	70	CN39
Murray Pl, (Barr.) G78	74	AZ41
Murray Rd, (Both.) G71	85	CQ42
Murray St, Pais. PA3	44	AS31
Murray St, Renf. PA4	31	AY26
Murrin Av, (Bishop.) G64	24	BZ20
Murroes Rd, G51	47	BF30
Muslin St, G40	51	BV33
Mybster Rd, G51	47	BF30
Myers Cres, (Udd.) G71	85	CQ40
Myreside Pl, G32	53	BZ31
Myreside St, G32	52	BZ31
Myres Rd, G53	61	BF37
Myroch Pl, G34	42	CL38
Myrtle Hill La, G42	64	BS37
Myrtle Pk, G42	64	BR36
Myrtle Pl, G42	64	BS36
Myrtle Rd, (Udd.) G71	71	CR37
Myrtle Sq, (Bishop.) G64	24	BW21
Myrtle St, (Blan.) G72	84	CM44
Myrtle Vw Rd, G42	64	BS37
Myrtle Wk, (Camb.) G72	67	CB39

N

Naburn Gate, G5	50	BS33
Nairn Av, (Blan.) G72	84	CL43
Nairnside Rd, G21	24	BY22
Nairn St, G3	8	BM28
Naismith St, G32	68	CE36
Nansen St, G20	36	BQ26
Napier Dr, G51	34	BK29
Napier Pl, G51	34	BK29
Napier Rd, G51	34	BK29
Napier Rd, G52	32	BB28
Napiershall La, G20	9	BP27
Napiershall Pl, G20	9	BP27
Napiershall St, G20	9	BP27
Napier St, Clyde. G81	17	AY22
Napier Ter, G51	34	BK29
Naseby Av, G11	34	BH26
Naseby La, G11	34	BH26
Nasmyth Pl, G52	47	BC30
Nasmyth Rd, G52	47	BC30
Nasmyth Rd N, G52	47	BC30
Nasmyth Rd S, G52	47	BC30
Navar Pl, Pais. PA2	59	AW35
Naver St, G33	39	CA28
Neidpath, (Baill.) G69	55	CJ33
Neilsland Oval, G53	61	BF37
Neilsland Sq, G53	61	BF36
Neilston Av, G13	75	BE40
Neilston Ct, G53	75	BE40
Neilston Rd, Pais. PA2	44	AU34
Neil St, Pais. PA1	44	AS33
Neil St, Renf. PA4	18	AZ24
Neilvaig Dr, (Ruther.) G73	80	BY42
Neistpoint Dr, G33	39	CC29
Nelson Mandela Pl, G2	10	BS29
Nelson Pl, (Baill.) G69	55	CK33
Nelson St, G5	13	BQ31
Nelson St, (Baill.) G69	55	CK33
Neptune St, G51	48	BK30
Ness Dr, (Blan.) G72	84	CN44
Ness Rd, Renf. PA4	31	AX25
Ness St, G33	39	CA28
Nethan St, G51	34	BJ29
Nether Auldhouse Rd, G43	63	B
Netherburn Av, G44	78	Bl
Nether Pl, (Both.) Dr, G41	49	BN
Nethercairn Rd, G43	77	B
Nethercliffe Av, G44	78	Bl
Nethercommon Harbour, Pais. PA3	44	A
Nethercraigs Dr, Pais. PA2	58	A
Netherdale Dr, Pais. PA1	46	B
Netherfield St, G31	52	B
Nethergreen Cres, Renf. PA4	31	A)
Nethergreen Rd, Renf. PA4	31	A)
Nethergreen Wynd, Renf. PA4	31	A.
Netherhill Av, G44	78	B
Netherhill Cres, Pais. PA3	45	AV
Netherhill Rd, (Mood.) G69	28	C
Netherhill Rd, Pais. PA3	45	A
Netherhill Way, Pais. PA3	45	A.
Netherhouse Pl, G34	42	Cl
Netherhouse Rd, (Baill.) G69	56	Cl
Netherlee Pl, G44	78	B
Netherlee Rd, G44	78	B
Netherpark Av, G44	78	B
Netherplace Cres, G53	61	Bl
Netherplace Rd, G53	61	B
Netherton Av, G13	20	B
Netherton Ct, G45	79	B
Netherton Dr, (Barr.) G78	74	A
Netherton Fm La, (Bears.) G61	20	B
Netherton Rd, G13	20	Bl
Netherton St, G13	20	Bl
Nethervale Av, G44	78	B
Netherview Rd, G44	78	B
Netherway, G44	78	B
Neuk Av, (Muir.) G69	28	C
Neuk Way, G32	68	C
Nevis Ct, (Barr.) G78	73	A
Nevis Rd, G43	77	B
Nevis Rd, Renf. PA4	31	A
Nevis Way, (Abbots.) Pais. PA3	30	A
Newark Dr, G41	49	BN
Newark Dr, Pais. PA2	58	A
Newbank Ct, G31	53	C
Newbank Gdns, G31	53	B
Newbank Rd, G31	53	C
Newbattle Ct, G32	68	C
Newbattle Gdns, G32	68	C
Newbattle Pl, G32	68	C
Newbattle Rd, G32	67	C
Newbold Av, G21	23	B
Newburgh St, G43	63	BF
New City Rd, G4	10	Bl
Newcroft Dr, G44	79	B
New Edinburgh Rd, (Udd.) G71	71	C
New Edinburgh Rd, Bell. ML4	71	C
Newfield La, (Both.) G71	85	C
Newfield Pl, (Thornlie.) G46	76	Bl
Newfield Pl, (Ruther.) G73	65	Bl
Newfield Sq, G53	60	Bl
Newgrove Gdns, (Camb.) G72	67	C
Newhall St, G40	51	Bl
Newhaven Rd, G33	40	Cl
Newhaven St, G32	53	C
Newhills Rd, G33	55	Cl
New Inchinnan Rd, Pais. PA3	44	A
Newington St, G32	53	C
Newlandsfield Rd, G43	63	BF
Newlands Rd, G43	63	B

Street	Page	Grid
wlands Rd, G44	64	BQ39
wlands Rd, (Udd.) G71	71	CP37
w Luce Dr, G52		
mins Rd, Renf. PA4	31	AX27
wmill Rd, G21	24	BP39
milns Dr, G53	60	BB39
nham Rd, Pais. PA1	46	AJ33
w Rd, (Camb.) G72	82	CG41
shot Dr, Ersk. PA8	16	AS30
w Sneddon St, Pais. PA3	44	AU32
wstead Gdns, G23	21	BN20
t St, Pais. PA1	44	AU33
wton Av, (Camb.) G72	68	CF39
wton Av, (Barr.) G78	73	AY44
wton Brae, (Camb.) G72	69	CG39
wton Dr, (Udd.) G71	72	CQ38
wton Dr, (Camb.) G72	69	CH38
wtongrange Av, G32	54	CD35
wtongrange Gdns, G32	68	CD35
wton Rd, G3	9	BP28
wton Sta Rd, (Camb.) G72	83	CG41
wton St, Pais. PA1	44	AS33
wton Ter La, G3	9	BP29
wtyle Dr, G53	60	BB36
wtyle Pl, G53	60	BB36
wtyle Pl, (Bishop.) G64	24	BZ20
wtyle Pl, Renf. PA1	45	AS32
w Wynd, G1	14	BS31
mh Ct, (Inch.) Renf. PA4	16	AS22
holas St, G1	15	BT30
holson St, G5	14	BR31
olson Ct, (Stepps) G33	26	CG24
drie Rd, G42	64	BP35
drie Sq, G42	64	BP35
dry St, Pais. PA3	44	AV32
tel Gdns, G41	63	BM36
Pl, G34	41	CJ29
mo Dr, G51	48	BG30
bet St, G31	52	BZ32
sen Pl, G53	60	BB36
n Dr, Renf. PA4	32	BA27
nsdale Dr, G41	64	BP35
nsdale Pl, G41	64	BP35
nsdale Rd, G41	64	BP35
n St, G33	38	BZ28
shill Rd, (Thornlie.) G46	75	BF42
shill Rd, G53	60	BB39
en St, G20	21	BL23
drum Av, G32	68	CE37
breck Dr, (Giff.) G46	77	BJ41
by Rd, G11	34	BH26
field Dr, G44	64	BR38
field St, G41	14	BS32
ham St, G41	36	BM36
man St, G40	51	BV34
se Pl, G14	33	BE25
se Rd, G14	33	BE25
thampton Dr, G12	20	BK23
thampton La, G12	20	BK23
th Av, (Camb.) G72	67	CB39
thbank Av, (Camb.) G72	68	CF39
th Bk Pl, Clyde. G81	17	AY21
th Bk St, Clyde. G81	17	AY21
th Brae Pl, G13	19	BD22
th British Rd, (Udd.) G71	71	CP39
th Calder Gro, (Udd.) G71	69	CK35
th Calder Pl, (Udd.) G71	69	CK35
th Calder Rd, (Udd.) G71	71	CS36
th Canal Bk, G4	10	BS27
th Canal Bk St, G4	10	BS27
th Claremont St, G3	8	BN28

Street	Page	Grid
North Corsebar Rd, Pais. PA2	58	AS35
North Ct La, G1	14	BS30
Northcroft Rd, G21	37	BV25
North Cft St, Pais. PA3	44	AV32
North Dean Pk Av, (Both.) G71	85	CQ42
North Douglas St, Clyde. G81	14	BR30
North Dr, G1	14	BR30
North Elgin Pl, Clyde. G81	17	AY22
North Elgin St, Clyde. G81	17	AY22
North Frederick St, G1	14	BS30
North Gardner St, G11	35	BK27
Northgate Quad, G21	24	BY23
Northgate Rd, G21	24	BY22
North Gower St, G51	49	BL32
North Hanover St, G1	35	BS29
Northinch St, G14	33	BF27
Northland Av, G14	18	BE24
Northland Dr, G14	19	BE24
North Lo Rd, Renf. PA4	31	AY25
North Pk Av, (Thornlie.) G46	76	BH41
North Pk Av, (Barr.) G78	73	AX42
Northpark St, G20	21	BN25
North Portland St, G1	15	BT30
North St, G3	9	BP29
North St, Pais. PA3	44	AU31
North Wallace St, G4	11	BT28
Northway, (Blan.) G72	84	CL44
North Woodside Rd, G20	21	BN26
Norval St, G11	34	BJ27
Norwood Dr, G12	21	BK24
Norwood Dr, (Giff.) G46	76	BJ44
Norwood Ter, (Udd.) G71	71	CQ38
Novar Dr, G12	34	BJ25
Nuneaton St, G40	52	BW34
Nuneaton St Ind Est, G40	52	BW34
Nurseries Rd, (Baill.) G69	55	CH31
Nursery La, G41	64	BP35
Nutberry Ct, G42	64	BR36

O

Street	Page	Grid
Oakbank Ind Est, G20	36	BR26
Oak Cres, (Baill.) G69	55	CJ33
Oakdene Av, (Udd.) G71	71	CR38
Oak Dr, (Camb.) G72	82	CE41
Oakfield Av, G12	8	BN27
Oakfield La, G12	8	BN27
Oakhill Av, (Baill.) G69	55	CH34
Oakley Dr, G44	78	BP42
Oakley Ter, G31	51	BV30
Oak Pk, (Bishop.) G64	24	BX20
Oak Pl, (Udd.) G71	71	CS38
Oakridge Rd, (Baill.) G69	57	CO31
Oak Rd, Pais. PA2	59	AW36
Oakshaw Brae, Pais. PA1	44	AT32
Oakshawhead, Pais. PA1	44	AT32
Oakshaw St E, Pais. PA1	44	AT32
Oakshaw St W, Pais. PA1	44	AT32
Oak St, G2	13	BQ30
Oaktree Gdns, G45	79	BV45
Oakwood Cres, G34	42	CM28
Oakwood Dr, G34	42	CM29
Oak Wynd, (Camb.) G72	83	CH42
Oatfield St, G21	38	BX25
Oban Dr, G20	21	BN25
Oban La, G20	21	BN25
Observatory Rd, G12	20	BL26
Ochil Dr, (Barr.) G78	73	AX44
Ochil Dr, Pais. PA2	58	AU37
Ochil Pl, G32	53	CC33
Ochil Rd, (Bishop.) G64	24	BY20
Ochil Rd, Renf. PA4	31	AX28
Ochil St, G32	53	CC33

Street	Page	Grid
Ochiltree Av, G13	20	BH22
Ochil Vw, (Udd.) G71	71	CO37
Ogilvie Pl, G31	53	BZ33
Ogilvie St, G31	53	BZ33
Old Bothwell Rd, (Both.) G71	85	CR44
Old Castle Gdns, G44	64	BR39
Old Castle Rd, G44	64	BR39
Old Ch Gdns, (Baill.) G69	57	CO32
Old Dalmarnock Rd, G40	51	BV33
Old Dumbarton Rd, G3	35	BL28
Old Edinburgh Rd, (Udd.) G71	70	CN36
Old Edinburgh Rd, Bell. ML4	71	CQ38
Old Fm La, (Bears.) G61	20	BH21
Old Fm Rd, Pais. PA2	60	AZ36
Old Gartloch Rd, (Gart.) G69	42	CP25
Old Glasgow Rd, (Udd.) G71	70	CM37
Old Govan Rd, Renf. PA4	32	BB26
Old Greenock Rd, (Inch.) Renf. PA4	16	AT22
Oldhall Rd, Pais. PA1	45	AY32
Old Manse Rd, G32	54	CF33
Old Mill Rd, (Both.) G71	85	CQ44
Old Mill Rd, (Udd.) G71	84	CP40
Old Mill Rd, (Camb.) G72	68	CF39
Old Rutherglen Rd, G5	51	BS33
Old Shettleston Rd, G32	53	CC32
Old Sneddon St, Pais. PA3	44	AU32
Old Sta Ct, (Both.) G71	85	CQ43
Old Wd Rd, (Baill.) G69	55	CJ34
Old Wynd, G1	14	BS31
Olifard Av, (Both.) G71	85	CR42
Olive Bk, (Udd.) G71	71	CS36
Olive St, G33	39	BZ25
Olympia St, G40	51	BV32
O'Neill Av, (Bishop.) G64	24	BX21
Onslow Dr, G31	52	BW30
Onslow Sq, G31	52	BW30
Oran Gdns, G20	21	BN24
Oran Gate, G20	21	BN24
Oran Pl, G20	35	BN25
Oran St, G20	21	BN24
Orbiston Gdns, G32	53	CC32
Orcades Dr, G44	78	BR41
Orchard Av, (Both.) G71	85	CR44
Orchard Ct, G32	72	CD37
Orchard Ct, (Thornlie.) G46	76	BJ42
Orchard Ct, Renf. PA4	32	AZ25
Orchard Dr, (Giff.) G46	77	BK42
Orchard Dr, (Ruther.) G73	65	BV37
Orchard Gro, (Giff.) G46	76	BK41
Orchard Pk, (Giff.) G46	77	BL42
Orchard Pk Av, (Giff.) G46	76	BJ41
Orchard St, (Baill.) G69	55	CH34
Orchard St, Pais. PA1	44	AU33
Orchard St, Renf. PA4	32	AZ25
Orchy Dr, (Clark.) G76	77	BP44
Orchy Gdns, (Clark.) G76	78	BP44
Orchy St, G44	64	BQ39
Oregon Pl, G5	51	BS33
Orion Way, (Camb.) G72	67	CC39
Orkney St, G51	48	BK30
Orleans Av, G14	34	BG26
Orleans La, G14	34	BG26
Ormiston Av, G14	33	BE25
Ormonde Av, G44	78	BP42
Ormonde Ct, G44	77	BN42
Ormonde Cres, G44	78	BP42
Ormonde Dr, G44	78	BP42
Ornsay St, G22	23	BT22
Orr Sq, Pais. PA1	44	AU32

Orr St, G40		51	BV32
Orr St, Pais. PA1		44	AT32
Orr St, Pais. PA2		44	AU34
Orton Pl, G51		48	BJ31
Osborne St, G1		14	BS31
Osprey Dr, (Udd.) G71		71	CQ38
Ossian Av, Pais. PA1		46	BB32
Ossian Rd, G43		63	BN39
Oswald St, G1		14	BR31
Otago La, G12		8	BN27
Otago St, G12		8	BN27
Otterburn Dr, (Giff.) G46		77	BL43
Otterswick Pl, G33		40	CE27
Oval, The, (Clark.) G76		78	BP44
Oval, The, (Glenb.)			
Coat. ML5		29	CS23
Overdale Av, G42		64	BP37
Overdale Gdns, G42		64	BP37
Overdale St, G42		64	BP37
Overlea Av, (Ruther.) G73		67	BZ39
Overnewton Pl, G3		8	BM29
Overnewton St, G3		8	BM28
Overton Rd, (Camb.) G72		82	CF41
Overton St, (Camb.) G72		82	CF41
Overtoun Dr,			
(Ruther.) G73		66	BW38
Overtown Av, G53		61	BC39
Overtown Pl, G31		52	BW32
Overtown St, G31		52	BW32
Overwood Dr, G44		64	BS39
Oxford La, G5		14	BR32
Oxford La, Renf. PA4		31	AY26
Oxford Rd, Renf. PA4		31	AY26
Oxford St, G5		14	BR31
Oxton Dr, G52		47	BD32

P

Pacific Dr, G51		49	BL31
Pacific Quay, G51		12	BM30
Paisley Rd, G5		13	BQ31
Paisley Rd, (Barr.) G78		73	AX40
Paisley Rd, Renf. PA4		31	AX28
Paisley Rd W, G51		49	BL32
Paisley Rd W, G52		48	BJ32
Paladin Av, G13		19	BD21
Palmer Av, G13		19	BF20
Palm Pl, (Udd.) G71		71	CR36
Pandora Way, (Udd.) G71		71	CQ38
Panmure Cl, G22		36	BU25
Panmure St, G20		36	BU25
Park Av, G3		9	BP27
Park Av, (Barr.) G78		73	AX44
Park Av, Pais. PA2		58	AS36
Park Brae, Ersk. PA8		16	AS21
Parkbrae Gdns, G20		22	BQ23
Parkbrae Pl, G20		22	BQ23
Park Circ, G3		8	BN28
Park Circ La, G3		8	BN28
Park Circ Pl, G3		9	BP28
Park Ct, (Giff.) G46		77	BL43
Park Cres, (Inch.) Renf. PA4		16	AS22
Park Dr, G3		8	BN27
Park Dr, (Ruther.) G73		66	BW38
Park Dr, Ersk. PA8		16	AS21
Park Gdns, G3		8	BN28
Park Gdns La, G3		8	BN28
Park Gate, G3		8	BN28
Park Gro, Ersk. PA8		16	AS21
Parkgrove Av, (Giff.) G46		77	BM42
Parkgrove Ct, (Giff.) G46		77	BM42
Parkgrove Ter, G3		8	BN28
Parkhead Cross, G31		52	BZ32
Parkhill Dr, (Ruther.) G73		66	BW38

Parkhill Rd, G43		63	BM37
Parkhouse Rd, G53		74	BB41
Parkhouse Rd, (Barr.) G78		74	BB41
Parkinch, Ersk. PA8		16	AS21
Parklands Rd, G44		78	BP42
Parklands Vw, G53		60	BB35
Parkneuk Rd, G43		77	BL41
Park Quad, G3		8	BN28
Park Rd, G4		8	BN27
Park Rd, G32		68	CE37
Park Rd, (Giff.) G46		77	BL43
Park Rd, (Baill.) G69		57	CP32
Park Rd, (Muir.) G69		28	CL21
Park Rd, Pais. PA2		58	AT36
Park Rd, (Inch.) Renf. PA4		16	AT22
Parksail, Ersk. PA8		16	AS22
Parksail Dr, Ersk. PA8		16	AS21
Parkside Gdns, G20		22	BQ23
Parkside Pl, G20		22	BQ23
Park St S, G3		8	BN28
Park Ter, G3		8	BN28
Park Ter, (Giff.) G46		77	BL43
Park Ter E La, G3		8	BN28
Park Ter La, G3		8	BN28
Park Top, Ersk. PA8		16	AS20
Parkvale Av, Ersk. PA8		16	AT20
Parkvale Cres, Ersk. PA8		16	AT21
Parkvale Dr, Ersk. PA8		16	AT21
Parkvale Gdns, Ersk. PA8		16	AT20
Parkvale Pl, Ersk. PA8		16	AT21
Parkvale Way, Ersk. PA8		16	AT21
Park Vw, Pais. PA2		58	AT35
Parkview Dr, (Stepps) G33		26	CG23
Park Winding, Ersk. PA8		16	AS21
Park Wd, Ersk. PA8		16	AS20
Parnie St, G1		14	BS31
Parsonage Row, G1		15	BT30
Parsonage Sq, G4		15	BT30
Parson St, G4		11	BU29
Partick Br St, G11		35	BL27
Partickhill Av, G11		35	BK27
Partickhill Ct, G11		35	BK26
Partickhill Rd, G11		34	BK26
Paterson St, G5		13	BQ32
Pathhead Gdns, G33		25	CB23
Patna St, G40		52	BX34
Paton St, G31		52	BX30
Patrick St, Pais. PA2		44	AV34
Patterton Dr, (Barr.) G78		73	AZ43
Payne St, G4		10	BS27
Pearce St, G51		34	BJ29
Pearson Dr, Renf. PA4		32	AZ27
Peathill Av, (Chry.) G69		27	CK20
Peathill St, G21		37	BS26
Peat Rd, G53		61	BD39
Peebles Dr, (Ruther.) G73		66	BZ38
Peel La, G11		35	BK27
Peel Pl, (Both.) G71		85	CQ42
Peel St, G11		35	BK27
Peinchorran, Ersk. PA8		16	AS22
Pembroke St, G3		9	BP29
Pencaitland Dr, G32		53	CC34
Pencaitland Gro, G32		67	CC35
Pencaitland Pl, G23		21	BN20
Pendale Ri, G45		79	BT42
Pendeen Cres, G33		54	CG32
Pendeen Pl, G33		55	CH31
Pendeen Rd, G33		55	CG32
Pendle Ct, (Gart.) G69		29	CP23
Penicuik St, G32		52	BZ31
Penilee Rd, G52		32	AZ29
Penilee Rd, Pais. PA1		46	BA32
Penilee Ter, G52		46	BA31
Peninver Dr, G51		33	BF29
Penman Av, (Ruther.) G73		66	BV37
Pennan Pl, G14		19	BC24
Penneld Rd, G52		46	BB32
Penrith Av, (Giff.) G46		77	BL42
Penrith Dr, G12		20	BJ23

Penryn Gdns, G32		54	CH34
Penston Rd, G33		40	CH28
Pentland Cres, Pais. PA2		58	AT37
Pentland Dr, (Barr.) G78		73	AX43
Pentland Dr, Renf. PA4		31	AX30
Pentland Pl, G43		77	BM41
Pentland Rd, (Chry.) G69		28	CM20
Percy Dr, (Giff.) G46		77	BM44
Percy Rd, Renf. PA4		31	AW30
Petershill Ct, G21		38	BV26
Petershill Dr, G21		38	BX26
Petershill Pl, G21		38	BX26
Petershill Rd, G21		37	BV26
Peterson Dr, G13		18	BA22
Peterson Gdns, G13		18	BA22
Petition Pl, (Udd.) G71		85	CQ40
Pettigrew St, G32		53	CC33
Peveril Av, G41		63	BM36
Peveril Av, (Ruther.) G73		80	BY40
Peveril Ct, (Ruther.) G73		80	BY41
Phoenix Ind Est, Pais. PA3		30	AU25
Piccadilly St, G3		13	BP30
Piershill St, G32		53	CE32
Pikeman Rd, G13		19	BE22
Pilmuir Av, G44		78	BP41
Pilrig St, G32		53	CA33
Pine Av, (Camb.) G72		83	CH39
Pine Gro, (Baill.) G69		57	CQ32
Pine Gro, (Udd.) G71		71	CR36
Pine Pl, G5		51	BS32
Pine St, Pais. PA2		59	AW36
Pinkerton Av, (Ruther.) G73		65	BU37
Pinkerton La, Renf. PA4		32	AZ28
Pinkston Dr, G21		11	BU26
Pinkston Rd, G4		37	BT26
Pinkston Rd, G21		37	BT26
Pinmore Pl, G53		60	BB38
Pinmore St, G53		60	BB38
Pinwherry Dr, G33		25	CB26
Pinwherry Pl, (Both.) G71		85	CQ42
Pitcairn St, G31		53	CA34
Pitcaple Dr, G43		62	BK39
Pitlochry Dr, G52		47	BD34
Pitreavie Pl, G33		40	CE28
Pitt St, G2		13	BQ30
Pladda Rd, Renf. PA4		32	AZ28
Plaintrees Ct, Pais. PA2		58	AU36
Plane Pl, (Udd.) G71		71	CR37
Plantation Pk Gdns, G51		12	BM30
Plantation Sq, G51		12	BN30
Plant St, G31		52	BY32
Playfair St, G40		52	BW34
Plean St, G14		18	BC24
Pleasance St, G43		63	BL37
Pleasance Way, G43		63	BM37
Pointhouse Rd, G3		12	BM30
Pollok Av, G43		63	BK40
Pollok Dr, (Bishop.) G64		23	BU20
Pollokshaws Rd, G41		64	BO36
Pollokshaws Rd, G43		63	BK40
Pollok Shop Cen, G53		61	BE38
Polmadie Av, G5		65	BT37
Polmadie Ind Est, G5		65	BU36
Polmadie Rd, G5		51	BU35
Polmadie Rd, G42		65	BS36
Polmadie St, G42		65	BS37
Polnoon Av, G13		19	BC24
Polquhap Ct, G53		60	BC37
Polquhap Gdns, G53		60	BC37
Polquhap Pl, G53		60	BC37
Polquhap Rd, G53		60	BC37
Polsons Cres, Pais. PA2		58	AT36
Polwarth La, G12		35	BK26
Polwarth St, G12		34	BK26
Poplar Pl, (Blan.) G72		84	CL44
Poplar Way, (Camb.) G72		83	CH39
Poplin St, G40		51	BV34
Porchester St, G33		40	CG28
Portal Rd, G13		19	BE21

rt Dundas Ind Est, G4	10	BS27
rt Dundas Pl, G2	10	BS29
rt Dundas Rd, G4	10	BR28
rt Dundas Trd Centres, G4	10	BS27
terfield Rd, Renf. PA4	31	AX26
ter St, G51	49	BN30
rters Well, (Udd.) G71	84	CN40
rtland St, Pais. PA2	45	AX34
rtman St, G41	12	BN32
rtsoy Pl, G13	18	BA21
rt St, G3	9	BP29
rtugal St, G5	14	BR32
ull Cross, G22	36	BS26
sdel Rd, G4	10	BR27
tassels Rd, (Muir.) G69	28	CL22
tter Cl, G32	53	CA34
tter Gro, G32	53	CA34
tterhill Av, Pais. PA2	58	AU37
tterhill Rd, G53	61	BD35
tter Pl, G32	53	CA34
tter St, G32	53	CA34
wfoot St, G31	53	BZ32
wrie St, G33	40	CE26
entice La, (Udd.) G71	71	CQ37
eston Pl, G42	64	BR35
estwick St, G51	60	BF39
esthill Av, G53	61	BE39
iesthill Cres, G53	61	BE39
iesthill Gdns, G53	61	BE39
iesthill Rd, G53	61	BE39
imrose Pl, (Udd.) G71	71	CS37
imrose St, G14	18	BE26
ince Albert Rd, G12	35	BK26
ince Edward St, G42	64	BQ35
ince's Dock, G51	49	BL30
inces Gdns, G12	35	BK26
inces Gate, (Both.) G71	84	CN41
inces Pl, (Ruther.) G73	66	BW37
inces Pl, G12	35	BL26
incess Av, Pais. PA1	45	AX32
incess Dr, (Baill.) G69	57	CQ32
incess Sq, (Barr.) G78	74	AZ42
incess St, (Ruther.) G73	66	BW37
inces Ter, G12	35	BL26
iorwood Ct, G13	19	BF23
iorwood Gdns, G13	19	BF23
iorwood Pl, G13	19	BF23
iory Av, Pais. PA3	45	AW30
iory Dr, (Udd.) G71	70	CM38
iory Pl, G13	19	BF22
iory Rd, G13	19	BF22
rofessors Sq, G12	8	BM27
rosen St, G32	53	CB34
rospect Av, (Udd.) G71	70	CN39
rospect Av, (Camb.) G72	67	CB39
rospecthill Circ, G42	65	BU37
rospecthill Cres, G42	65	BU37
rospecthill Dr, G42	64	BQ37
rospecthill Gro, G42	64	BQ37
rospecthill Pl, G42	65	BU37
rospecthill Rd, G42	64	BQ37
rospecthill Sq, G42	65	BU37
rospect Rd, G43	63	BM37
rovand Hall Cres, (Baill.) G69	55	CK34
rovanhill St, G21	37	BV28
rovanmill Rd, G33	39	BZ26
rovan Rd, G33	38	BY28
rovan Wk, G34	41	CL29
rovost Driver Ct, Renf. PA4	32	AZ27
urdon St, G11	35	BK27

Q

Quadrant Rd, G43	77	BN40
Quarrybrae St, G31	53	BZ32
Quarryknowe, (Ruther.) G73	65	BV38
Quarryknowe St, G31	53	CA32
Quarry Pl, (Camb.) G72	67	CA39
Quarry Rd, (Barr.) G78	73	AX41
Quarry Rd, Pais. PA2	59	AV36
Quarrywood Av, G21	38	BY25
Quarrywood Rd, G21	38	BZ25
Quay Rd, (Ruther.) G73	66	BW36
Quay Rd N, (Ruther.) G73	66	BW36
Quebec Wynd, G32	68	CE37
Queen Elizabeth Av, G52	46	BA36
Queen Elizabeth Gdns, G5	51	BS33
Queen Elizabeth Sq, G5	51	BT33
Queen Margaret Dr, G12	35	BM26
Queen Margaret Dr, G20	35	BM26
Queen Margaret Rd, G20	35	BN25
Queen Mary Av, G42	64	BR36
Queen Mary St, G40	52	BV33
Queens Av, (Camb.) G72	68	CD39
Queensbank Av, (Gart.)	28	CN22
Queensborough Gdns, G12	34	BJ25
Queensbury Av, G52	46	BB30
Queensby Dr, (Baill.) G69	55	CK31
Queensby Pl, (Baill.) G69	56	CL31
Queensby Rd, (Baill.) G69	55	CK31
Queens Cres, G4	9	BP27
Queen's Cres, (Baill.) G69	56	CP32
Queens Dr, G42	64	BR34
Queens Dr La, G42	64	BR34
Queensferry St, G5	65	BU35
Queensland Ct, G52	47	BE31
Queensland Dr, G52	47	BE31
Queensland Gdns, G52	47	BE31
Queensland La E, G52	47	BE31
Queensland La W, G52	47	BE31
Queenslie Ind Est, G33	40	CE29
Queenslie St, G33	39	BZ27
Queen St, G1	11	BS30
Queen St, (Ruther.) G73	66	BW37
Queen St, Pais. PA1	44	AS33
Queen St, Renf. PA4	32	AZ26
Queen Victoria Dr, G13	19	BE24
Queen Victoria Dr, G14	33	BE25
Queen Victoria Gate, G13	19	BE24
Quendale Dr, G32	53	CB34
Quentin St, G41	63	BN36
Quinton Gdns, (Baill.) G69	55	CJ32

R

Raasay Dr, Pais. PA2	58	AT38
Raasay Pl, G22	23	BS21
Raasay St, G22	23	BS21
Radnor St, G3	8	BM29
Raeberry St, G20	36	BP26
Raeburn Av, Pais. PA1	45	AW33
Raeswood Dr, G53	60	BB37
Raeswood Gdns, G53	60	BB37
Raeswood Pl, G53	60	BC37
Raeswood Rd, G53	60	BB37
Rafford St, G51	48	BJ30
Raglan St, G4	9	BQ27
Raithburn Av, G45	78	BS42
Raithburn Rd, G45	78	BS42
Ralston Av, G52	46	BB33
Ralston Av, Pais. PA1	46	BB34

Por-Rei 119

Ralston Ct, G52	46	BB33
Ralston Dr, G52	46	BB33
Ralston Path, G52	46	BB33
Ralston Pl, G52	46	BB33
Ralston Rd, (Barr.) G78	73	AY43
Ralston Rd, Pais. PA1	45	AW33
Rampart Av, G13	19	BC21
Ramsay Pl, Coat. ML5	57	CS32
Ram St, G32	53	CB32
Ranald Gdns, (Ruther.) G73	80	BZ42
Randolph Av, (Clark.) G76	78	BQ44
Randolph Dr, (Clark.) G76	78	BP44
Randolph Gdns, (Clark.) G76	78	BP44
Randolph Gate, G11	34	BH25
Randolph La, G11	34	BH26
Randolph Rd, G11	34	BH25
Ranfurly Rd, G52	46	BB32
Rankin Way, (Barr.) G78	74	AZ42
Rannoch Av, (Bishop.) G64	24	BX20
Rannoch Dr, Renf. PA4	31	AY25
Rannoch Pl, Pais. PA2	45	AW34
Rannoch Rd, (Udd.) G71	70	CN36
Rannoch St, G44	64	BQ39
Raploch Av, G14	33	BD25
Raploch La, G14	33	BD25
Rathlin St, G51	34	BJ29
Ratho Dr, G21	23	BU24
Rattray St, G32	53	CA34
Ravel Row, G31	52	BZ32
Ravelston St, G32	53	BZ31
Ravel Wynd, (Udd.) G71	71	CQ37
Ravenscliffe Dr, (Giff.) G46	76	BK42
Ravenscraig Av, Pais. PA2	58	AS35
Ravenscraig Dr, G53	61	BD39
Ravenshall Rd, G41	63	BL37
Ravenstone Dr, (Giff.) G46	77	BL40
Ravenswood Dr, G41	63	BM36
Ravenswood Rd, (Baill.) G69	56	CL33
Redan St, G40	51	BV32
Redcastle Sq, G33	40	CF28
Redford St, G33	38	BZ29
Redgate Pl, G14	33	BD25
Redlands La, G12	35	BL25
Redlands Rd, G12	35	BL25
Redlands Ter La, G12	35	BL25
Redlawood Pl, (Camb.) G72	69	CJ39
Redlawood Rd, (Camb.) G72	69	CJ39
Redmoss St, G22	22	BR24
Rednock St, G22	37	BS25
Redpath Dr, G52	47	BE32
Red Rd, G21	38	BX25
Red Rd Ct, G21	38	BX26
Redwood Cres, (Udd.) G71	71	CS37
Redwood Cres, (Camb.) G72	83	CH42
Redwood Dr, G21	38	BW26
Redwood Way, (Camb.) G72	83	CH42
Reelick Av, G13	18	BA21
Reelick Quad, G13	18	BA21
Reen Pl, (Both.) G71	85	CR41
Regent Moray St, G3	8	BM28
Regent Pk Sq, G41	64	BP35
Regents Gate, (Both.) G71	84	CM41
Regent St, Pais. PA1	45	AX32
Regwood St, G41	63	BM37
Reidhouse St, G21	37	BV25
Reid Pl, G40	51	BV33

Reid St, G40	51	BV34
Reid St, (Ruther.) G73	66	BX37
Reidvale St, G31	51	BV31
Renfield La, G2	14	BR30
Renfield St, G2	14	BR30
Renfield St, Renf. PA4	32	AZ25
Renfrew Ct, G2	14	BR29
Renfrew La, G2	10	BR29
Renfrew Rd, G51	33	BD29
Renfrew Rd, Pais. PA3	44	AV32
Renfrew Rd, Renf. PA4	32	BC28
Renfrew St, G2	10	BQ29
Renfrew St, G3	9	BP29
Renfrew St, Coat. ML5	57	CS33
Rennies Rd, (Inch.) Renf. PA4	16	AS24
Renshaw Dr, G52	47	BD31
Renton St, G4	10	BR28
Resipol Rd, (Stepps) G33	26	CG24
Reston Dr, G52	47	BD31
Reuther Av, (Ruther.) G73	66	BX38
Revoch Dr, G13	18	BC22
Rhannan Rd, G44	78	BQ40
Rhannan Ter, G44	78	BQ40
Rhindmuir Pl, (Baill.) G69	56	CM32
Rhindhouse Rd, (Baill.) G69	56	CM32
Rhindmuir Av, (Baill.) G69	56	CM32
Rhindmuir Ct, (Baill.) G69	56	CL32
Rhindmuir Cres, (Baill.) G69	56	CM31
Rhindmuir Dr, (Baill.) G69	56	CL31
Rhindmuir Gdns, (Baill.) G69	56	CM31
Rhindmuir Gro, (Baill.) G69	56	CM31
Rhindmuir Path, (Baill.) G69	56	CM31
Rhindmuir Pl, (Baill.) G69	56	CM31
Rhindmuir Rd, (Baill.) G69	56	CM31
Rhindmuir Vw, (Baill.) G69	56	CM31
Rhindmuir Wynd, (Baill.) G69	56	CM31
Rhinds St, Coat. ML5	57	CR33
Rhinsdale Cres, (Baill.) G69	56	CL32
Rhymer St, G21	11	BU28
Rhymie Rd, G32	54	CF34
Rhynie Dr, G51	48	BK32
Riccarton St, G42	64	BS35
Riccartsbar Av, Pais. PA2	44	AS34
Richard St, Renf. PA4	32	AZ25
Richmond Ct, (Ruther.) G73	66	BY37
Richmond Dr, (Camb.) G72	81	CA40
Richmond Dr, (Ruther.) G73	66	BY38
Richmond Gro, (Chry.) G69	27	CK20
Richmond Gro, (Ruther.) G73	66	BY38
Richmond Pl, (Ruther.) G73	66	BY37
Richmond St, G1	15	BT30
Richmond St, Clyde. G81	17	AY20
Riddon Av, G13	18	BA21
Riddon Av, Clyde. G81	18	BA21
Riddon Pl, G13	18	BA21
Riddrie Cres, G33	39	CA29
Riddrie Knowes, G33	39	CA29
Riddrievale Ct, G33	39	CA28
Riddrievale St, G33	39	CA28
Rigby St, G32	53	CA31
Rigg Pl, G33	55	CG30
Riggside Rd, G33	40	CE27

Riglands Gate, Renf. PA4	31	AY25
Riglands Way, Renf. PA4	31	AY25
Riglaw Pl, G13	19	BC22
Rigmuir Rd, G51	47	BE30
Rimsdale St, G40	52	BW32
Ringford St, G21	37	BV26
Ripon Dr, G12	20	BJ23
Ritchie St, G5	50	BO33
Riverbank St, G43	63	BL38
Riverford Rd, G43	63	BL38
Riverford Rd, (Ruther.) G73	66	BY36
River Rd, G32	68	CE37
Riversdale La, G14	33	BC25
Riverside Ct, G44	78	BP43
Riverside Ind Est, Clyde. G81	17	AW20
Riverside Pk, G44	78	BQ42
Riverside Pl, (Camb.) G72	68	CG39
Riverside Rd, G43	63	BN38
Riverview Dr, G5	13	BQ31
Riverview Gdns, G5	13	BQ31
Riverview Pl, G5	13	BQ31
Robert Dr, G51	34	BJ29
Roberton Av, G41	63	BL35
Robertson Av, Renf. PA4	31	AX26
Robertson Cl, Renf. PA4	31	AY26
Robertson Dr, Renf. PA4	31	AX26
Robertson La, G2	13	BQ30
Robertson's Gait, Pais. PA2	44	AU34
Robertson St, G2	14	BR30
Robertson St, (Barr.) G78	73	AX42
Robert St, G51	34	BJ29
Robert Templeton Dr, (Camb.) G72	82	CD40
Robin Way, G32	68	CE37
Robroyston Av, G33	39	CA26
Robroyston Av, G33	39	CA25
Robroyston Rd, G33	25	CA29
Robroyston Rd, (Bishop.) G64	25	CB20
Robslee Cres, (Giff.) G46	76	BJ42
Robslee Dr, (Giff.) G46	76	BK42
Robslee Rd, (Thornlie.) G46	76	BJ43
Robson Gro, G42	50	BR34
Rockall Dr, G44	78	BS41
Rockbank Pl, G40	52	BW32
Rockbank St, G40	52	BW32
Rockcliffe St, G40	51	BV34
Rockfield Pl, G21	24	BY24
Rockfield Rd, G21	24	BY24
Rockmount Av, (Thornlie.) G46	76	BJ41
Rockmount Av, (Barr.) G78	74	AZ44
Rock St, G4	36	BR26
Rockwell Av, Pais. PA2	58	AS37
Rodger Dr, (Ruther.) G73	66	BW39
Rodger Pl, (Ruther.) G73	66	BW39
Rodil Av, G44	78	BS41
Rodney St, G4	10	BR27
Roffey Pk Rd, Pais. PA1	46	AY44
Rogart St, G40	51	BV32
Rogerfield Rd, (Baill.) G69	56	CL30
Roman Av, G15	18	BC20
Roman Way, (Udd.) G71	71	CS39
Romney Av, G44	78	BS40
Ronaldsay St, G22	23	BS22
Rona St, G21	38	BX27
Rona Ter, (Camb.) G72	81	CB42
Ronay St, G22	23	BT21
Rooksdell Av, Pais. PA2	58	AS36
Rosebank Av, (Blan.) G72	84	CN44
Rosebank Dr, (Camb.) G72	82	CE41

Rosebank Gdns, (Udd.) G71	69	CK39
Rosebank Pl, (Udd.) G71	69	CK39
Rosebank Ter, (Baill.) G69	57	CP32
Roseberry St, G5	51	BU34
Rosedale Dr, (Baill.) G69	55	CJ32
Rosedale Gdns, G20	21	BL22
Rosefield Gdns, (Udd.) G71	70	CN37
Rose Knowe Rd, G42	65	BU35
Roselea Gdns, G13	20	BH23
Roselea Pl, (Blan.) G72	84	CL44
Rosemount Cres, G21	37	BV27
Rosemount Meadows, (Both.) G71	84	CP44
Rosemount St, G21	37	BV27
Roseness Pl, G33	39	CC27
Rosepark Av, (Udd.) G71	71	CS35
Rose St, G3	10	BR29
Roslea Dr, G31	38	BJ21
Rosewood St, G13	20	BG21
Roslea Dr, G31	52	BW35
Roslin Twr, (Camb.) G72	81	CA42
Roslyn Dr, (Baill.) G69	56	CP35
Rosneath St, G51	34	BJ29
Ross Av, Renf. PA4	31	AW26
Rossbank Dr, (Udd.) G71	71	CS33
Rossendale Ct, G43	63	BL38
Rossendale Rd, G41	63	BL38
Rossendale Rd, G43	63	BL38
Rosshall Av, Pais. PA1	45	AY37
Ross Hall Pl, Renf. PA4	32	AZ28
Rosshill Av, G52	46	BB33
Rosshill Rd, G52	46	BB33
Rossie Cres, (Bishop.) G64	24	BY23
Rosslea Dr, (Giff.) G46	77	BL44
Rosslyn Av, (Ruther.) G73	66	BY39
Rosslyn Ter, G12	35	BL21
Ross Pl, (Ruther.) G73	81	BZ40
Ross St, G40	15	BT30
Ross St, Pais. PA1	45	AV33
Rostan Rd, G43	77	BL44
Rosyth Rd, G5	65	BU33
Rosyth St, G5	65	BU33
Rotherwick Dr, Pais. PA1	46	BA36
Rotherwood Av, G13	19	BE22
Rotherwood Pl, G13	20	BG22
Rothes Dr, G23	21	BM22
Rottenrow, G4	11	BT29
Rottenrow E, G4	15	BT30
Roukenburn St, (Thornlie.) G46	76	BG44
Rouken Glen Pk, (Thornlie.) G46	76	BH44
Rouken Glen Rd, (Thornlie.) G46	76	BH44
Roundknowe Rd, (Udd.) G71	70	CL39
Rowallan Gdns, G11	34	BJ26
Rowallan La, G11	34	BJ26
Rowallan La E, G11	34	BJ26
Rowallan Rd, (Thornlie.) G46	76	BH43
Rowallan Ter, G33	40	CD25
Rowan Av, Renf. PA4	31	AY26
Rowan Ct, (Camb.) G72	83	CH41
Rowan Ct, Pais. PA2	58	AU35
Rowandale Av, (Baill.) G69	55	CJ33
Rowand Av, (Giff.) G46	77	BL43
Rowan Gdns, G41	48	BK33
Rowan Gate, Pais. PA2	58	AV35
Rowan Rd, (Giff.) G46	77	BM44
Rowanpark Dr, (Barr.) G78	73	AW40
Rowan Pl, (Camb.) G72	68	CE39
Rowan Rd, G41	48	BK33
Rowan Gdns, (Both.) G71	85	CH44
Rowan St, Pais. PA2	44	AU38

vantree Av, (Udd.) G71	71	CS38	
vantree Av, (Ruther.) G73	80	BX40	
vantree Gdns, (Ruther.) G73	80	BX40	
chester St, G40	52	BW32	
vena Av, G13	19	BF20	
burgh St, G12	35	BM26	
al Cres, G3	8	BN29	
al Ex Ct, G1	15	BS30	
al Ex Sq, G1	15	BS30	
al Gdns, (Both.) G71	84	CN43	
al Ter, G3	8	BN28	
al Ter La, G3	8	BN28	
stonhill, G21	37	BV28	
stonhill Pl, G21	37	BV28	
ston Rd, G21	11	BU28	
ston Sq, G21	11	BU28	
St, G21	37	BT26	
y St, G40	52	BW33	
hazie Pl, G33	39	CB29	
hazie Rd, G32	53	CB30	
hazie Rd, G33	53	CB30	
ill St, G20	21	BN24	
St, G44	64	BQ38	
lees Av, (Barr.) G78	74	AZ41	
by Av, G13	19	BD21	
on Pl, G33	39	CB29	
aford St, G40	51	BV34	
ert St, G4	9	BP27	
nyhill St, G21	38	BW25	
kin La, G12	35	BN26	
kin Pl, G12	35	BN26	
kin Ter, G12	35	BN26	
ge, (Bishop.) G64	24	BW20	
kin Ter, (Ruther.) G73	66	BX37	
sell Cres, (Baill.) G69	56	CM33	
sell St, Pais. PA3	44	AT30	
erglen Dr, G40	51	BV34	
erglen Dr, G42	51	BV34	
erglen Ind Est,			
erglen Rd, G5	51	BT34	
erglen Rd, (Ruther.) G73	51	BT34	
ven Av, (Giff.) G46	77	BM44	
ven Pl,			
(Bishop.) G64	24	BY21	
ven St, G12	35	BM26	
and Ct, G51	12	BN31	
and Cres, G51	12	BN31	
and Pl, G51	12	BN31	
Rd, (Bishop.) G64	24	BX20	
ide Rd, G21	24	BX24	
nds Dr, G32	54	CF33	
nds Gdns, G32	54	CG33	
es Cres, G52	46	BA31	
es Pl, G52	46	BA31	
es Rd, G52	46	BA31	
a Rd, G13	19	BF23	
ville Av, G13	20	BH24	
ville La, G13	20	BH23	
ndrew's Av,			
(Both.) G71	85	CQ44	

St. Andrews Cres, G41	49	BN33	
St. Andrews Cres, Pais. PA3	30	AS28	
St. Andrews Cross, G41	50	BQ34	
St. Andrews Dr, G41	49	BN33	
St. Andrews Dr, (Abbots.) Pais. PA3	30	AT29	
St. Andrews Dr W, (Abbots.) Pais. PA3	30	AS28	
St. Andrews Rd, G41	50	BP33	
St. Andrews Rd, Renf. PA4	31	AY26	
St. Andrews St, G1	15	BT31	
St. Annes Wynd, Ersk. PA8	16	AS21	
St. Anns Dr, (Giff.) G46	77	BL43	
St. Blanes Dr, (Ruther.) G73	65	BU39	
St. Brides Av, (Udd.) G71	71	CS38	
St. Brides Rd, G43	63	BM39	
St. Brides Way, (Both.) G71	85	CQ42	
St. Catherines Rd, (Giff.) G46	77	BL43	
St. Clair Av, (Giff.) G46	77	BL42	
St. Cyrus Gdns, (Bishop.) G64	24	BY20	
St. Cyrus Rd, (Bishop.) G64	24	BY20	
St. Enoch Av, (Udd.) G71	71	CS37	
St. Enoch Shop Cen, G1	14	BS31	
St. Enoch Sq, G1	14	BR31	
St. Fillans Rd, G33	25	CE24	
St. Francis Rigg, G5	51	BS33	
St. Georges Rd, G3	9	BQ27	
St. James Rd, G4	11	BT29	
St. James St, Pais. PA3	44	AU32	
St. John's Ct, G41	49	BN33	
St. John's Quad, G41	49	BN33	
St. John's Rd, G41	49	BN33	
St. Joseph's Ct, G21	37	BV28	
St. Joseph's Pl, G21	37	BV28	
St. Joseph's Vw, G21	37	BV28	
St. Kenneth Dr, G51	33	BF29	
St. Kilda Dr, G14	34	BG25	
St. Leonards Dr, (Giff.) G46	77	BL42	
St. Luke's Pl, G5	14	BS32	
St. Luke's Ter, G5	14	BS32	
St. Margaret's Av, Pais. PA3	45	AW30	
St. Margaret's Ct, Pais. PA3	45	AW30	
St. Mark Gdns, G32	53	CB32	
St. Mark St, G32	53	CA32	
St. Marnock St, G40	52	BW32	
St. Mary's Cres, (Barr.) G78	73	AY43	
St. Mary's Gdns, (Barr.) G78	74	AZ43	
St. Marys La, G2	14	BR30	
St. Michael's La, G31	52	BY32	
St. Mirren St, Pais. PA1	44	AU32	
St. Monance St, G21	23	BV24	
St. Mungo Av, G4	11	BS29	
St. Mungo Pl, G4	11	BT29	
St. Mungo St, (Bishop.) G64	23	BV21	
St. Ninians Cres, Pais. PA2	59	AV35	
St. Ninians Rd, Pais. PA2	59	AV35	
St. Ninian Ter, G5	14	BS32	
St. Peters La, G2	13	BQ30	
St. Peters St, G4	9	BQ27	
St. Roberts Gdns, G53	75	BF40	
St. Rollox Brae, G21	11	BU27	
St. Ronans Dr, G41	63	BM36	
St. Ronans Dr, (Ruther.) G73	66	BY39	
St. Stephens Av, (Ruther.) G73	80	BZ42	
St. Stephens Cres, (Ruther.) G73	81	CA42	
St. Valentine Ter, G5	51	BT33	

Row-Sca 121

St. Vincent Cres, G3	8	BM29	
St. Vincent Cres La, G3	8	BM29	
St. Vincent La, G2	9	BQ29	
St. Vincent Pl, G1	14	BS30	
St. Vincent St, G2	9	BQ29	
St. Vincent St, G3	9	BP29	
St. Vincent Ter, G3	9	BP29	
Salamanca St, G31	52	BZ32	
Salen St, G52	48	BH32	
Salisbury Pl, G5	50	BR33	
Salisbury St, G5	50	BR33	
Salkeld St, G5	50	BR33	
Salmona St, G22	36	BR25	
Saltaire Av, (Udd.) G71	85	CQ40	
Salterland Rd, G53	74	BA40	
Salterland Rd, (Barr.) G78	74	BA40	
Saltmarket, G1	14	BS31	
Saltoun La, G12	35	BM26	
Saltoun St, G12	35	BL26	
Salvia St, (Camb.) G72	67	CB39	
Sandaig Rd, G33	54	CG31	
Sanda St, G20	35	BN25	
Sandbank Av, G20	21	BM22	
Sandbank Cres, G20	21	BM23	
Sandbank Dr, G20	21	BM22	
Sandbank St, G20	21	BM22	
Sandbank Ter, G20	21	BM22	
Sandend Rd, G53	60	BC38	
Sanderling Rd, Pais. PA3	30	AT29	
Sandfield St, G20	21	BN24	
Sandgate Av, G32	54	CF34	
Sandhaven Rd, G53	60	BC38	
Sandholes St, Pais. PA1	44	AS33	
Sandholm Pl, G14	18	BB24	
Sandholm Ter, G14	18	BB24	
Sandiefield Rd, G5	51	BS33	
Sandielands, Ersk. PA8	16	AT22	
Sandilands St, G32	54	CD32	
Sandmill St, G21	38	BW28	
Sandwood Cres, G52	46	BC32	
Sandwood Rd, G52	46	BC33	
Sandyford Pl La, G3	8	BN29	
Sandyford Rd, Pais. PA3	31	AV29	
Sandyford St, G3	35	BL29	
Sandyhills Cres, G32	54	CD34	
Sandyhills Dr, G32	54	CD34	
Sandyhills Gro, G32	68	CE35	
Sandyhills Pl, G32	54	CD34	
Sandyhills Rd, G32	54	CD34	
Sandy Rd, G11	34	BJ28	
Sannox Gdns, G31	38	BX29	
Sanquhar Dr, G53	60	BC37	
Sanquhar Gdns, G53	60	BC37	
Sanquhar Gdns, (Blan.) G72	83	CK43	
Sanquhar Pl, G53	60	BC37	
Sanquhar Rd, G53	60	BC37	
Saracen St, G22	36	BS26	
Sardinia La, G12	35	BM26	
Saucelhill Ter, Pais. PA2	44	AV34	
Saucel St, Pais. PA1	44	AU33	
Sauchiehall La, G2	9	BQ29	
Sauchiehall St, G2	9	BQ29	
Sauchiehall St, G3	8	BM28	
Saughs Av, G33	25	CB23	
Saughs Dr, G33	25	CB23	
Saughs Gate, G33	25	CB23	
Saughs Pl, G33	25	CB23	
Saughs Rd, G33	25	CA24	
Saughton St, G32	53	CA30	
Savoy St, G40	51	BV33	
Sawmillfield St, G4	10	BR27	
Saxon Rd, G13	19	BF22	
Scalpay Pas, G22	23	BT22	

Street	Page	Grid
Scalpay Pl, G22	23	BT22
Scalpay St, G22	23	BS22
Scapa St, G23	21	BN21
Scaraway Dr, G22	23	BT21
Scaraway Pl, G22	23	BT21
Scaraway St, G22	23	BS21
Scaraway Ter, G22	23	BT21
Scarba Dr, G43	76	BK40
Scarrel Dr, G45	80	BW41
Scarrel Gdns, G45	80	BW41
Scarrel Rd, G45	80	BW41
Scarrel Ter, G45	80	BW41
Schaw Dr, Pais. PA3	45	AW31
School Av, (Camb.) G72	82	CD40
School St, (Stepps) G33	26	CG23
School Rd, Pais. PA1	46	BA32
School Wynd, Pais. PA1	44	AU32
Scioncroft Av, (Ruther.) G73	66	BY38
Scone St, G21	37	BS26
Scone Wk, (Baill.) G69	55	CJ34
Sconser St, G23	21	BN20
Scotland St, G5	13	BP32
Scotland St W, G41	12	BN32
Scotsburn Rd, G21	38	BY25
Scotstoun St, G14	33	BE26
Scott Rd, G52	32	BB29
Scotts Rd, Pais. PA2	45	AY34
Scott St, G3	9	BQ29
Scott St, (Baill.) G69	55	CK33
Seafield Dr, (Ruther.) G73	80	BZ42
Seaforth Cres, (Barr.) G78	73	AX40
Seaforth Rd, G52	46	BC30
Seaforth Rd, Clyde. G81	17	AX20
Seaforth Rd N, G52	46	BC30
Seaforth Rd S, G52	46	BC30
Seagrove St, G32	53	BZ31
Seamill St, G53	74	BB40
Seamore St, G20	9	BP27
Seath Rd, (Ruther.) G73	66	BW36
Seath St, G42	64	BS35
Seaward La, G41	12	BN31
Seaward Pl, G41	49	BN33
Seaward St, G41	13	BP32
Second Av, (Millerston) G33	26	CD24
Second Av, G44	64	BR39
Second Av, (Kirk.) G66	29	CE20
Second Av, (Udd.) G71	70	CN36
Second Av, Renf. PA4	31	AY27
Second Gdns, G41	48	BJ33
Second St, (Udd.) G71	70	CP37
Seedhill, Pais. PA1	44	AV33
Seedhill Rd, Pais. PA1	45	AV33
Seggielea Rd, G13	19	BF23
Seil Dr, G44	78	BR41
Selborne Pl La, G13	20	BG24
Selborne Rd, G13	20	BG24
Selkirk Av, G52	47	BE33
Selkirk Dr, (Ruther.) G73	66	BY38
Selvieland Rd, G52	46	BB32
Seton Ter, G31	51	BV30
Seventh Av, (Udd.) G71	70	CP37
Seyton Av, (Giff.) G46	77	BL44
Shaftesbury St, G3	9	BP29
Shafton Pl, G13	20	BG21
Shafton Rd, G13	20	BG21
Shakespeare St, G20	21	BN24
Shamrock St, G4	20	BQ28
Shandwick St, G34	41	CJ29
Shanks Av, (Barr.) G78	73	AY43
Shanks Ind Pk, (Barr.) G78	73	AY40
Shanks St, G20	21	BN24
Shannon St, G20	22	BP24
Shapinsay St, G22	23	BT21
Sharp Av, Coat. ML5	57	CS33
Shawbridge St, G43	63	BK38
Shawfield Dr, G5	65	BU35
Shawfield Ind Est, (Ruther.) G73	65	BV35
Shawhill Rd, G5	51	BV34
Shawhill Rd, G41	63	BL37
Shawhill Rd, G43	63	BL37
Shawholm Cres, G43	63	BK38
Shawlands Arc, G41	63	BN37
Shawlands Sq, G41	63	BM37
Shawmoss Rd, G41	63	BL36
Shawpark St, G20	21	BN23
Shaw St, G51	34	BJ29
Sheddens Pl, G32	53	CB32
Sheepburn Rd, (Udd.) G71	70	CN38
Sheila St, G33	39	CA25
Shelley Ct, G12	20	BJ24
Shelley Dr, (Both.) G71	85	CR42
Shelley Rd, G12	20	BH24
Sherbrooke Av, G41	49	BL34
Sherbrooke Dr, G41	49	BL33
Sherbrooke Gdns, G41	49	BL34
Sherburn Gdns, (Baill.) G69	55	CH33
Sheriff Pk Av, (Ruther.) G73	66	BW38
Sherry Hts, (Camb.) G72	67	CC39
Sherwood Av, (Udd.) G71	85	CQ40
Sherwood Av, Pais. PA1	45	AW31
Sherwood Dr, (Thornlie.) G46	76	BJ42
Shetland Dr, G44	78	BR41
Shettleston Rd, G31	52	BY31
Shettleston Rd, G32	53	CC32
Shettleston Sheddings, G31	53	CA32
Shieldaig Dr, (Ruther.) G73	80	BX41
Shieldaig Rd, G22	22	BR21
Shieldburn Rd, G51	47	BE30
Shieldhall Gdns, G51	47	BE30
Shieldhall Rd, G51	33	BE29
Shields Rd, G41	13	BP32
Shiel Rd, (Bishop.) G64	25	BX20
Shilford Av, G13	18	BC22
Shillay St, G22	23	BU21
Shilton Dr, G53	75	BE40
Shinwell Av, Clyde. G81	18	AZ20
Shiskine Dr, G20	21	BL22
Shiskine Pl, G20	21	BL21
Shiskine St, G20	21	BL21
Shore St, G40	65	BV35
Shortridge St, G20	21	BN24
Shortroods Av, Pais. PA3	44	AT30
Shortroods Cres, Pais. PA3	44	AT30
Shortroods Rd, Pais. PA3	44	AT30
Shotts St, G33	40	CF29
Showcase Leisure Pk, (Baill.) G69	57	CR33
Shuna Gdns, G20	22	BP24
Shuna Pl, G20	21	BN24
Shuna St, G20	21	BN23
Shuttle St, G1	15	BT30
Shuttle St, Pais. PA1	44	AU33
Sidland Rd, G21	38	BY24
Sielga Pl, G34	41	CJ29
Siemens Pl, G21	38	BX27
Siemens St, G21	38	BX27
Silkin Av, Clyde. G81	18	AZ20
Silk St, Pais. PA1	44	AV32
Silver Birch Dr, G51	47	BF30
Silver Birch Gdns, G51	47	BF30
Silverburn St, G33	39	CA29
Silverdale St, G31	52	BY33
Silverfir Ct, G5	51	BT34
Silverfir Pl, G5	51	BT34
Silverfir St, G5	51	BT34
Silvergrove St, G40	15	BU33
Silverwells, (Both.) G71	85	CS41
Silverwells Ct, (Both.) G71	85	CS41
Silverwells Cres, (Both.) G71	85	CS41
Simons Cres, Renf. PA4	18	AS18
Simpson St, (Udd.) G71	71	CJ37
Simpson Gdns, (Barr.) G78	73	AX43
Simpson St, G20	36	BP26
Simshill Rd, G44	78	BS39
Sinclair Dr, G42	64	BR39
Sinclair Gdns, (Bishop.) G64	24	BW20
Sinclair St, Clyde. G81	18	AX18
Sir Michael Pl, Pais. PA1	44	AT33
Sixth Av, Renf. PA4	31	AY29
Sixth St, (Udd.) G71	70	CP37
Skaethorn Rd, G20	21	BL23
Skaterigg Dr, G13	20	BH23
Skaterigg Gdns, G13	20	BH23
Skaterigg La, G13	20	BH23
Skelbo Pl, G34	42	CF29
Skene Rd, G51	48	BJ31
Skerray Quad, G22	22	BS21
Skerray St, G22	22	BS21
Skerryvore Pl, G33	40	CD29
Skerryvore Rd, G33	40	CD29
Skibo Dr, (Thornlie.) G46	76	BH42
Skibo La, (Thornlie.) G46	76	BH42
Skipness Dr, G51	34	BG30
Skye Av, Renf. PA4	31	AY28
Skye Cres, Pais. PA2	58	AV38
Skye Rd, (Ruther.) G73	80	BZ42
Slakiewood Av, (Gart.) G69	28	CL22
Slatefield St, G31	52	BV32
Slenavon Av, (Ruther.) G73	81	BX41
Sloy St, G22	37	BS25
Smeaton Gro, G20	22	BN22
Smeaton St, G20	22	BN22
Smith Cl, (Bishop.) G64	25	BX20
Smith Gdns, (Bishop.) G64	25	BX20
Smith Gro, (Bishop.) G64	25	BX20
Smithhills St, Pais. PA1	44	AV33
Smiths La, Pais. PA3	44	AU32
Smith St, G14	34	BH27
Smith Ter, (Ruther.) G73	66	BW37
Smith Way, (Bishop.) G64	25	BY20
Smithycroft Rd, G33	39	CC27
Snaefell Av, (Ruther.) G73	80	BX41
Snaefell Cres, (Ruther.) G73	80	BX41
Snuff Mill Rd, G44	78	BS39
Society St, G31	52	BX32
Sollas Pl, G13	18	BB22
Solway Pl, (Chry.) G69	28	CK21
Solway St, G40	65	BV35
Somerford Rd, (Bears.) G61	20	BH19
Somerled Av, Pais. PA3	31	AV29
Somerset Pl, G3	9	BP28
Somerset Pl Ms, G3	9	BP28
Somervell St, (Camb.) G72	67	CB39
Somerville Dr, G42	64	BS38
Sorby St, G31	52	BY32
Sorn St, G40	52	BX34
Southampton Dr, G12	20	BG23
Southampton La, G12	20	BG23
South Annandale St, G42	64	BS36
South Av, Pais. PA2	58	AV37
South Av, Renf. PA4	32	AZ26
Southbank St, G31	52	BY32
South Bk St, Clyde. G81	17	AX21

Street	Page	Grid
outhbar Av, G13	18	BC22
outhbrae Dr, G13	19	BE24
outh Campbell St, Pais. PA2	44	AU34
outh Chester St, G32	53	CC32
outhcroft Rd, (Ruther.) G73	65	BQ36
outhcroft St, G51	49	BK30
outh Crosshill Rd, (Bishop.) G64	24	BW20
outh Dean Pk Av, (Both.) G71	85	CQ43
outh Douglas St, Clyde. G81	17	AY21
outh Elgin Pl, Clyde. G81	17	AY22
outh Elgin St, Clyde. G81	17	AY22
outhern Av, (Ruther.) G73	80	BX40
outh Ex Ct, G1	14	BS30
outhfield Av, Pais. PA2	58	AU37
outhfield Cres, G53	61	BE37
outh Frederick St, G1	14	BS30
outh Hallhill Rd, G32	54	CD32
outhhill Av, (Ruther.) G73	80	BY40
outhinch Av, G14	18	BA23
outhinch La, G14	18	BA23
outhlea Av, (Thornlie.) G46	76	BJ42
outh Ln, (Chry.) G69	28	CN21
outhloch Gdns, G21	37	BV26
outhloch St, G21	37	BV26
outh Medrox St, (Glenb.) Coat. ML5	29	CS22
outhmuir Pl, G20	21	BM24
outh Nitshill Ind Est, G53	74	BC40
outhpark Av, G12	8	BM27
outh Pk Av, (Barr.) G78	73	AX42
outh Pk Dr, Pais. PA2	58	AU35
outhpark La, G12	8	BN27
outh Portland St, G5	14	BR32
outh Scott St, (Baill.) G69	55	CK33
outhside Cres, G5	50	BR33
outh St, G11	33	BF27
outh St, G14	33	BF27
outh Vw, (Blan.) G72	84	CL44
outhview Av, (Gart.) G69	28	CN23
outhview Ter, (Bishop.) G64	23	BV22
outhwold Rd, Pais. PA1	46	BA33
outhwood Dr, G44	79	BS40
outh Woodside Rd, G4	8	BN27
outh Woodside Rd, G20	8	BP26
outra Pl, G33	40	CD29
bean St, G4	64	BQ39
beirsfield Ct, Pais. PA2	44	AT34
beirsfield Dr, Pais. PA2	44	AU34
beirshall St, G14	18	BA23
beirshall Ter, G14	18	BA23
bencer St, G13	20	BH22
bence St, G20	21	BL21
bey Dr, Renf. PA4	32	BA27
bey St, G33	39	CB29
biersbridge Av, (Thornlie.) G46	76	BH42
biersbridge La, (Thornlie.) G46	76	BG42
biersbridge Rd, (Thornlie.) G46	76	BH42
biersbridge Ter, (Thornlie.) G46	76	BG42
biersbridge Toll, (Thornlie.) G46	76	BH43
biers Gro, (Thornlie.) G46	76	BH43
biers Wf, G4	10	BR27
bindlehowe Rd, (Udd.) G71	71	CP39
bittal Rd, (Ruther.) G73	79	BV41
bittal Ter, (Camb.) G72	83	CJ43
Spoolers Rd, Pais. PA1	44	AS34
Spoutmouth, G1	15	BT31
Springbank Rd, Pais. PA3	44	AT30
Springbank St, G20	36	BP25
Springbank Ter, Pais. PA3	44	AT30
Springboig Av, G32	54	CE31
Springboig Rd, G32	54	CE30
Springburn Rd, G21	11	BU27
Springburn Rd, (Bishop.) G64	23	BU24
Springburn Shop Cen, G21	37	BV25
Springburn Way, G21	37	BV25
Springcroft Av, (Baill.) G69	55	CK31
Springcroft Cres, (Baill.) G69	55	CK31
Springcroft Dr, (Baill.) G69	55	CJ31
Springcroft Gdns, (Baill.) G69	56	CL31
Springcroft Gro, (Baill.) G69	55	CK31
Springcroft Rd, (Baill.) G69	55	CK31
Springcroft Wynd, (Baill.) G69	55	CK31
Springfield Av, (Bishop.) G64	24	BW21
Springfield Av, (Udd.) G71	85	CP40
Springfield Av, Pais. PA1	45	AX33
Springfield Ct, G1	14	BS30
Springfield Cres, (Bishop.) G64	24	BW21
Springfield Dr, (Barr.) G78	74	BA44
Springfield Pk Rd, (Ruther.) G73	66	BY39
Springfield Quay, G5	13	BP31
Springfield Rd, G31	52	BX31
Springfield Rd, G40	52	BX34
Springfield Rd, (Bishop.) G64	24	BW20
Springfield Sq, (Bishop.) G64	24	BW21
Springhill Av, Coat. ML5	57	CS33
Springhill Dr N, (Baill.) G69	55	CJ30
Springhill Dr S, (Baill.) G69	55	CJ30
Springhill Fm Gro, (Baill.) G69	55	CJ31
Springhill Fm Pl, (Baill.) G69	55	CJ31
Springhill Fm Rd, (Baill.) G69	55	CJ31
Springhill Fm Way, (Baill.) G69	55	CJ31
Springhill Gdns, G41	63	BN36
Springhill Parkway, (Baill.) G69	55	CJ31
Springhill Pl, Coat. ML5	57	CS33
Springhill Rd, (Baill.) G69	55	CH32
Springhill Rd, (Barr.) G78	73	AX43
Springkell Av, G41	49	BL34
Springkell Dr, G41	62	BK35
Springkell Gdns, G41	63	BL35
Springkell Gate, G41	63	BM35
Springvale Ter, G21	37	BU25
Spring Wynd, G5	51	BS33
Spruce Dr, (Camb.) G72	83	CH41
Spruce St, G22	23	BR24
Spruce Way, (Camb.) G72	83	CH41
Squire St, G14	33	BF27
Staffa Av, Renf. PA4	31	AY28
Staffa Dr, Pais. PA2	58	AU38
Staffa Rd, (Camb.) G72	81	CB42
Staffa St, G31	38	BX29
Staffa Ter, (Camb.) G72	81	CB42
Staffin Dr, G23	21	BM20
Staffin Path, G23	21	BN20
Staffin St, G23	21	BN20
Stafford St, G4	11	BT28
Stag St, G51	49	BK30
Stair St, G20	36	BP25
Stamford Pl, G31	52	BX32
Stamford Rd, G31	52	BX32
Stamford St, G31	52	BX32
Stamford St, G40	52	BX32
Stamperland Gdns, (Clark.) G76	78	BP44
Stanalane St, (Thornlie.) G46	76	BH41
Standburn Rd, G21	24	BY22
Stanely Dr, Pais. PA2	58	AS36
Stanely Rd, Pais. PA2	58	AS36
Stanford St, Clyde. G81	17	AY20
Stanhope Dr, (Ruther.) G73	80	BZ40
Stanley Pl, (Blan.) G72	84	CM44
Stanley St, G41	12	BN32
Stanley St La, G41	12	BN32
Stanmore Rd, G42	64	BR37
Startpoint St, G33	39	CC29
Station Pk, (Baill.) G69	56	CL33
Station Rd, G20	21	BL21
Station Rd, (Millerston) G33	25	CC24
Station Rd, (Stepps) G33	26	CF24
Station Rd, (Baill.) G69	56	CL33
Station Rd, (Muir.) G69	28	CL23
Station Rd, (Both.) G71	85	CQ43
Station Rd, (Udd.) G71	70	CN39
Station Rd, (Blan.) G72	84	CN44
Station Rd, Renf. PA4	32	AZ25
Station Way, (Udd.) G71	71	CP39
Staybrae Dr, G53	60	BB36
Staybrae Gro, G53	60	BB36
Steel St, G1	15	BT31
Stenhouse Av, (Muir.) G69	28	CL22
Stenton St, G32	53	CA30
Stepford Pl, G33	55	CH30
Stepford Rd, G33	55	CH30
Stephen Cres, (Baill.) G69	55	CH32
Stephenson St, G52	32	BA29
Steppshill Ter, G33	26	CE24
Stepps Rd, G33	40	CE28
Stevenson St, G40	15	BU31
Stevenson St, Pais. PA2	44	AU34
Stewart Av, Renf. PA4	31	AX28
Stewart Ct, (Ruther.) G73	66	BY38
Stewart Cres, (Barr.) G78	74	AZ41
Stewart Dr, (Baill.) G69	57	CR31
Stewarton Dr, (Camb.) G72	81	CA40
Stewarton Rd, (Thornlie.) G46	76	BG43
Stewart Rd, Pais. PA2	58	AV37
Stewart St, G4	10	BR28
Stewart St, (Barr.) G78	74	AZ41
Stewartville St, G11	35	BK27
Stirling Dr, (Ruther.) G73	80	BX42
Stirlingfauld Pl, G5	14	BR32
Stirling Rd, G4	11	BT29
Stirrat St, G20	21	BL23
Stobcross Rd, G3	8	BM29
Stobcross Rd, G3	13	BP30
Stobcross Wynd, G3	35	BL29
Stobhill Rd, G21	23	BV22
Stobs Dr, (Barr.) G78	73	AX40
Stobs Pl, G34	42	CL28
Stock Av, Pais. PA2	44	AU34
Stockholm Cres, Pais. PA2	44	AU34
Stock St, Pais. PA2	44	AU34
Stockwell Pl, G1	14	BS31
Stockwell St, G1	14	BS31
Stonebank Gro, G45	79	BT42

Name	Page	Grid
Stonefield Av, G12	21	BK23
Stonefield Av, Pais. PA2	58	AV36
Stonefield Cres, Pais. PA2	58	AV36
Stonefield Dr, Pais. PA2	59	AV36
Stonefield Gdns, Pais. PA2	58	AV36
Stonefield Grn, Pais. PA2	58	AU36
Stonefield Gro, Pais. PA2	58	AU36
Stonefield Pk, Pais. PA2	58	AU37
Stonelaw Dr, (Ruther.) G73	66	BX38
Stonelaw Rd, (Ruther.) G73	66	BX38
Stonelaw Twrs, (Ruther.) G73	66	BY39
Stoneside Dr, G43	62	BJ39
Stoneside Sq, G43	62	BJ39
Stoney Brae, Pais. PA1	44	AU32
Stoney Brae, Pais. PA2	58	AU37
Stonyhurst St, G22	36	BR25
Storie St, Pais. PA1	44	AU33
Stormyland Way, (Barr.) G78	73	AY43
Stornoway St, G22	23	BS21
Stow Brae, Pais. PA1	44	AU33
Stow St, Pais. PA1	44	AU33
Strachur St, G22	22	BQ22
Straiton St, G32	53	CA30
Stranka Av, Pais. PA2	44	AS34
Stratford St, G20	21	BM24
Strathallan Gdns, G13	20	BH21
Strathbran St, G31	52	BZ33
Strathcarron Cres, Pais. PA2	59	AX36
Strathcarron Dr, Pais. PA2	59	AX36
Strathcarron Pl, Pais. PA2	59	AX36
Strathcarron Rd, Pais. PA2	59	AX37
Strathcarron Way, Pais. PA2	59	AX36
Strathclyde Dr, (Ruther.) G73	66	BW38
Strathclyde Path, (Udd.) G71	70	CN39
Strathclyde St, G40	66	BW35
Strath Clyde Vw, (Both.) G71	85	CR44
Strathcona Dr, G13	20	BH22
Strathcona Gdns, G13	20	BJ22
Strathcona St, G13	20	BH22
Strathdee Rd, G44	77	BN43
Strathdon Av, G44	78	BP43
Strathdon Av, Pais. PA2	58	AS35
Strathdon Dr, G44	78	BP43
Strathendrick Dr, G44	77	BN41
Strathmore Av, (Blan.) G72	84	CL44
Strathmore Av, Pais. PA1	46	AZ33
Strathmore Gdns, (Ruther.) G73	81	BZ41
Strathmore Rd, G22	22	BR22
Strathord St, G32	53	CC34
Strathtay Av, G44	78	BP43
Strathview Gro, G44	77	BN43
Strathview Pk, G44	77	BN43
Strathyre St, G41	63	BN37
Stratton Dr, (Giff.) G46	77	BK43
Strauss Av, Clyde. G81	18	BA20
Stravanan Av, G45	79	BU43
Stravanan Ct, G45	79	BU43
Stravanan Gdns, G45	79	BT43
Stravanan Pl, G51	79	BT43
Stravanan Rd, G45	79	BT43
Stravanan St, G45	79	BT43
Stravanan Ter, G45	79	BT43
Streamfield Gdns, G33	25	BZ22
Streamfield Lea, G33	25	BZ22
Streamfield Pl, G33	25	BZ22
Strenabey Av, (Ruther.) G73	80	BZ41
Striven Gdns, G20	36	BP26
Stroma St, G21	38	BX27
Stromness St, G5	50	BQ33
Stronend St, G22	22	BR24
Strone Rd, G33	54	CD30
Stronsay St, G21	38	BX27
Stronvar Dr, G14	33	BD25
Strowan Cres, G32	54	CD33
Strowan St, G32	54	CD33
Struan Av, (Giff.) G46	77	BK42
Struan Gdns, G44	78	BQ40
Struan Rd, G44	78	BQ40
Struie St, G34	41	CJ29
Stuart Av, (Ruther.) G73	80	BX40
Stuart Dr, (Bishop.) G64	23	BU21
Succoth St, G13	20	BH22
Sugworth Av, (Baill.) G69	55	CK32
Suisnish, Ersk. PA8	16	AS32
Sumburgh St, G33	39	CB29
Summer St, G40	52	BV32
Summerfield Cotts, G14	34	BG27
Summerfield St, G40	66	BX35
Summerlea Rd, (Thornlie.) G46	76	BH41
Summerlee St, G33	40	CE29
Summer St, G40	52	BV32
Summertown Rd, G51	48	BK30
Sunart Av, Renf. PA4	31	AX25
Sunart Gdns, (Bishop.) G64	24	BY20
Sunart Rd, G52	48	BZ32
Sunart Rd, (Bishop.) G64	24	BY20
Sunningdale Rd, G23	21	BM21
Sunningdale Wynd, (Both.) G71	84	CN42
Sunnybank St, G40	52	BX34
Sunnylaw St, G22	36	BR25
Sunnyside Av, (Udd.) G71	85	CP40
Sunnyside Dr, G15	19	BC20
Sunnyside Dr, (Baill.) G69	57	CP32
Sunnyside Oval, Pais. PA2	58	AU36
Sunnyside Pl, G15	19	BC20
Sunnyside Pl, (Barr.) G78	73	AX43
Sunnyside Rd, Pais. PA2	58	AT35
Surrey St, G5	50	BR33
Sussex St, G41	12	BN32
Sutcliffe Rd, G13	20	BG22
Sutherland Av, G41	49	BK34
Sutherland Av, (Giff.) G46	77	BM44
Sutherland La, G12	35	BL27
Sutherland Rd, Pais. PA1	44	AT32
Sutherness Dr, G33	53	CC30
Swallow Gdns, G13	18	BB22
Swanston St, G40	66	BW35
Swan St, G4	10	BS28
Sween Av, G44	78	BQ41
Sweethope Gdns, (Both.) G71	85	CR43
Sweethope Pl, (Both.) G71	85	CQ42
Swift Cres, G13	18	BB22
Swinton Av, (Baill.) G69	56	CL32
Swinton Cres, (Baill.) G69	56	CL32
Swinton Cres, Coat. ML5	57	CL33
Swinton Dr, G52	47	BD32
Swinton Path, (Baill.) G69	56	CM32
Swinton Pl, G52	47	BD32
Swinton Pl, (Baill.) G69	56	CL32
Swinton Vw, (Baill.) G69	56	CL32
Swordale Pl, G34	41	CJ29
Sword St, G31	51	BV31
Sycamore Av, (Udd.) G71	71	CS37
Sycamore Way, (Camb.) G72	83	CH41
Sydenham Rd, G12	35	BL26
Sydney St, G31	15	BU31
Sylvania Way S, Clyde. G81	17	AX21
Syriam St, G21	37	BV21

T

Name	Page	Grid
Tabard Pl, G13	19	BE21
Tabard Rd, G13	19	BE21
Tabernacle La, (Camb.) G72	81	CC40
Tabernacle St, (Camb.) G72	81	CC40
Tain Pl, G34	42	CM29
Tait Av, (Barr.) G78	74	AZ41
Talbot Ct, G13	19	BD21
Talbot Dr, G13	19	BD21
Talbot Pl, G13	19	BD21
Talbot Ter, (Udd.) G71	70	CN33
Talisman Rd, G13	19	BE22
Talla Rd, G52	47	BD33
Tamarack Cres, (Udd.) G71	71	CS33
Tambowie St, G13	20	BG21
Tamshill St, G20	22	BP22
Tanar Av, Renf. PA4	32	BB22
Tanera Av, G44	79	BS44
Tanfield St, G32	54	CE33
Tankerland Rd, G44	64	BQ38
Tannadice Av, G52	47	BE33
Tanna Dr, G52	48	BH33
Tannahill Rd, G43	64	BP38
Tannochside Business Pk, (Udd.) G71	71	CQ37
Tannochside Dr, (Udd.) G71	71	CQ37
Tannock St, G22	36	BR22
Tantallon Dr, Coat. ML5	43	CS29
Tantallon Rd, G41	63	BN33
Tantallon Rd, (Baill.) G69	55	CJ33
Tanzieknowe Av, (Camb.) G72	82	CD40
Tanzieknowe Dr, (Camb.) G72	82	CD40
Tanzieknowe Pl, (Camb.) G72	82	CD40
Tanzieknowe Rd, (Camb.) G72	82	CD40
Taransay St, G51	34	BJ29
Tarbert Av, (Blan.) G72	84	CL44
Tarbolton Rd, G43	63	BM38
Tarfside Gdns, G52	47	BE33
Tarfside Oval, G52	47	BE33
Tarland St, G51	48	BH33
Tarn Gro, G53	75	BC42
Tarras Dr, Renf. PA4	32	BA22
Tarras Pl, (Camb.) G72	82	CE40
Tassie St, G41	63	BM38
Tattershall Rd, G33	40	CE32
Tavistock Dr, G43	77	BM40
Tay Av, Renf. PA4	32	BA22
Tay Cres, G33	39	CA28
Tay Cres, (Bishop.) G64	24	BY20
Taylor Pl, G4	11	BT21
Taylor St, G4	15	BT31
Taylor St, Clyde. G81	17	AY21
Taymouth St, G32	54	CD33
Taynish Dr, G44	78	BR44
Tay Rd, (Bishop.) G64	24	BY20
Tay St, Coat. ML5	43	CS32
Teal Dr, G13	18	BC21
Tealing Av, G52	47	BE33
Tealing Cres, G52	47	BE33
Teasel Av, G53	75	BD44
Teith Av, Renf. PA4	32	BB22
Teith Pl, (Camb.) G72	82	CF40
Teith St, G33	39	CA28
Telephone La, G12	35	BL26

mplar Av, G13 19 BF21
mple Gdns, G13 20 BH22
mpleland Av, G53 61 BE35
mpleland Rd, G53 61 BE35
mple Locks Ct, G13 20 BH22
mple Locks Pl, G13 20 BH22
mple Rd, G13 20 BH22
mpletons Business Centre, G40 15 BU32
mpleton St, G40 15 BU32
nnant St, Renf. PA4 32 AZ25
nnyson Dr, G31 53 CA33
rrace Pl, (Camb.) G72 82 CG40
rregles Av, G41 63 BK35
rregles Cres, G41 63 BL35
rregles Dr, G41 63 BL35
viot Pl, (Camb.) G72 82 CF40
viot St, G3 35 BN32
ane Rd, G13 19 BE23
arsis St, G21 37 BV28
ird Av, (Millerston) G33 26 CD24
ird Av, G44 64 BR38
ird Av, (Kirk.) G66 26 CF20
ird Av, Renf. PA4 31 AY27
irdpart Cres, G13 18 BA22
istle St, G5 14 BS32
istle St, Pais. PA2 58 AS35
istle Ter, G5 50 AS33
omas Muir Av, (Bishop.) G64 24 BW21
omson Dr, G31 52 BZ30
omson St, G31 52 BZ30
ornbank St, G3 35 BL28
ornbridge Gdns, (Baill.) G69 55 CJ32
ornbridge Rd, (Baill.) G69 55 CJ32
orncliffe Gdns, G41 63 BN35
orncliffe La, G41 63 BN35
orncroft Dr, G44 79 BT41
ornden La, G14 33 BV25
orn Dr, (Ruther.) G73 80 BY41
orniewood Gdns, (Udd.) G71 71 CQ38
orniewood Rd, (Udd.) G71 71 CP37
ornlea Dr, (Giff.) G46 77 BM41
ornley Av, G13 19 BD23
ornliebank Ind Est, (Thornlie.) G46 76 BG42
ornliebank Rd, G43 76 BJ40
ornliebank Rd, (Thornlie.) G46 76 BJ41
ornly Pk Av, Pais. PA2 58 AV37
ornly Pk Rd, Pais. PA2 58 AV37
ornly Pk Gdns, Pais. PA2 58 AU36
ornly Pk Rd, Pais. PA2 58 AU36
ornton La, G20 21 BN22
ornton St, G20 21 BN22
orntree Way, (Both.) G71 85 CR42
ornwood Av, G11 34 BJ27
ornwood Cres, G11 34 BH26
ornwood Dr, G11 34 BH27
ornwood Gdns, G11 34 BJ27
ornwood Pl, G11 34 BJ26
ornwood Rd, G11 34 BH27
ornyburn Dr, (Baill.) G69 56 CM33
ornyburn Pl, (Baill.) G69 56 CL33
eestonehill Av, G32 54 CD31
ums Av, (Bishop.) G64 24 BY20

Thrums Gdns, (Bishop.) G64 24 BY20
Thrushcraig Cres, Pais. PA2 58 AV35
Thurso St, G11 35 BL28
Thurston Rd, G52 47 BC32
Tianavaig, Ersk. PA8 16 AS22
Tibberton Rd, G11 34 BJ26
Tillet Oval, Pais. PA3 44 AT30
Tillie St, G20 36 BP26
Tillycairn Av, G33 40 CF27
Tillycairn Dr, G33 40 CF27
Tillycairn Pl, G33 40 CG27
Tillycairn Rd, G33 40 CG27
Tillycairn St, G33 40 CG27
Tilt St, G33 39 CA27
Tinto Dr, (Barr.) G78 73 AX44
Tinto Gro, (Baill.) G69 57 CR31
Tinto Rd, G43 77 BL40
Tinto Rd, (Bishop.) G64 24 BY20
Tinwald Path, G52 47 BC32
Tiree Av, Pais. PA2 58 AT38
Tiree Av, Renf. PA4 31 AY29
Tiree St, G21 38 BY27
Tirry Av, Renf. PA4 32 BB27
Titwood Rd, G41 63 BN36
Tiverton Av, G32 54 CF34
Tobago Pl, G40 15 BU32
Tobago St, G40 15 BU32
Tobermory Rd, (Ruther.) G73 80 BZ43
Todburn Dr, Pais. PA2 58 AV37
Todd St, G31 52 BY30
Todholm Cres, Pais. PA2 59 AX35
Todholm Rd, Pais. PA2 59 AX35
Todholm Ter, Pais. PA2 59 AW35
Toll Ct, G51 12 BN31
Tollcross Pk Vw, G32 53 CA34
Tollcross Rd, G31 52 BZ32
Tollcross Rd, G32 53 CA33
Tolsta St, G23 21 BN20
Tontine La, G1 14 BS31
Tontine Pl, (Ruther.) G73 81 CA41
Torbreck St, G52 48 BH32
Torburn Av, (Giff.) G46 77 BK41
Torgyle St, G23 21 BM20
Tormore St, G51 47 BF31
Tormusk Dr, G45 80 BW41
Tormusk Gdns, G45 80 BW41
Tormusk Gro, G45 80 BW41
Tormusk Rd, G45 80 BW41
Torness St, G11 35 BL27
Torogay Pl, G22 23 BU21
Torogay St, G22 23 BS21
Torogay Ter, G22 22 BS21
Toronto Wk, G32 68 CE37
Torphin Cres, G32 53 CC30
Torphin Wk, G32 54 CD31
Torrance St, G21 37 BV25
Torran Dr, (Ersk.) PA8 16 AU22
Torran Rd, G33 55 CH30
Torr Gdns, G22 37 BS25
Torridon Av, G41 48 BK34
Torrington Cres, G32 54 CF34
Torrin Rd, G23 21 BM20
Torrisdale St, G42 64 BP35
Torr Pl, G22 37 BT25
Torr St, (Bishop.) G64 24 BZ20
Torryburn Rd, G21 38 BY25
Toryglen Rd, (Ruther.) G73 65 BU37
Toryglen St, G5 65 BS35
Toward Ct, (Blan.) G72 84 CN44
Toward Rd, G33 54 CE30
Tower Av, (Barr.) G78 74 AZ41
Tower Cres, Renf. PA4 31 AX27
Tower Dr, Renf. PA4 31 AX27
Towerhill Rd, G13 19 BE20

Towerside Cres, G53 61 BC35
Towerside Rd, G53 61 BC35
Tower St, G41 12 BN32
Tower Ter, Pais. PA1 44 AT33
Towie Pl, (Udd.) G71 71 CP39
Townhead Pl, (Udd.) G71 71 CQ37
Townhead Rd, Coat. ML5 43 CQ28
Townhead Ter, Pais. PA1 44 AT33
Townmill Rd, G31 37 BV29
Townsend St, G4 10 BS28
Tradeston St, G5 13 BQ32
Trafalgar St, G40 51 BV34
Trainard Av, G32 53 CB33
Tranent Pl, G33 39 CA29
Traquair Dr, G52 47 BD33
Treeburn Av, (Giff.) G46 76 BK42
Trees Pk Av, (Barr.) G78 73 AX41
Trefoil Av, G41 63 BM37
Tresta Rd, G23 22 BP21
Trinity Av, G52 47 BE33
Trinity Dr, (Camb.) G72 82 CE42
Trinley Brae, G13 19 BE20
Trinley Rd, G13 19 BF20
Trondra Path, G34 41 CH29
Trondra Pl, G34 55 CH30
Trondra Rd, G34 41 CH29
Trongate, G1 14 BS31
Troon St, G40 52 BX34
Trossachs Rd, (Ruther.) G73 80 BZ43
Trossachs St, G20 36 BQ26
Truce Rd, G13 19 BD21
Tudor Rd, G14 34 BG26
Tudor St, (Baill.) G69 55 CH34
Tullis Ct, G40 51 BU33
Tullis St, G40 51 BU33
Tulloch St, G44 64 BQ39
Tummel St, G33 39 CA27
Tunnel St, G3 12 BN30
Tureen St, G40 51 BV31
Turnberry Dr, (Ruther.) G73 79 BV41
Turnberry Rd, G11 34 BJ26
Turnberry Wynd, (Both.) G71 84 CN42
Turnbull St, G1 15 BT31
Turner Rd, G21 37 BV27
Turner Rd, Pais. PA3 31 AV29
Turnlaw Rd, (Camb.) G72 81 CC43
Turnlaw St, G5 51 BT33
Turret Cres, G13 19 BE21
Turret Rd, G13 19 BE21
Turriff St, G5 50 BR33
Tweed Cres, G33 39 BZ28
Tweed Cres, Renf. PA4 32 BA26
Tweedsmuir Rd, G52 47 BD33
Tweedvale Av, G14 18 BA23
Twinlaw St, G34 42 CM28
Tylney Rd, Pais. PA1 46 AZ32
Tyndrum St, G4 10 BS28
Tynecastle Cres, G32 54 CD30
Tynecastle Pl, G32 54 CD30
Tynecastle St, G32 54 CD30
Tyne St, G14 33 BF27
Tynwald Av, (Ruther.) G73 80 BZ41

U

Uddingston Rd, (Both.) G71 85 CP42
Uig Pl, G33 55 CG32
Uist Cres, (Stepps) G33 40 CG25
Uist St, G51 48 BH30
Ulva St, G52 48 BH32

Street	Area	Page	Grid
Umachan, Ersk. PA8		16	AS22
Underwood Ct, Pais. PA3		44	AT32
Underwood La, Pais. PA1		44	AT32
Underwood Rd, (Ruther.) G73		66	BY39
Underwood Rd, Pais. PA3		44	AS32
Union Ct, Pais. PA2		58	AU35
Union St, G1		14	BR30
Union St, Clyde. G81		17	AY21
Union St, Pais. PA2		58	AU35
Unity Pl, G4		9	BQ27
University Av, G12		8	BM27
University Gdns, G12		8	BM27
University of Glasgow, G12		8	BM27
University Pl, G12		8	BM27
Unsted Pl, Pais. PA1		45	AW33
Uphall Pl, G33		39	CA29
Upland Rd, G14		33	BE25
Upper Bourtree Ct, (Ruther.) G73		80	BY41
Upper Bourtree Dr, (Ruther.) G73		80	BX41
Urquhart Cres, Renf. PA4		31	AY27
Urrdale Rd, G41		49	BK32

V

Street	Area	Page	Grid
Vaila Pl, G23		22	BQ22
Vaila St, G23		22	BP22
Valeview Ter, G42		64	BO37
Vale Wk, (Bishop.) G64		24	BY21
Vallantine Cres, (Udd.) G71		71	CQ37
Vallay St, G22		23	BT21
Valley Vw, (Camb.) G72		68	CE39
Vancouver Rd, G14		33	BE25
Vanguard Way, Renf. PA4		31	AY28
Varna La, G14		34	BG26
Varna Rd, G14		34	BG25
Vasart Pl, G20		22	BP24
Vennacher Rd, Renf. PA4		31	AW25
Vennard Gdns, G41		63	BN35
Vermont Av, (Ruther.) G73		66	BW38
Vermont St, G41		12	BN32
Verona Av, G14		33	BE25
Verona Gdns, G14		33	BE25
Verona La, G14		33	BE25
Vesalius St, G32		53	CC32
Vicarfield St, G51		48	BK30
Vicarland Pl, (Camb.) G72		81	CC41
Vicarland Rd, (Camb.) G72		81	CC40
Vicars Wk, (Camb.) G72		82	CD40
Victoria Br, (Barr.) G78		73	AX41
Victoria Br, G1		14	BS31
Victoria Br, G5		14	BS31
Victoria Circ, G12		35	BL26
Victoria Cres, (Barr.) G78		73	AX41
Victoria Cres La, G12		35	BL26
Victoria Cres Rd, G12		35	BL26
Victoria Cross, G42		64	BO35
Victoria Dr, (Barr.) G78		73	AX41
Victoria Dr E, Renf. PA4		31	AY27
Victoria Dr W, Renf. PA4		31	AX26
Victoria Gdns, Pais. PA2		58	AS35
Victoria Gro, (Barr.) G78		73	AX41
Victoria Pk Cor, G14		33	BF25
Victoria Pk Dr N, G14		33	BF25
Victoria Pk Dr S, G14		33	BE26
Victoria Pk Gdns N, G11		34	BH26
Victoria Pk Gdns S, G11		34	BH26
Victoria Pk La N, G14		33	BF26
Victoria Pk St, G14		33	BF26
Victoria Pl, (Barr.) G78		73	AY41
Victoria Rd, (Stepps) G33		26	CF24
Victoria Rd, G42		64	BO36
Victoria Rd, (Ruther.) G73		66	BX39
Victoria Rd, (Barr.) G78		73	AX41
Victoria Rd, Pais. PA2		58	AS35
Victoria St, (Ruther.) G73		66	BW37
Victory Way, (Baill.) G69		55	CK33
Viewbank, (Thornlie.) G46		76	BJ42
Viewfield Av, (Bishop.) G64		23	BU21
Viewfield Av, (Baill.) G69		55	CH32
Viewfield Av, (Blan.) G72		84	CN44
Viewfield Dr, (Bishop.) G64		23	BU21
Viewfield Dr, (Baill.) G69		55	CH32
Viewfield La, G12		8	BN27
Viewfield Rd, (Bishop.) G64		23	BU21
Viewfield Rd, Coat. ML5		57	CR33
Viewglen Ct, G45		79	BT44
Viewmount Dr, G20		21	BM22
Viewpark Av, G31		38	BX29
Viewpark Dr, (Ruther.) G73		66	BX39
Viewpark Gdns, Renf. PA4		31	AX27
Viewpoint Pl, G21		23	BV23
Viewpoint Rd, G21		23	BV23
Viking Rd, (Thornlie.) G46		76	BH41
Village Gdns, (Blan.) G72		84	CN44
Village Rd, (Camb.) G72		83	CG40
Vine St, G11		34	BK27
Vinicombe La, G12		35	BM26
Vinicombe St, G12		35	BM26
Vintner St, G4		10	BS27
Violet St, Pais. PA1		45	AW33
Virginia Pl, G1		14	BS30
Virginia St, G1		14	BS30
Viscount Av, Renf. PA4		31	AY28
Viscount Gate, (Both.) G71		84	CN40
Voil Dr, G44		78	BQ41

W

Street	Area	Page	Grid
Waddell Ct, G5		15	BT32
Waddell St, G5		51	BT33
Waldemar Rd, G13		19	BE22
Waldo St, G13		20	BH22
Walkerburn Rd, G52		60	BD33
Walker Ct, G11		35	BK28
Walker Path, (Udd.) G71		71	CQ37
Walker St, G11		35	BK28
Walker St, Pais. PA1		44	AT33
Walkinshaw Rd, Renf. PA4		30	AS26
Walkinshaw St, G40		52	BW33
Wallace Av, (Bishop.) G64		25	BZ21
Wallace Gate, (Bishop.) G64		25	BZ21
Wallace Pl, (Bishop.) G64		25	BZ21
Wallace Rd, Renf. PA4		31	AW28
Wallace St, G5		13	BQ31
Wallace St, (Ruther.) G73		66	BW38
Wallace St, Clyde. G81		17	AX21
Wallace St, Pais. PA3		44	AU31
Wallacewell Cres, G21		24	BX24
Wallacewell Pl, G21		24	BX24
Wallacewell Quad, G21		24	BY23
Wallacewell Rd, G21		24	BX24
Wallneuk Rd, Pais. PA3		44	AV32
Walls St, G1		15	BT30
Walmer Cres, G51		49	BL31
Walnut Cres, G22		23	BT24
Walnut Cres, (Camb.) G72		83	CH41
Walnut Pl, G22		23	BT24
Walnut Pl, (Udd.) G71		71	CS36
Walnut Rd, G22		23	BT24
Walter St, G31		52	BX...
Walton Ct, (Giff.) G46		77	B...
Walton St, G41		63	BN...
Walton St, (Barr.) G78		73	A...
Wamba Av, G13		20	BG...
Wamba Pl, G13		20	BG...
Wanlock St, G51		34	B...
Warden Rd, G13		19	B...
Wardhill Rd, G21		24	B...
Wardhouse Rd, Pais. PA2		58	A...
Wardie Path, G33		55	C...
Wardie Pl, G33		55	C...
Wardie Rd, G33		55	C...
Wardie Rd, G34		41	C...
Wardlaw Av, (Ruther.) G73		66	B...
Wardlaw Dr, (Ruther.) G73		66	B...
Wardlaw Rd, (Bears.) G61		20	B...
Wardrop St, G51		34	B...
Wardrop St, Pais. PA1		44	A...
Ware Path, G34		55	C...
Ware Rd, G34		55	C...
Warnock St, G31		11	B...
Warren St, G42		64	B...
Warriston Cres, G33		39	B...
Warriston Pl, G32		54	C...
Warriston St, G33		38	B...
Warroch St, G3		13	A...
Washington Rd, Pais. PA3		31	A...
Washington St, G3		13	B...
Waterfoot Av, G53		61	B...
Waterford Rd, (Giff.) G46		77	B...
Waterhaughs Gdns, G33		24	B...
Waterhaughs Gro, G33		24	B...
Waterhaughs Pl, G33		24	B...
Waterloo La, G2		14	B...
Waterloo St, G2		13	B...
Water Rd, (Barr.) G78		73	A...
Water Row, G51		34	B...
Waterside Gdns, (Camb.) G72		82	C...
Waterside Pl, G5		51	B...
Waterside St, G5		51	B...
Watling St, (Udd.) G71		70	C...
Watson Av, (Ruther.) G73		65	B...
Watson St, G1		15	B...
Watson St, (Udd.) G71		85	C...
Watt Av, G33		27	C...
Watt Low Av, (Ruther.) G73		65	B...
Watt Rd, G52		46	B...
Watt St, G5		13	B...
Waukglen Av, G53		75	B...
Waukglen Cres, G53		75	B...
Waukglen Dr, G53		75	B...
Waukglen Gdns, G53		75	B...
Waukglen Pl, G53		75	B...
Waukglen Rd, G53		75	B...
Waulkmill Av, (Barr.) G78		74	A...
Waulkmill St, (Thornlie.) G46		76	B...
Waverley Ct, (Both.) G71		85	C...
Waverley Dr, (Ruther.) G73		66	B...
Waverley Gdns, G41		63	B...
Waverley St, G41		63	B...
Weardale La, G33		40	C...
Weardale St, G33		40	C...
Weaver St, G4		15	B...
Weaver Ter, Pais. PA2		45	AV...
Webster St, G40		52	BV...
Webster St, Clyde. G81		18	B...
Wedderlea Dr, G52		47	B...
Weensmoor Rd, G53		74	B...
Weighhouse Cl, Pais. PA1		44	A...
Weir Av, (Barr.) G78		73	A...
Weir St, Pais. PA3		44	A...
Weirwood Av, (Baill.) G69		55	C...
Weirwood Gdns, (Baill.) G69		55	C...
Welbeck Rd, G53		75	C...

elfare Av, (Camb.) G72 82 CF41
ellcroft Pl, G5 50 BR33
ellfield Av, (Giff.) G46 79 BR42
ellfield St, G21 37 BV25
ell Grn, G43 63 BL37
ellhouse Cres, G33 54 CG30
ellhouse Gdns, G33 55 CH30
ellhouse Gro, G33 55 CH30
ellhouse Path, G34 55 CH30
ellhouse Rd, G33 41 CH29
ellington La, G2 13 BQ30
ellington Pl, Coat. ML5 57 CS32
ellington St, G3 14 BR30
ellington St, Pais. PA3 44 AT32
ellmeadow Rd, G43 62 BJ39
ellmeadow St, Pais. PA1 44 AT33
ellpark St, G31 15 BU30
ellshot Rd, G32 52 CB34
ellside Dr, (Camb.) G72 82 CE41
ell St, Pais. PA1 44 AS32
emyss Gdns, (Baill.) G69 55 CJ34
enlock Rd, Pais. PA2 59 AV35
est Av, (Stepps) G33 26 CF39
est Av, (Udd.) G71 71 CF39
est Av, Renf. PA4 32 AZ26
estbank Ct, G12 8 BN27
estbank La, G12 8 BN27
estbank Quad, G12 8 BN27
estbourne Gdns La, G12 35 BL25
estbourne Gdns N, G12 35 BL25
estbourne Gdns S, G12 35 BL25
estbourne Gdns W, G12 35 BL25
estbourne Rd, G12 35 BK25
estbourne Shop Cen, (Barr.) G78 73 AX43
est Brae, Pais. PA1 44 AT33
estbrae Dr, G14 34 BG25
estburn Av, (Camb.) G72 68 CF39
estburn Cres, (Ruther.) G73 65 BV38
estburn Dr, (Camb.) G72 68 CD38
estburn Fm Rd, (Camb.) G72 68 CD38
estburn Rd, (Camb.) G72 68 CE39
est Campbell St, G2 13 BQ30
estcastle Cres, G45 79 BT42
estcastle Gdns, G45 79 BT42
estclyffe St, G41 63 BN36
est Coats Rd, (Camb.) G72 81 CB40
est Cotts, (Gart.) G69 41 CK26
est End Pk St, G3 9 BP28
esterburn St, G32 53 CB31
ester Carriagehill, Pais. PA2 58 AU35
ester Common Dr, G22 22 BQ24
ester Common Rd, G22 36 BQ24
ester Common Ter, G22 36 BR25
estercraigs, G31 51 BV30
esterhouse Rd, G34 41 CJ28
esterkirk Dr, G23 21 BN20
estern Av, (Ruther.) G73 65 BV37
estern Rd, (Camb.) G72 81 CA41
ester Rd, G32 54 CF33
esterton Av, (Bears.) G61 20 BF38
estfield Av, (Ruther.) G73 65 BV38
estfield Rd, (Thornlie.) G46 76 BJ43
estfield Vil, (Ruther.) G73 65 BV38
est George La, G2 9 BP29
est George St, G2 9 BQ29
est Graham St, G4 9 BP29
est Greenhill Pl, G3 8 BN29
esthorn Dr, G32 67 CC36

Westhouse Av, (Ruther.) G73 65 BU38
Westhouse Gdns, (Ruther.) G73 65 BU38
Westknowe Gdns, (Ruther.) G73 80 BX40
Westland Dr, G14 33 BF26
Westlands Gdns, Pais. PA2 58 AT26
West Lo Rd, Renf. PA4 31 AX25
Westmoreland St, G42 64 BQ35
Westmuir Pl, (Ruther.) G73 65 BU37
Westmuir St, G31 53 BZ32
West Nile St, G1 14 BR30
West Princes St, G4 9 BP27
Westray Circ, G22 23 BT23
Westray Pl, G22 23 BT23
Westray Sq, G22 23 BS22
Westray St, G22 22 BS22
West Regent La, G2 10 BR29
West Regent St, G2 9 BQ29
Westside Gdns, G11 35 BK27
West St, G5 13 BQ32
West St, Clyde. G81 18 BA31
West St, Pais. PA1 44 AS33
West Whitby St, G31 52 BY33
Westwood Av, (Giff.) G46 77 BK42
Westwood Quad, Clyde. G81 18 AZ20
Westwood Rd, G43 62 BK39
Weymouth St, G20 23 BJ23
Whamflet Av, (Baill.) G69 56 CL30
Wheatley Ct, G32 53 CC32
Wheatley Dr, G32 53 CC32
Wheatley Ln, (Bishop.) G64 24 BY21
Wheatley Pl, G32 53 CC32
Wheatley Rd, G32 53 CC32
Whin Av, (Barr.) G78 73 AW41
Whinhill Gdns, G53 47 BC34
Whinhill Pl, G53 47 BC34
Whinhill Rd, G53 47 BC34
Whinhill Rd, Pais. PA2 59 AX35
Whins Rd, G41 63 BL36
Whirlow Gdns, (Baill.) G69 55 CJ32
Whirlow Rd, (Baill.) G69 55 CJ32
Whitacres Rd, G53 74 BB41
Whitburn St, G32 53 CB30
Whitecrook St, Clyde. G81 17 AX21
Whitefield Av, (Camb.) G72 81 CC42
Whitefield Rd, G51 49 BL32
Whiteford Rd, (Stepps) G33 27 CH24
Whitehall Rd, Pais. PA2 59 AW35
Whitehall St, G3 13 BP30
Whitehaugh Av, Pais. PA1 45 AX32
Whitehaugh Cres, G53 75 BC41
Whitehaugh Dr, Pais. PA1 45 AX32
Whitehaugh Rd, G53 75 BC41
Whitehill Ct, G31 52 BW30
Whitehill Fm Rd, (Stepps) G33 26 CF24
Whitehill Gdns, G31 52 BW30
Whitehill Pl, G31 52 BW30
Whitehill Rd, (Kirk.) G66 26 CF22
Whitehill St, G31 52 BW30
Whitehill St La, G31 52 BW30
Whitehill Ter, (Gart.) G69 43 CP25
Whitelaw St, G20 21 BL22
Whiteloans, (Both.) G71 85 CR42
White St, G11 35 BK27
White St, Clyde. G81 18 AZ22
Whitevale St, G31 52 BW31
Whithope Rd, G53 74 BB40
Whithope Ter, G53 74 BB41

Whitlawburn Av, (Camb.) G72 81 CA41
Whitlawburn Rd, (Camb.) G72 81 CA41
Whitlawburn Ter, (Camb.) G72 81 CA41
Whitriggs Rd, G53 74 BB40
Whitslade Pl, G34 41 CH28
Whitslade St, G34 41 CJ28
Whittingehame Dr, G12 20 BH24
Whittingehame Dr, G13 20 BH24
Whittingehame Gdns, G12 20 BJ24
Whittingehame La, G13 20 BH24
Whittingehame Pk, G12 20 BH24
Whittliemuir Av, G44 78 BP41
Whitton Dr, (Giff.) G46 77 BM41
Whitton St, G20 21 BL21
Whitworth Dr, G20 22 BQ23
Whitworth Gdns, G20 22 BQ23
Whitworth Gate, G20 22 BQ23
Whyte Av, (Camb.) G72 67 CA39
Wickets, The, Pais. PA1 45 AW34
Wilfred Av, G13 19 BF22
Wilkie Rd, (Udd.) G71 85 CQ40
Williamson St, G31 52 BY33
William St, G3 9 BP29
William St, Pais. PA1 44 AS33
Williamwood Dr, G44 78 BP43
Williamwood Pk, G44 78 BP43
Williamwood Pk W, G44 78 BP43
Willock Pl, G20 21 BN22
Willoughby Dr, G13 20 BH23
Willow Av, (Bishop.) G64 24 BW21
Willowbank Cres, G3 9 BP27
Willowbank St, G3 9 BP27
Willowdale Cres, (Baill.) G69 55 CJ33
Willowdale Gdns, (Baill.) G69 55 CJ33
Willowford Rd, G53 74 BB41
Willow La, G32 68 CD35
Willow St, G13 20 BH22
Wilmot Rd, G13 19 BF23
Wilson St, G1 14 BS30
Wilson St, Pais. PA1 44 AS33
Wilson St, Renf. PA4 32 AZ25
Wiltonburn Rd, G53 75 BC41
Wilton Cres, G20 36 BP26
Wilton Cres La, G20 36 BP26
Wilton Dr, G20 36 BP26
Wilton Gdns, G20 36 BP26
Wilton St, G20 35 BN26
Wilverton Rd, G13 20 BG21
Winchester Dr, G12 20 BK23
Windhill Cres, G43 77 BK40
Windhill Rd, G43 77 BK40
Windlaw Ct, G45 79 BT43
Windlaw Gdns, G44 78 BP42
Windlaw Pk Gdns, G44 78 BP41
Windlaw Rd, G45 79 BT44
Windmillcroft Quay, G5 50 BQ31
Windsor Cres, Pais. PA1 45 AW31
Windsor Rd, Renf. PA4 31 AY27
Windsor St, G20 36 BQ27
Windsor St, G32 54 CE31
Windsor Ter, G20 36 BQ27
Windsor Wk, (Udd.) G71 71 CR38
Windyedge Cres, G13 19 BE24
Windyedge Pl, G13 19 BE24
Winifred St, G33 38 BZ25
Winning Ct, (Blan.) G72 84 CN44
Winning Row, G31 53 BZ32
Winton Av, (Giff.) G46 77 BL43
Winton Dr, G12 21 BL24
Winton Gdns, (Udd.) G71 70 CP38

Winton La, G12	21	BL24
Wirran Pl, G13	18	BA21
Wishart St, G31	15	BU30
Wisner Ct, (Thornlie.) G46	76	BH42
Wiston St, (Camb.) G72	82	CF40
Woddrop St, G40	66	BX35
Wolseley St, G5	51	BT34
Woodburn Ct, (Ruther.) G73	66	BX39
Woodburn Rd, G43	77	BM40
Woodcroft Av, G11	34	BH26
Woodend Ct, G32	68	CG35
Woodend Dr, G13	20	BG24
Woodend Dr, Pais. PA1	46	AZ33
Woodend Gdns, G32	68	CG35
Woodend La, G13	20	BG24
Woodend Rd, G32	68	CF35
Woodend Rd, (Ruther.) G73	80	BX41
Wood Fm Rd, (Thornlie.) G46	76	BJ43
Woodfield, (Udd.) G71	71	CS39
Woodfield Av, (Bishop.) G64	24	BX20
Woodfoot Quad, G53	75	BD41
Woodfoot Rd, G53	75	BC41
Woodford St, G41	63	BN38
Woodgreen Av, G44	64	BR39
Woodhall St, G40	66	BX35
Woodhead Cres, (Udd.) G71	71	CP38
Woodhead Ind Est, (Chry.) G69	27	CK23
Woodhead Rd, G53	74	BB40
Woodhead Rd, (Chry.) G69	27	CK24
Woodhead Ter, (Chry.) G69	27	CK22
Woodhill Gro, (Bishop.) G64	24	BY21
Woodhill Rd, G21	24	BX23
Woodhill Rd, (Bishop.) G64	24	BY20
Woodholm Av, G44	64	BS39
Woodhouse St, G13	20	BG22
Woodland Av, Pais. PA2	58	AU37
Woodland Cres, (Camb.) G72	82	CD41
Woodlands Av, (Gart.) G69	28	CN22
Woodlands Av, (Both.) G71	85	CQ42
Woodlands Ct, (Thornlie.) G46	76	BH43
Woodlands Cres, (Thornlie.) G46	76	BH43
Woodlands Cres, (Both.) G71	85	CP42
Woodlands Dr, G4	9	BP27
Woodlands Gdns, (Both.) G71	85	CP41
Woodlands Gate, G3	9	BP28
Woodlands Gate, (Thornlie.) G46	76	BH42
Woodlands Pk, (Thornlie.) G46	76	BH43
Woodlands Rd, G3	9	BP27
Woodlands Rd, (Thornlie.) G46	76	BH43
Woodlands Ter, G3	8	BN28
Woodlands Ter, (Both.) G71	85	CP42
Woodlea Dr, (Giff.) G46	77	BM41
Woodlinn Av, G44	78	BR40
Woodneuk La, (Gart.) G69	29	CQ24
Woodneuk Rd, G53	75	BD41
Woodneuk Rd, (Gart.) G69	29	CP24
Woodneuk Ter, (Gart.) G69	29	CP24
Wood Quad, Clyde. G81	18	BA21
Woodrow Circ, G41	49	BM33
Woodrow Pl, G41	49	BL33
Woodrow Rd, G41	49	BM33
Woodside Av, (Thornlie.) G46	76	BJ42
Woodside Av, (Ruther.) G73	66	BY38
Woodside Cres, G3	9	BP28
Woodside Cres, (Barr.) G78	74	AZ43
Woodside Cres, Pais. PA1	44	AS33
Woodside Gro, (Ruther.) G73	66	BY38
Woodside Pl, G3	9	BP28
Woodside Pl, (Udd.) G71	71	CS37
Woodside Pl La, G3	9	BP28
Woodside Ter, G3	9	BP28
Woodside Ter La, G3	9	BP28
Woodstock Av, G41	63	BM37
Wood St, G31	38	BX29
Wood St, Pais. PA2	45	AX34
Woodville Pk, G51	48	BK31
Woodville St, G51	48	BK31
Wordsworth Way, (Both.) G71	85	CR42
Works Av, (Camb.) G72	82	CG40
Wraes Av, (Barr.) G78	74	AZ41
Wraes Vw, (Barr.) G78	73	AV44
Wright Av, (Barr.) G78	73	AW43
Wrightlands Cres, Ersk. PA8	16	AU21
Wright St, Renf. PA4	31	AW28
Wykeham Pl, G13	19	BE23
Wykeham Rd, G13	19	BE23
Wyndford Dr, G20	21	BM24
Wyndford Rd, G20	21	BL24
Wyndham St, G12	35	BM25
Wynford Ter, (Udd.) G71	71	CR38
Wyper Pl, G40	52	BW31
Wyvil Av, G13	20	BG20
Wyvis Av, G13	18	BA21
Wyvis Pl, G13	18	BB21
Wyvis Quad, G13	18	BB21

Y

Yair Dr, G52	46	BC31
Yarrow Gdns, G20	36	BP26
Yate Gro, G31	52	BX32
Yate Rd, G31	52	BX32
Yate St, G31	52	BX32
Yew Dr, G21	38	BW26
Yokerburn Ter, Clyde. G81	18	AZ22
Yoker Ferry Rd, G14	18	BA23
Yoker Mill Gdns, G13	18	BA22
Yoker Mill Rd, G13	18	BA22
York Dr, (Ruther.) G73	81	BZ40
Yorkhill Par, G3	35	BL28
Yorkhill Quay, G3	35	BK29
Yorkhill St, G3	8	BM29
York St, G2	13	BQ31
York Way, Renf. PA4	32	AZ28
Young Pl, (Udd.) G71	71	CQ37
Young Ter, G21	38	BW25

Z

Zambesi Dr, (Blan.) G72	84	CL44
Zena Cres, G33	38	BY25
Zena Pl, G33	38	BZ25
Zena St, G33	38	BZ25
Zetland Rd, G52	32	BB29